The Sibold Effect

*Beyond Science, History, Ghosts, and
the Appalachian Supernatural*

John David Miller

Table of Contents

1. The Setup

2. The Canvas

3. The Passage

4. Retribution

5. The Feud

6. Price's Mill

7. Greenville

8. Summer of Love

9. The Search

10. The Seventh Step

11. The Faces of Clover Hollow

12. The Sibold Effect

Chapter 1 The Setup

'Where there is an open mind, there will always be a frontier' Dorthea Brown

Is this my destiny? Is this my predetermined path for the rest of my life? Growing up exploring the Saltpeter Caves in Greenville, West Virginia, instilled in me an overwhelming passion, or more like a compulsion, to research and investigate this curious kinship we share with Mother Earth.

It was the fall of 2002 and the group of us were sitting on the deck of the 'Golden Dawn' anchored in the harbor off Port Moresby, Papua New Guinea. We were waiting for dusk so that we could shimmy down the anchor line with our lights off hoping to get a glimpse of flashlight fish erupting out of the cargo hold of an old fishing trawler sitting on the bottom of the harbor one-hundred feet down. Flashlight fish only come out on moonless nights about twenty minutes after dusk when it becomes pitch black. It was our last dive on this trip before we had to pack up and head home half a world away.

The discussion on the deck at the time was how the Motuan, the indigenous people of Port Moresby, Papua New Guinea, were treated by the British, much like the American Indian during the British colonializing of America. At 10 am on February 20, 1873, almost one-hundred years after the American Revolution, the English captain, John Moresby of the HMS Basilisk, claimed the land of Papua New Guinea for Britain and named it after his father, Admiral Sir Fairfax Moresby. He called the inner reach 'Fairfax Harbor' and the other 'Port Moresby.'

The Motuan were considered savages and uncivilized heathens that had no right to the land of their ancestors. These discussions always got lively and entertaining among my travel buddies who were a very diverse bunch. They were political opposites and geographically separated by oceans. From China to California, from the Appalachian Mountains to the English countryside, we had it all pretty much covered. I was the hillbilly of the group.

It had been a successful and rewarding dive trip to the Coral Sea, located between northern Australia and Papua New Guinea. It was a somewhat unusual dive trip in that we were diving sea mounts in the rain all week and never saw any land. These sea mounts were the tops of underwater mountains covered with coral heads and lava tubes.

The flashlight fish showed up right on cue and it was amazing. They came out all at once and like water from a fire hose, exploded out of the hold. When they came out on that moonless night they were lit up like it was Christmas. Flashlight fish are two or three inches long and have pockets under their eyes that are filled with bioluminescent bacteria which produces their bright glow. Not unlike squid, cuddle fish, and other creatures of light, they can sync and resonate with Earth's hidden energy as if they were all connected wirelessly.

Is this what I am supposed to be doing, exploring faraway places, looking for the unknown, searching for the obscure, chasing encounters with wild animals? This compulsion to make that connection to the natural universe has been with me all my life. Even though it has not been exactly clear, there has always been the presence of a higher spirit, or maybe a guardian angel, that always seems to be close by. It seemed important to always listen to that inner voice, that sudden revelation of intuition, it has never let me down.

It was now nearing the end of the trip and the next hurdle was to figure out how to make a satellite phone call back to Virginia. The fifteen-second delay made the call very difficult so I had to wait till I arrived in Cairns, Australia, to make a clear call home. The gang of us on the boat for the last night were already discussing where our next adventure might be. In the running were the

Andaman Islands off the coast of India, or maybe a livaboard trip traveling around the Island of Borneo and a visit with the orangutans. Little did I know that the world I knew was getting ready to flip on its axis and everything known was going to change forever.

It wasn't until my arrival in Cairns that I was able to make a clear phone call back home. My girlfriend had just started Vet School at Virginia Tech in Blacksburg, Virginia, and we were looking for a house for her to live in while she was in school. We had a realtor looking around for quite a while and hadn't seen much, until that day when he called out of the blue and said he had a realtor friend who was going to list a property tomorrow, and it just might be the place we are looking for. Well, being in Australia at the time and not seeing the place first, I told my girlfriend that if she likes it, go on and put a low offer on it and we would see what happens. The plan was to call back tomorrow from Sydney.

This was the age before the cell phone and there was only a small window of opportunity to find that bank of pay phones somewhere in the international terminal before my flight left for the sixteen hour flight back to LAX and then on to Richmond. Only having a couple of minutes to talk, it was conveyed to me that there were three other offers on the property already and the realtor had not yet put our offer in. The only thing my girlfriend mentioned was that it had a decent view; she was not very persuasive either way. But, something deep inside me said go ahead and make another offer and this time at one thousand dollars over the asking price. The phone call ended and I ran like OJ to my departure gate.

These long plane rides were not too bad anymore as some of my travel friends were emergency room doctors and have access to sleeping pills that will knock you out cold for eight to ten hours. And, if you sync the sleep time to California time, the jet lag heading east isn't so bad. During the long layover at LAX and upon arrival, I looked for a pay phone to check in back home.

Well, my bid was the high bid, I now own an old house somewhere in the Appalachian Mountains of Virginia and I knew absolutely nothing about it. I don't really believe in coincidences, so I was wondering what I might find when I finally get to see it. This just might get interesting. The only thing known about the house was that it sat in a rural area near Blacksburg, Virginia, called Clover Hollow. Some of these places can really be run down and need a lot of work to get up and running so I braced myself and was prepared for anything.

The first time I saw the place, I could not believe my eyes. It was a beautiful country house with a wrap around covered porch and a tin roof. Walking up on the porch, the strong surge of chill bumps started to form along my spine as I gazed out over Sinking Creek flowing west, over a dam, and then heading northwestwardly through the Appalachian Mountains. If you close your eyes you could easily mistake the water falling over the dam and hitting the rocks below for ocean waves crashing on the beach. Nothing but a natural wonderland in all directions and a dream come true. I had died and gone to Heaven. The Earth's natural energy emanating around me was palpable.

This did not seem real. Before me was a place more beautiful than I have ever seen in all my travels. It was the strongest of notions that I had been summoned here for a very specific reason and purpose, and it looked like it was going to take a lot of ciphering to unlock the secrets buried deep inside Clover Hollow. From that moment on, I kept my camera close by, just in case.

Just a week or so after closing, I received a letter in the mail from the insurance company stating they had an issue with insuring the place because their records show that the property was sitting in the one-hundred year flood plain. This sounded strange since the house and property sit up on the side of a mountain. I found a copy of the plat to see where the problem may lie. Turns out that the bottom of the driveway where the mailbox stands, sits down next to the creek which of course is in a flood plain. That wasn't the jaw-dropper that made me go find a chair, it was the name written down at the bottom right corner of the plat; Frank W. Sibold.

Sibold is not a very common name, but it did happen to be my mother's maiden name. I did know that some Sibold's were from the Blacksburg area and I did know they had something to do with Virginia Tech. Oh yeah, I also spent every summer as a kid in Greenville, West Virginia, not thirty miles northwest of Clover Hollow as the crow flies. It is where both sets of my grandparents, the Millers and Sibold's, lived across the street from each other. All the thoughts of purpose and why I am here came rushing back to me. What does all this mean? Believing there are no coincidences, everything happens for a reason, and everything is connected, I wanted to know the reason I was brought here, what am I supposed to find, and where am I supposed to look?

It didn't take long to find out that of the first five women to graduate Virginia Tech in 1925, two of them, Lucy Lee Lancaster and Carrie Sibold, were cousins of mine. Lucy Lee became the librarian at Virginia Tech for the next fifty-two years. Her interest lay in travel and genealogy, and her papers are now archived at the Virginia Tech Library. She

Lucy Lee Lancaster   Carrie Sibold

left forty boxes, or forty cubic feet of genealogical documents in her collection.

It took over ten years to piece together the history associated with this little piece of land and it's mostly unbelievable. The house sits on the side of the hill and was built before 1890. It was built with two rooms on two rooms and built as the miller's house, the house where the mill manager lived. Price's Mill and dam sat about one-hundred yards down the hill on Sinking Creek. Only the dam and house remain today.

One of the first white settlers to the area, who chose this strategic piece of property for a mill site, was John Michael Price, my first-generation grandfather, one of three first-generation grandfathers that came to the New World together on the ship Winter Galley in 1738. They became founding fathers of the German New River Settlement in 1740 when they settled around the horseshoe bottoms on the New River. The other two first-generation grandfathers were John Phillip Harless and John Phillip Sibold. They too, have a connection to this little piece of Earth in Clover Hollow.

This place also has a direct connection to Paleo-Indians, Cherokee Indians, Draper's Meadow Massacre, French and Indian War, American Revolution, Daniel Boone, George Washington, and William Preston, among many others. The historical imprint on this specific spot has been heavy.

One would think the story ends there but that would be a mistake. When the last renter moved out and I took my chance to move in, the strangest of all things began. It wasn't but a few weeks before bizarre supernatural activity in the house commenced after the start of a remodeling project. It really would not have been mentioned, had it not been all caught on film. During the next year, there were visitors who manifested themselves in a variety of ways; like orbs, ectoplasm, mist, and shape shifting glowing sparkly's. Was the house I now live in haunted by the ghosts of my ancestors, or was this place being visited by ancient Indian spirits who had once roamed these parts?

Explanations for these events suggested the real possibility of visitors who may represent; ghosts, Indian spirits, or some other supernatural phenomena. Ruled out were insects, snowflakes, and figments of my imagination, thanks to the photographic evidence. My sense at the time was that this phenomenon was mischievous and playful by nature and they were deliberately, almost purposely, letting me photograph them. It was like they were trying to show me something, or tell me something, and I knew that if I kept my eyes open, my camera close, and followed the clues, I would surely find out what's going on.

During my investigations of the property, strange and mysterious electromagnetic field disruptions occurred in specific areas which could be measured using gauss-meters, dowsing rods, and they would make my compass needle rotate on it's axis. This was clear evidence to me of an active geodesic zone, meaning an active geological energetic site.

Sinking Creek out front flows west and empties into the New River. Sinking Creek is a major tributary along with many other creeks and springs running off the mountains into the New. The name Sinking Creek comes from the fact that the creek travels at times underground through limestone bedrock on its journey to the New River.

The New River is known to be one of the oldest rivers in the world in par with the Nile in Egypt. It is thought to be over sixty-five million years old and probably preceded the mountain building process that created the Appalachian Mountains. This may be a factor in the prehistoric nature and ancient feel of Clover Hollow and Sinking Creek.

Over time, watching the property on a day to day basis, it was noticed that every time there was a weather event like rain or snow, there would be some sort of off-gassing of Sinking Creek and the creek would erupt like a bubbling witches cauldron. I began photographing and videotaping the creek during these events. Video screenshots in this book will show strange light forms and odd creatures traveling through and above the water. Again, it would not have been mentioned without the abundant documented evidence. It was clear Clover Hollow was being visited by strange and mysterious entities whose messages have not yet been deciphered.

Bob Dylan might say a 'Simple Twist of Fate' occurred that day in February 2013 when I gazed out over the dam after a light snow. Because of the contrast between the snow and the dead brown leaves, a recognizable outline of an old trail crossing over the side of the mountain and running right across my yard clearly came into view. This would turn out to be the same trail that twenty Shawnee warriors retreated across with Mary Ingles, four hostages, and Phillip Barger's head in a burlap sack. They crossed my property on July 8, 1755, just one day before General Braddock's Defeat and the unofficial start of the French and Indian War, when Colonel James Patton was assassinated at Draper's Meadow, not seven miles down the Indian trail from my property in Clover Hollow.

It was known an old Indian trail was located nearby but believed to have been completely covered up when the Price mill in the 1840s was built and a road was cut in down beside the creek. A closer look revealed a small piece of the trail cuts right across my property and then comes to an abrupt stop on the side of the mountain overlooking the road and dam below. At the edge of the trail, where it looked like nobody had stood for over two-hundred years, was a very strange rock that looked like it might be some sort of pioneering or survey trail-marker. It had markings of some type carved all over the entire surface. It turns out

that rock was no eighteenth century trail-marker, but just one of a whole complex of petroglyphs of unknown origin, more than likely thousands of years old. These newly discovered stone panels, megaliths, and portable artifacts, are abstract, creative, unique, artistic, clever, crumbling, and alien in nature.

Because of a trip to Peru and a hike to Machu Picchu, I started putting some of the pieces of the puzzle called Clover Hollow back in Virginia together. After finding a connection between the ruins of Saksayhuaman, Ollantaytambo, and Machu Picchu to Clover Hollow, I was able to formulate some possible explanations that might unlock some of the mysteries at the Price Mill site.

It became quite clear to me early on that there were no experts in the academic community that had the knowledge or interest in what is happening in Clover Hollow. As many archaeologist and university department heads that could be found were contacted, including the State Archaeologist at the Virginia Department of Historical Resources. All the American Indian experts that could be found were also contacted, but no one had the prehistoric expertise that I needed.

It looks like I am completely alone in my investigation and the clues that I have been given are all pointing to the unknown. The documented evidence collected falls into three categories; natural, supernatural, and the historical record. The answers to some of the mysteries at Clover Hollow might lie somewhere in the historical record and may provide some clues as to why I was brought here in the first place. The first place I visited was the library at Virginia Tech where the Lucy Lee Lancaster Collection was stored. After studying the forty boxes of genealogical documents, much pertaining to eight generations of three of my bloodlines, I got the overwhelming notion that the information put into those cardboard boxes were specifically put there for me to find.

The conclusions that have emerged I believe are true. They are both unconventional and controversial, yet they are the only theories that can be supported by the documented evidence consisting of high resolution photographs, videos, and the historical record. My research goes back to the beginning of time and has been sewn into a quite unbelievable storyline that is absolutely true according to my research. What appears to be thousands of random coincidences and pieces of a giant puzzle, actually fit tightly together, connected with purpose and a reason for their existence. The answers to this puzzle were eventually found buried deep into the roots of my religious and spiritual beliefs.

The most important clue that I have been given is so profound that it shakes me to the core. It is the simple fact that I purchased a piece of property sight unseen while out of the country, and that it is directly connected to three of my first generation grandfathers. There are only two explanations as to how this could happen. First, you would have to believe that buying this property and the three bloodline connections are all purely coincidental, almost a statistical impossibility as far as I can tell. If it wasn't coincidental, then it would mean that it must have happened for a reason. Therein lies the spiritual conundrum; have I been contacted by my ancestors from beyond the grave? If so, why?

This opens up a myriad of unanswered questions and a collection of seemingly unrelated clues:

1. *Why was I brought here?*
2. *What is my connection to this place?*
3. *What is the historical imprint of this property?*
4. *Who carved the petroglyphs?*
5. *What's the connection between the petroglyphs and my ancestors?*
6. *What's the connection between the petroglyphs and the American Indian?*
7. *What is the geological footprint of this little piece of energetic property?*
8. *What are the unidentified flying objects shooting around the property?*
9. *What are the unidentified swimming objects darting around Sinking Creek?*
10. *Have my ancestors returned as ghosts and made contact with me from beyond the Grave?*

The only thing I know for certain is that there are no coincidences, everything happens for a reason, and everything is connected.

Chapter 2 The Canvas

First and foremost, there is no doubt in my mind that the universe was created with God's design. But, according to scientific scholars, the universe was created by the 'Big Bang.' One second there was nothing and then '*POOF*' the entire universe appeared out of nowhere. They don't use any scientific facts to back this up, however, it's the only thing that works when you don't believe in a supreme being who has created it all. Seems to me 'The Big Bang Theory' would require a whole lot more magic to achieve than any providence of God. Every culture on Earth originally had a creation story that involved a supreme entity. This is not at odds with science as these early civilizations also believed that their god created the science (*i.e.* Sacred Geometry) that supported the physical dimension we call the natural universe.

As far as Earth goes, It is believed that some four-hundred million years ago, Pangea, the super continent, started to form during the Devonian Period. By the late

Triassic period, two-hundred million years ago, Pangea had started to split apart. By the Middle and Late Jurassic, 145 million years ago, enough plate movement had occurred to separate South America from southern Africa. Laurasia (which consisted of North America and Eurasia) also moved away from Africa and South America, helping to create the Atlantic Ocean and the Gulf of Mexico. This was the age of the reptiles. Much of the Jurassic world was warm and moist, with a greenhouse climate.

The Appalachian orogeny is one of the geological mountain-forming events that created the Appalachian Mountains. This orogeny occurred about 325 million to 260 million years ago. The orogeny was caused by Africa colliding with North America. At the time, these continents did not exist in their current forms. It applied massive stress on what is today the Eastern Seaboard of North America, forming a wide and high mountain chain. Evidence of the Appalachian orogeny stretches for hundreds of miles on the surface from Alabama to New Jersey. The Appalachians likely once reached elevations similar to those of the Alps and the Rocky Mountains before they were eroded down to what they are today. Subsequent erosion wore down the mountain chain and spread sediment both to the east and to the west. The sedimentary rock in the eastern Appalachian Basin region was pinched into great folds that ran perpendicular to the direction of forces. The greatest amount of deformation associated with the Appalachian orogeny occurred in the Southern Appalachians (North Carolina, Tennessee, Virginia, and West Virginia). A series of great faults developed along with the folds. As the two continents collided, large belts of rock forced by thrust faults, piled one on top of another building up pressure and energy. This is a prime example of pent up energy confined deep inside the Earth that can manifest itself in many different forms.

About sixty-six million years ago, the Appalachian Mountains had been eroded to an almost flat plain. It was not until the region was uplifted during the Cenozoic Era (sixty-five million years ago to the present) that the distinctive topography of the Appalachian Mountains formed. Some believe that the New River existed before

this second mountain building process began. This era is known as the Age of the Mammals. This uplifting rejuvenated the streams, which rapidly responded by cutting downward into the ancient bedrock. Some streams flowed along weak layers that define the folds and faults created many millions of years earlier. Sinking Creek, a tributary of the New River, is an example of this process.

A look at rocks exposed in today's Appalachian Mountains reveals elongated belts of folded and thrust, faulted marine sedimentary rocks, volcanic rocks, and slivers of ancient ocean floor which provides strong evidence that these rocks were deformed during plate collision. Limestone is among the rocks derived from old marine sediments in the Appalachian region. Some believe that limestone, once the shells of living organisms, still retain a spiritual essence or vibration.

Highly susceptible to chemical weathering, a significant factor in the heavily vegetated humid climate, limestone often erodes more rapidly than more resistant layers of sandstone. In the Valley-and-Ridge Province, for example, sandstone and other durable layers often compose the ridges, while the worn-down valleys are commonly underlain by limestone. Caves and caverns, as well as natural rock bridges and arches, are widespread in Appalachian limestone country. Natural Bridge in Virginia, for example, is a ninety foot corridor of Paleozoic-era

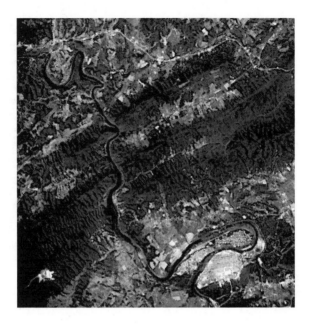

limestone standing more than two-hundred feet above Cedar Creek.

The area of interest in this book is the New River Valley in western Virginia. It lies in the Valley-and-Ridge Province of the Appalachian Mountains. This part of the Appalachians is strung with gaps, which are small passes in the mountain front. Those with streams flowing through them are called water gaps. Because of the layout of drainage in the folded layers in much of the Appalachians, stream piracy, where one watercourse captures the headwaters of another, is a common phenomenon. Therefore, so-called wind gaps representing old drainages whose waters have been diverted away, are also widely scattered about.

This special piece of property in Clover Hollow lies directly on top of an ancient water gap cutting between Spring Run Mountain and Clover Hollow Mountain containing the waters of Sinking Creek. Sinking Creek is an ancient tributary running west into the New River. The New River is an ancient river system, the oldest on the North American continent and second only to the Nile River in Africa, the oldest river in the world. It begins as two streams in the Blue Ridge Mountains of North Carolina before merging into the New River four miles from the Virginia line. Therein lays another quirk of this ancient river. It flows northward rather than southward like most of the other major rivers along the eastern seaboard. The New River, part of the Mississippi River watershed, is a tributary of the Kanawha River and about 320 miles long. The New River is one of the oldest rivers in the world. It may have been on its present course for at least sixty-five million years. In the geologic past, the New River was a much longer stream and geologists have named it the Teays. It flowed through present-day central Ohio, Indiana, and Illinois before emptying into the Mississippi River. The last advance of Pleistocene continental glacial ice buried most of this river. Then, the waters of the New were diverted into rivers (the present-day Ohio and Kanawha Rivers) created by the glaciers.

The New River flows directly across the Appalachian Plateau, not around or from it, as most other streams of this region do. The river had to exist before the mountains formed as it has carved through more than ten-thousand feet (about two miles) of their strata. It is believed that the New River cut through the mountains at the same rate the mountains would erode.

Today, most streams in the central Appalachians, southeast of the Appalachian Plateau, drain eastward to the Atlantic Ocean. Yet, evidence from Paleozoic rocks indicates that the sediments that constitute them were deposited by streams flowing to the northwest. How was the direction of stream flow reversed after the end of the late Paleozoic mountain-building? The concept of plate tectonics gives clues to the answer. The pulling apart of the North American Plate and the African Plate, which occurred during the Mesozoic, explains. When plates separate, the crust near their margins usually subsides. This subsidence may explain how streams can reverse their direction of flow. The New River is the only river that still drains westward in this region. It cuts across three topographic/physiographic provinces of the Appalachians. It is easily the oldest river system in North America with origins at the end of the Paleozoic Era. Water coming off the ridges form streams, springs, and creeks, as they find

21

the path of least resistance on the surface through gaps or passes, or find their way through the bedrock as they flow into other streams, creeks, and rivers.

The Appalachian Mountains created a formidable barrier for east west travel. The New River Valley is a great example of a mountain *pass*. A mountain pass is a route through a mountain range or over a ridge. Mountain passes make use of a gap, saddle, notch, or the low point in a ridge. Passes have been important since before recorded history and have played a key role in trade, war, and migration. The New River Valley was an ancient passage way and migration route to or from the Ohio River Valley. Passes are often found just above the source of a river, constituting a drainage divide. Passes may be very short, consisting of steep slopes to the top of the pass, or valleys of many miles, whose highest point is only identifiable by surveying. There are many words for pass in the English-speaking world. In the United States, pass is very common in the West, the word gap, is common in the southern Appalachians. If water flows through the gap it is known as a water gap, if no water, it's a wind gap.

~ ~ ~ ~ ~ ~

We have covered four-hundred million years and now it comes down to the question of who were the first humans to visit Virginia. The mainstream scientific community thinks that the first people entered the Western

Hemisphere from Asia over land that connected Siberia and Alaska at the end of the last great Ice, or Pleistocene Age. A huge glacier more than mile thick covered large areas of land in what is now Canada. The glaciers lowered the sea level by three-hundred feet, exposing an immense one-thousand mile-wide plain between Siberia and Alaska known as Beringia. Especially along the coast, the tundra-like plain teemed with animal and plant life, and the ocean provided abundant marine life. The early immigrants were unaware they entered a new continent as they hunted Beringia's game and gathered plants for food.

When did the first people arrive and what was their culture like? While Native Americans believe that they have always been here, the first documented Paleo-Indian culture was found at an archaeological site near Folsom, New Mexico, in 1927. There, a distinctive spear point was found between the ribs of a type of bison that had been extinct since the end of the last Ice Age. Five years later near Clovis, New Mexico, a woolly mammoth kill and associated stone tools were uncovered, dating to 11,200 years ago. The hallmark of the Clovis culture is the lance shaped fluted point. Although Clovis points are found across the continent, an especially large number of them are found in Virginia. Other stone tools found with the Clovis point include scrapers, gravers, perforators, wedges, and knives. Evidence uncovered so far in Virginia suggests that these tools were used to spear game, cut up meat, scrape and cut hides, and split and carve bone of deer, bison, and rabbit. Caribou, elk, moose, and possibly mastodon also may have been hunted.

The effects of the glaciers made for long, hard winters and short, cool summers. In the Appalachian region, the mountain slopes were bare and tundra-like. People in the Shenandoah Valley and northern Virginia lived among grasslands, open forests of conifers such as pine, fir, spruce, hemlock, and occasional islands of deciduous trees. Slightly warmer weather south of present-day Richmond encouraged the growth of more deciduous trees such as birch, beech, and oak. The first people lived in groups which anthropologists today call bands and camped along streams that flowed through the tundra-like grasslands and the open spruce, pine, and fir forests that covered Virginia.

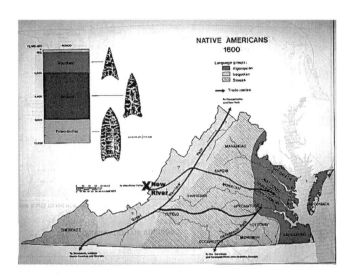

A band was like an extended family. Due to the harsh climate, each band moved seasonally within a set territory to hunt and forage.

According to the Virginia Department of Historical Resources, the term archaic, meaning old, signals a series of new adaptations by the early people that occurred between 8000 and 1200 B.C. As the cold, moist climate of the Pleistocene Age changed to a warmer, drier one, the warming winds melted the glaciers to the north and warmed the ocean water. The sea level rose, spreading water across the Coastal Plain of Virginia and creating the Chesapeake Bay. Many of the places where early humans lived were eroded and covered by the rising water. Grassland and open forests of conifers gave way to thick forests of pine, oak, and hickory. As the flora changed, the mastodon, the last of the large Pleistocene animals, became extinct and other animals such as bison, caribou, and moose moved away. People now hunted widely the abundant deer, elk, bear, turkey, and small game such as rabbit and fox. As the vegetation became profuse, they gathered more plant foods such as fruit, acorns, and hickory nuts.

The people of the Archaic period began to vary the size and shape of their lithic (stone) points. Stone spear points, knives, scrapers, gravers, and drills were still used;

however, the hunter-gatherers fashioned them differently, with side or corner notches. Notching tells us how the points were attached to the spear or knife handle.

In their quest for food and raw materials, the people ventured into every section of Virginia. Soapstone, commonly found along the eastern foothills of the Blue Ridge, was one of the most sought-after materials around 2000 B.C. because it was a type of soft rock that carved easily and did not break when heated, it made excellent cooking pots. The people quarried large mushroom shaped pieces of soapstone from outcroppings, and with stone and bone tools, hollowed out bowls. When people started making heavy soapstone cooking vessels, they were probably more settled, as the vessels were too heavy to move often. Archaeologists have found fragments of soapstone vessels across Virginia, sometimes hundreds of miles from a quarry.

In a similar fashion, cobbles of quartzite along the Fall Line, and outcrops of quartzite and rhyolite in the mountains were mined for the production of large points and knives. These tools, like the soapstone bowls, also found their way across Virginia, confirming the widespread trading in Virginia between people living in the mountains and along the coast.

As increasingly more groups sought the abundant environment along the rivers, they merged through marriage and trade, to form small settlements, called hamlets. Each series of hamlets began to take on a simple tribal identity. Elders guided the groups, along with members whose talents made them leaders in specific tasks. This structure was unlike that of earlier bands in which each member held equal standing.

Indian populations grew in Virginia so that diverse tribes now lived in scattered, settled hamlets, along major rivers that wound through the mountain valleys and down through the Piedmont and the Coastal Plain. One example of the great diversity can be found in the Stone Mound Burial culture in the northern Shenandoah Valley. This culture, dating from 400 B.C. to 200 A.D. placed hundreds of low stone mounds in clusters on ancient bluff-like river terraces overlooking the floodplain. Only a few people were buried with great ceremony in each mound.

Sometimes, the Stone Mound people placed rare and sacred objects made from exotic materials in the graves. These objects included tubular and platform pipes, copper beads, hematite cones, pendants, basalt celts, spear-throwing stones, and caches of projectile points. The people placed the objects within the mound for the deceased to use on their afterlife journeys. The few graves within each mound, the few clusters of mounds, and the special objects, suggest that the Stone Mound Burial culture gave only higher-ranking people this preferential treatment. This was strong evidence that spiritualism played a great role in the lives of these early inhabitants of Virginia.

During the Middle Woodland period, the people slowly replaced their spears with the bow and arrow as a hunting weapon. Evidence for this change is found in smaller projectile points, particularly the triangular shapes. Further advances came as people redesigned the grooved axe and used what is called a celt, or un-grooved axe. Sleek and polished, the celt enabled people to refine their woodworking techniques.

Starting in the Middle Woodland, and continuing into the Historic Period, people lavished their artistic ability on their tobacco pipes. Tobacco pipes in the Early Woodland Period resembled large, straight cigars. Later pipes were fashioned into exquisite effigy carvings of birds and animals. Most of the Late Woodland pipes were a short-stemmed elbow type, into which wood or reed stems were inserted. Tobacco introduced during the Late Woodland Period and considered a gift from the gods, was reserved for reverent use in medicinal and spiritual applications. In later times, particularly after contact with the Europeans, smoking for pleasure developed among the Indians and pipes became commonplace.

Recent excavations at a number of sites, including Cactus Hill, located along the Nottoway River south of Richmond, Virginia, have provided new evidence and raised new questions about when people first ventured into Virginia. For many years, archaeologists thought that people arrived approximately eleven thousand years ago. However, stone artifacts, charcoal, and soil, plant and animal remains, point to human habitation at Cactus Hill at least eighteen-thousand years ago during the late Ice Age.

Cactus Hill is an archaeological site in southeastern Virginia, located on sand dunes above the Nottoway River, about forty-five miles south of Richmond. The site receives its name from the prickly pear cactus that can be found growing abundantly onsite in the sandy soil. Cactus Hill is one of the oldest archaeological sites in the Americas, and was inhabited as long as eighteen-thousand to twenty-thousand years ago. The site has yielded multiple levels of prehistoric inhabitance with two discrete levels of early Paleo-Indian activity. The Cactus Hill site furnished evidence of a pre-Clovis population in North America. Finds at Cactus Hill are considered highly significant as they address important questions such as, 'When did humans populate the Americas?' and 'Where did they come from?'

The entire theory concerning the first inhabitants being the Clovis culture was re-evaluated following the discoveries at Cactus Hill in the mid-1990s. With the emergence of new evidence, the hypothesis for a pre-Clovis human occupation began to surface. With excavation revealing evidence dating as old as eighteen-thousand to twenty-thousand years ago, it may mean that humans had occupied the Americas long before migration was possible across the Bering land bridge.

~ ~ ~ ~ ~ ~

By the time of the first European contact with the Indians, there were multiple tribes located all over Virginia with widely different cultures and dialect. When the Indians were asked, when did you first arrive in Virginia? They would respond 'we have always been here.' By the 1600s, the Virginia Indian tribes had developed sophisticated trails, establishing a major trade route through their sacred hunting grounds around the New River Valley, traveling west to the Ohio River Valley. The New River Valley was considered common and sacred hunting grounds shared by the neighboring tribes. Among these were the Cherokee to the south and the Shawnee and Iroquois to the west. The tribes in the Ohio River Valley at that time were in a constant state of warfare.

Before humans had entered Virginia, the property in Clover Hollow sat directly on or adjacent to, an ancient animal migration route and water gap cutting through the Appalachian Mountains. This migration passageway would also have been traveled by any humans heading east or west across the Appalachians. This spot also developed into a major Indian trail and a segment of the 'New River Trail.' This particular trail segment started near my property and headed west along Sinking Creek until it branched off near its mouth on the New River.

Chapter 3 The Passage

Winter Galley

Debarkation- Philadelphia, Pa.
September 5, 1738
Passengers

1st Gen.	John Phillip Sibold		John Michael Price		John Phillip Harless
2nd Gen.	John Phillip Sibold Jr		Michael Price Jr		Phillip Harless Jr
3rd Gen.	John Phillip Sibold III		Lewis Price	married	Peggy Harless
4th Gen.	Jacob Franz Sibold		John Price		
5th Gen.	James William Sibold	married	Mary Elizabeth Price		
5th Gen.	(James William Sibold's brother)	George Washington Sibold			
6th Gen.		John Franz Sibold			
7th Gen.		Annie May Sibold			
6th Gen.	John Arlington Sibold	married 7th Gen.	Annie May Sibold		
	(son of James William Sibold, 5th Gen.)		(daughter of John Franz Sibold, 6th Gen.)		
7th and 8th Gen. Sibold		Ann Lorraine Sibold			
8th and 9th Gen. Sibold		John David Miller			

Johan Michael Preisch 19 years old
Johan Phillip Halass 22 years old
Johan Phillip Seiboltt 26 years old

On September 5, 1738, the Winter Galley arrived in the Port of Philadelphia with three of my first-generation grandfathers and their families. If any one of the three had missed that boat, stayed in Germany, or not survived the crossing, I would not have ever existed. They were best friends and family, and had escaped with whatever they could carry, including the family bibles and their choir books written in German.

War, poverty, and religious persecution were rampant in Western Europe in the 1600s and into the early 1700s. With the Protestant Reformation, Roman Catholics were making it difficult for the Lutherans. In 1572, the French Catholics conducted the St. Bartholomew's Day massacre in which hundreds of Huguenot Lutherans were killed. For a period of over one-hundred and fifty years, the

Protestants suffered cruel persecutions in which an untold number of lives were sacrificed.

The religious 'Thirty Years War,' with its bloodshed, murder, robbery, and pillage, raged on from 1619 to 1648, and was disastrous to the Palatinate region in Germany. Although the war 'ended' in 1648, the repressive effects lasted for a century. One report states that the persecution reduced the population of the German Palatinate from some half-million to fewer than fifty-thousand. By the time the early 1700s had come along, the Palatine Germans had had enough of poverty, sickness, starvation, freezing, and being caught in the middle between the warring French and German troops. The Palatines had enough. They looked westward. They packed up, floated down the Rhine to Rotterdam, and headed for America.

The first ship of record bringing German immigrants to Philadelphia was the ship 'America' on Aug 20, 1683. The Germans, as well as the immigrants from other nations, looked forward to being free on their own land, out from under the cruel reign of their former masters. Little did they know the cost that freedom would entail. If they signed an 'Oath of Allegiance' to the King of England, they would have the opportunity to settle, clear, farm, and own land on the edge of the western frontier of the English colonies. Even though they were not English and only spoke German, they were white, and Germany was not at war with England at the time, so they would be acceptable as land owners. They may have heard stories of the savages and hardships that lay ahead of them on their journey into the wilderness.

William Penn was born into a wealthy family in England in 1644, but was expelled from Oxford University for associating with religious 'radicals.' Penn's father, Admiral Sir William Penn, was deeply disappointed in his son and sent him to Ireland in an attempt to separate him from this group. In Ireland, however, Penn met and joined the most radical and persecuted of all the Protestant sects, the Society of Friends, or 'Quakers.' It was this persecution, and later imprisonment, that drove Penn to seek freedom in the New World.

William Penn 'acquired' part of Pennsylvania in 1681 in payment of a debt that King Charles II owed his father,

Admiral Penn. He came to America on the ship 'Welcome' in 1682, at the age of thirty-eight. He used the king's land grant to establish his 'holy experiment,' a colony dedicated to religious tolerance. He purchased additional land on the Delaware River from the Delaware Indians.

It is interesting that William Penn's mother, Margaret Jasper of Rotterdam, Netherlands, had German cousins. This relationship may have played a part in why William Penn was offering Pennsylvania as a haven for the beleaguered German Protestants. William Penn lived in Pennsylvania from 1682 to 1684, and again from 1699 to 1701. He died in England in 1718.

Initially, all this land was known as 'Penn's Woods.' This was a tract of land of forty-five thousand square miles; Penn owned more land than any other commoner of that day. William Penn suggested that this large tract of land be called 'New Wales.' King Charles objected to such a name for this unsettled wilderness, so Penn suggested 'Sylvania' a Latin word meaning 'forest.' The King decided to honor the Penn family name and so coined the name 'Penn's Sylvania.'

Penn returned to Europe shortly after that. In Germany, he met with King Charles to encourage the beleaguered Protestants to come to Pennsylvania. He preached the beauty of the Poconos and Alleghenies, and assured the Germans that there were many similarities between Pennsylvania and Der Pfalz. His territorial mission was a beckoning light to the downtrodden Palatinate peasants. They must have felt that the potential hell of the voyage and wilderness were preferable to the real hell in which they were already living.

From the book 'Pennsylvania, The Keystone State' Stevens the author wrote; 'Pennsylvania began its history as a holy experiment with basic principles of democracy and ideals of human liberty as its foundation stones.'

The cost of passage from Rotterdam fluctuated from five to ten pounds Sterling, a great sum in those days. Children were half-price, although few under the age of seven survived the voyages. The trip down the Rhine River from the Palatinate to Rotterdam sometimes lasted for several weeks, much of the time being spent in complying with the regulations of the various German principalities which existed along that great river valley through which they were obliged to pass.

The sailing time for crossing the Atlantic from England to Philadelphia was from eight to sixteen weeks. Ships usually left in early summer to take advantage of calmer seas and balmy weather over the North Atlantic. Conditions on board the ships were usually horrible, with many passengers sick and dying. As many as one-hundred-and-fifty to four-hundred passengers were stuffed into the hold spaces of these small ships. Rarely was there sufficient food for the trip. Starvation and death stalked amidst stench, vermin, and filth. 'Ship fever' (typhus), dysentery, smallpox, and scurvy ravaged the passengers. Many vessels were lost at sea in storms.

When the ships landed, a doctor came on board to decide who was sick and who was well. Often the diagnosis was made by whether a person had a 'furry tongue' (which was considered an indicator of disease) or a 'clean tongue.' Those who had furry tongues were sent back to Europe.

Most of the ships arrived in the fall, with the hardships of the winter staring the pioneers in the face. But, in spite of all difficulties and hardships, new settlers continued to come. The wonder is not that so many succumbed, but that so many faced all hardships uncomplainingly and after a few years of service emerged from all difficulties as successful farmers, who made the country blossom. These pioneers were made of sturdy stuff.

For the love of family, friends, and the desire for religious freedom, my German ancestors banded together and headed across the Atlantic Ocean to settle the wild frontier. Something deep within their hearts compelled them to give up everything to make this incredible journey, all for the slight hope to be able to have a piece of land where they can raise their families in peace and worship how they saw fit.

Ship owners were actively recruiting German emigrants to settle in the colonies. England needed many souls to settle this new world. The more land that was settled, cleared, and farmed, the more it benefitted the King. He could officially claim land in England's name when his subjects would settle and live on the land. He could also build a population who could fight those other countries like Spain and France, who were also trying to acquire the same land.

The ship owners were bringing large quantities of cargo back to Europe from the colonies. To make the system more profitable, they needed cargo for the western journey also. It wasn't so much about bringing in money from the human cargo, but about the weight and ballast they could use to 'speed up' the sailings back to America. The faster the crossing, the more profits they could make.

The Port of Philadelphia showed the results of the German recruitment. In 1735, 268 German immigrants arrived at this port. In 1736, it was up to 736, and it rose to 1528 in 1737. Expectations were high for 1738, but even these high expectations were shattered by the large numbers who arrived, beginning earlier in the season than usual. To meet the higher demand, shipping companies contracted for extra ships. One company named Hope, provided eight ships, one of which was the Winter Galley.

The journey normally takes sixty to ninety days. The English ship Winter Galley was under the command of Edward Paynter and the ship sailed from Rotterdam, Holland. The Winter Galley would have to make a stop first at the English port of Deal to get customs clearance before they set sail to the English colonies to arrive on September 5, 1738.

The passengers used the 'redemptioner' system to help pay for the journey. What they would have to do was sign a contract to pay the fare within a certain period after arrival. They could also sell possessions, find friends or family already here to pay, or indenture themselves for payment. This system was working well for everyone. The ships could return to England with their cargo holds full of exported goods like tobacco, and the shipping firms were happy to have this extra ballast for the return trip.

The 1738 sailing season was dubbed the 'Year of Destroying Angels' because of the large number of emigrants who died making the crossing. This was a reference to Psalm 79-49. An epidemic swept over the fleets and it was estimated that sixteen-thousand people died on the crossing made by fifteen ships. Until this time, loss of life was minimal.

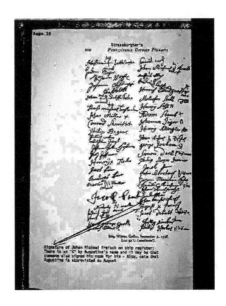

There were at least 360 passengers on the Winter Galley, however, Captain Paynter only claimed 252. These 252 were probably the adult men who had to take an oath of Fidelity and Abjuration to the King, and paid a twenty shilling fee.

It must have been bad back in Germany, for someone to give up everything and sail away into the unknown. It must have been something they felt they had to do to survive. They would have to rely on their family, friends, intuition, creativity, resourcefulness, Mother Nature, and the belief that God was always with them to help guide them along the way.

By 1738, the Colonies had been settled by more than twenty-thousand Germans. The first and largest German community was Germantown, Pennsylvania. This was the starting off point for all Germans entering through the Port of Philadelphia. The German settlement philosophy was all about the family. They would take care of all the German immigrants as soon as they arrived until they could get on their feet and search for their own land to settle.

You might have noticed that all three grandfathers had the first name of Johan, which would later become John in America. Saint John was the Patron Saint of the Home and in Germany, it was customary to name all your sons John and distinguishing each one by their middle names. After some time in America, their English names had evolved to:

John Michael Price
John Phillip Sibold
John Phillip Harless

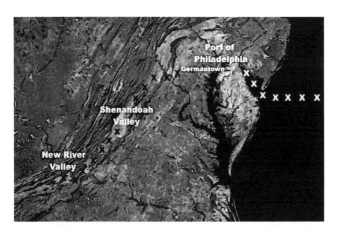

These German families had a unique balance of skill sets; they were young, strong, and had a thorough understanding of Mother Nature. They knew how to harness the Earths energy by building mills on creeks and farming rich fertile land to provide food and sustenance.

When they left Germantown, they continued west until they reached the 'Great Wagon Road' or as the Indians called it, the 'Great Valley Road.' It lay on the ancient Indian trail once known as the 'Great Warriors Path' and is now known as the 'I-81' Corridor. The furthermost German settlement at the time lay along this path and was located in the Shenandoah Valley of Virginia. This is as far west as the German community had ventured so far.

The first Europeans to settle in the Valley of Virginia was the German settlement led by Adam Miller (Muller) at Massanutten in 1726. In 1732, Joist Hite (Heydt) and other Germans, settled in the lower Shenandoah near Winchester and a little later another settlement of Germans was made at Peaked Mountain, not far from the town of Elkton on the Shenandoah River. Sixteen families from Pennsylvania made up this tiny colony. This became the western outpost for those who were looking for land they could call their own. These Germans were known for their 'untiring industry and love of rich lands.' It is said that these emigrants had no sooner heard of the fertility of the soil in the Shenandoah Valley, they began to spread themselves along that stream and its tributaries.

By 1736, the Germans were having legal difficulties with Lord Fairfax who had a large land survey covering much of the territory of Virginia and later West Virginia, as drained by the waters of the Potomac. This dispute was such as to make land titles insecure, especially for the German people. This led to the emigration of many Germans to southwest Virginia. Induced by the insecurity of titles in the lower Shenandoah, they crossed the Appalachians and started to build cabins in the New, Greenbrier, and the Kanawha River valleys around 1740. Michael Price and his group of Germans spent valuable time on Peaked Mountain researching everything they could on how to acquire land and where would the best places be to start looking. They were farmers, builders, and millers, who no doubt spent a couple of years fielding expeditions, exploring the wilderness, and looking for fertile farmland with fast creeks to run their grist mills. The Indians did not immediately object to the Pennsylvanians settling among them. For twenty years after the settlement in the Shenandoah Valley, the natives inhabiting the surrounding mountains and intervening valleys remained in comparative peacefulness.

There is no doubt in my mind that my ancestors were drawn by a higher power to the land that they would finally settle. The land that brought them here was as fertile as they had ever seen. It was sitting on a plateau valley of waist high grass next to a river flowing in the wrong direction, all nestled between beautiful mountains with numerous creeks, streams, and springs, running down from them. They knew God had guided them here safely, but now needed his protection more than ever.

The Price, Sibold, and Harless tribe started their settlement on the New River by 1740. It was in the deep wilderness and the vast unknown domain of Augusta County, and the furthest west anyone in the Colonies had attempted to settle permanently. Sometimes called 'West Augusta' Augusta County stretched from the top of the Appalachians westward to the Mississippi River, if not to the uttermost sea.

Before 1738, all that part of Virginia lying west of the Blue Ridge Mountains was included in the County of Orange, but in the fall of that year this territory was divided into the counties of Frederick and Augusta. Frederick County was becoming the next area in sight of the land operators and speculators, leaving Augusta to the brave and adventurous.

At this time, the area was a vast unexplored wilderness in which the people east of the Appalachians had very little knowledge. Immediately in and around this valley, about, or a little before the white people came, the Canawhay tribe of Indians occupied the valley and plateau now in Carroll and Floyd Counties. Some believe the Indians chose the name Canawhay from the names of the New and Kanawha Rivers.

Tradition tells us the first survey of the Horseshoe bottom area of the New River was made in the year 1738 and that the first owner was a Mr. Robinson who traded the same for a shotgun. There are other traditions that the Horseshoe was sold for a yoke of oxen, and at another time, for a horse, saddle, and bridle. It was clear that there were a number of owners for all, or part of the same, until it was finally owned by Jacob Harman.

Phillip Harless and Michael Price, both family and friends, acquired together a tract of land that was to be known as the Price and Harless Bottoms around the Horseshoe area of the New River. To get to this point, they had survived a very dangerous journey and now they had to start a settlement from scratch, in uncultivated terrain, on the edge of the frontier.

Michael Price and John Harless located their homesteads along Thoms Creek, nestled between the rolling countryside of the New River Valley plateau and the adjacent mountains of the Appalachians. They first had to build log cabins for cover and protection. For the first few years these early pioneers had to sleep on bear skin rugs on dirt floors in front of the fire place. Survival was of the utmost importance. Crops had to be planted and harvested, and game had to be hunted for their meat and fur. Furs were used for warmth, money, barter and trade.

This German colony became self sufficient over time, running a gristmill, tannery, and the production of gunpowder. Later, a stone fort was built around a spring on Michael Price's homestead so they would have protection from Indian attacks and a source of clean water. This fort was also used as a staging area for families to stay until they could find their own homestead somewhere in the area. This was only sustainable because they had found a balance between man, God, and nature.

The fort was also used as a staging area for the local militia during the French and Indian War and on through the Revolutionary War. The fort was strategically located near two major trade routes and Indian trails. One headed to southern Virginia and on to Tennessee and was called the Great Valley Road, and one south into North Carolina, called the Catawba and Northern Trail. There was another headed west toward the Ohio River Valley, by way of the New River, or the shortcut to Sinking Creek and across Clover Hollow called the New River and Southern Trail.

The Germans here were a godly people. They left the Palatinate area in Germany because of the religious persecution that tried to take away their spirit. All they wanted was to be able to worship as they so desired. Hence, before churches in the community could be built, the Price homestead was where the first members of three Protestant denominations worshiped. The denominations included the German Reformed (also known as German

Presbyterian), Lutheran and Methodist. They worshipped on rotating Sundays in a small log cabin on the property. The Germans seemed to have found a balance between their physical hardships and their faith.

This German settlement which centered around the Price homestead was very close knit. They traveled and settled closely next to each other. Somewhat what fish do when they swim in a tight proximity, as to enlarge their silhouette to scare off predators. The German New River Settlement banded together and settled the New River Valley from Stroubles Creek on up to Sinking Creek, with some Scotch-Irish scattered about.

The Price name is still used around this area, for example, Prices Fork, Price's Fork Road, and Price's Mountain. Michael Price's homestead was the nucleus of the settlement in which this community grew. Price's Fork became the community center and an outpost for expeditions heading south or west. No doubt Daniel Boone passed this way many times on his way to explore and settle 'The Great Valley Road.'

Other passengers on the Winter Galley that 5 of September, 1738, who also settled in the area were Adam Wall who developed the Wall bottoms of the New River, and Casper Barger, who settled the area with everyone else sometime after 1740.

~ ~ ~ ~ ~ ~

On August 26, 1738, ten days before the Winter Galley docked in Philadelphia, the 'Warpole' captained by James Patton, arrived in Belhaven near Alexandria, Virginia, on the Potomac River, with a human cargo of fifty-six passengers. It is believed that thirty of them were imported to settle a thirty-thousand acre tract, one-thousand acres each. This was part of a joint venture to obtain land from the Council of Virginia between James Patton and William Beverly.

James Patton brought with him on that trip, his wife and two daughters, John Preston and his wife Elizabeth Patton Preston (James Patton's sister), and their three daughters and son, William Preston, age nine. Others included John Buchanan and John Preston's sister, Mary Preston, who later married Phillip Barger. The Patton's and

Preston's settled next to Tinkling Springs in the southern part of Beverly Manor (near what is now Staunton, Virginia). Patton later built on the upper waters of the James River, two villages and two forts. One was called Pattonsburg and the other, Buchanan. These two villages remain to this day.

James Patton was born on July 8, 1692, in Newton, Limavaddy. The younger son of a ship builder and owner, not slated to inherit any of the Patton estates, went to sea when very young and became an Irish sea captain. It is said that Patton, a man of great stature at six feet two inches, took part in the War with France, called 'Queen Anne's War' which ended in 1713. He is described as a very impressive ship's master.

It is believed that James Patton became a ship captain for his father, but some would call him a privateer. He didn't enter the historical record until he was forty-five years old. It is believed that he made over twenty-five crossings to America, taking Scotch-Irish immigrants one way, and bringing tobacco back to Scotland the other. A little bit of smuggling was certainly not out of the question. It is also believed James Patton imported the first Arabian horse to the colonies.

The collaboration between William Beverly of Essex County and James Patton, the Scotch-Irish sea captain, was deemed of considerable significance for Virginia's westward movement and early settlement of the Shenandoah Valley. It took more than one-hundred years from the founding of Jamestown, for colonial Virginians to start exploiting the Shenandoah Valley. In the year 1716, an expedition party, history calls them 'The Knights of the Golden Horseshoe' traveled over the Blue Ridge Mountains. The party consisted of fifty people led by Governor Alexander Spotswood, Robert Beverly, including leading Virginians, rangers, and Meherrin Indians. They reached the Shenandoah River near present day Elkton in Rockingham County, where they celebrated and toasted King George I and his family's health with several 'sorts of liquors.'

It is not known If Robert Beverley's only son William Beverly (1696-1756) was on that expedition, however, we do know he became a prominent figure in the settling of the Shenandoah Valley two decades later. As his father's only child, William Beverly received a huge inheritance. He married Elizabeth Bland in 1725 and moved to a plantation he called Blandfield in honor of his wife. The plantation produced much of the tobacco that was shipped directly from its own wharves across the Atlantic.

By 1722, the settlement of Virginia's western frontier regions had become a matter of colonial policy. It was a somewhat improbable colonial policy that encouraged valley settlement by Scotch-Irish, German, and other non-English immigrants who were very unlike the English derived population long established in eastern Virginia. These settlers practiced different faiths, rarely held slaves, and did not raise tobacco.

It appears that the frontier settlements were used as buffers serving British Imperial policy that would check French expansion, extend English dominion, secure the region destabilized by Indian conflict and occupy mountainous terrain that provided refuge for runaway slaves and indentured servants. But, for the Germans and Scotch-Irish, it was a godsend and an opportunity they could not refuse.

William Beverly was a Virginia oligarch and a member of the Virginia elite. He received his first land grant in 1732. It was part of the 385,000 acres of the Shenandoah Valley controlled by Governor William Gooch. To ensure the desired settlement, grantees were required by Governor Gooch to place one family on every thousand acres of their grant. By 1735, Virginia had issued eighty-seven land grants and about 160 families had settled the region reaching fifty miles southwest down the valley from the Potomac River.

As his father before him, William Beverly was a Virginia aristocrat. He generated his wealth from his land holdings and plantations. In 1745, a partial inventory of his estate listed 119 tenants in five different counties and sixty-one slaves at four different plantations. Ships trading through Blandfield carried tobacco, slaves, sugar, rum, corn, and other goods.

He was politically based out of Essex County where he served in the lucrative position of Clerk. Beverly represented Orange County in the House of Burgesses

(1736-1740) and Essex County (1742-1749). The Beverly Manor grant of 118,491 acres, about fourteen square miles, centered where Staunton stands today and was conveyed in 1736.

Unlike William Beverly, James Patton didn't hit the historical record until he was forty-five years old. That record came in the way of two letters sent to James Patton from William Beverly in 1737. The letters imply that the two men had a long standing and close relationship. The first letter, written on August 8, 1737, that Beverly sent Patton, as requested by him a copy of the order of the Virginia Council granting Beverly western land. Beverly told Patton 'I should be very glad if you could import families enough to take the whole off from our hands at a reasonable price and although the order mentions families from Pennsylvania, yet families from Ireland will do as well.' On August 22, Beverly added in a second letter that the grant was for thirty-thousand acres of land and offering Patton one-quarter of it in exchange for Patton exerting his 'utmost endeavor to procure families to come in and settle it.' In the second letter, Beverly also wrote, 'I heartily wish you success and safe return to us.' James Patton took him up on his offer and brought his family to America on August 26, 1738. In that same year, 1738, Thomas Jefferson and George Washington were primary-school aged, and the Revolutionary War was still almost four decades in the future.

Chapter 4 Retribution

Colonel James Patton

After the organization of Augusta County, James Patton became a land speculator and operator. He also became County Lieutenant, Commander of the Virginia Militia, President of the Augusta Court, President of the Augusta Vestry, Commissioner of the Tinkling Spring congregation, County Coroner, County Escheator, Customs Collector, County Sheriff, member of the House of Burgesses, County Surveyor, and Colonel in the Augusta Militia.

James Patton made his last Atlantic voyage in 1740. He then proceeded to settle in the Shenandoah Valley and started managing his lucrative and vast land holdings and grants. The western Virginia frontier court system, like every colonial American court system, favored the interest and voices of the powerful and affluent over those of ordinary inhabitants. In colonial Augusta County, Virginia, no one was more powerful than the real estate speculators who both promoted and controlled initial settlement.

Throughout the eighteenth century, the social and economic elite, carefully managed access to land on the Virginia frontier. They were trying to replicate essential pieces of the social structure which they had become accustomed to in Tidewater, Virginia. Acquiring clear title to a piece of frontier Virginia usually required a cooperative deferential stance, not just the price paid for the land.

As newcomers quickly learned, claiming and occupying land was not the same as owning it. In western Virginia, the process of transforming land into private property or real estate began with an authorization to survey. Individuals could obtain such authorizations, known as warrants or entries, directly from the county surveyor if the tract encompassed no more than four hundred acres. Larger tracts required a grant from the Virginia Council, which took direction from the Crown.

Regardless of the form of authorization, the next step toward ownership was a survey, which produced a literal marking of the tract's borders, as well as a scaled drawing, or plat, depicting the specific parcel of land. Prospective landowners would then file the plat with the colonial government and eventually receive a freehold patent. Only then, were they liable for taxes, known as quitrents, on the land. This process took anywhere from two years up to a generation. Delays were normal as settlers took their time in securing a patent, holding off the payment of quitrents. The survey represented a significant but still incomplete, or provisional claim on a specific piece of land. Colonial Virginians would buy and sell grants, entries, and surveys, but such transactions conveyed only a claim, not an actual parcel of land. To own land was to own a patented freehold, everything else was an assertion.

Most large grants in early Augusta County remained abstractions, rather than defined real estate, gray areas of imperfect claims in which elite speculators enjoyed de facto ownership without the formality of a patent. These masters of this shadow land exercised the rights of ownership, but without holding clear title. They traded in surveys, buying and selling provisional claims on land that was not yet liable for quitrents. Colonial Virginia's grants to speculators thus conveyed not ownership, but official permission to create a market in individual claims that eventually could transform land into property. Of course, the original inhabitants of the land, the American Indian, had absolutely no say in the matter.

In 1740, the Virginia Council awarded one of these permissions to five speculators, one hundred thousand acres, lying 'on the river and branches of the Roanoke and the branches of the James River.' The Council revised and reissued the award in the spring of 1745, to include the New River Valley west. The five speculators made a sixth partner of Augusta County's senior magistrate, and senior militia officer, Colonel James Patton, empowering him 'as agent to survey, settle, and sell the land, and do all and every other act or acts, thing or things, for the interest of the company about the premises.'

These James, Roanoke, and New River Valley grants were never surveyed as a single tract, nor was it patented as a single piece of real estate. Instead, under Colonel Patton's supervision, the grant was converted piecemeal into property. Governor Francis Fauquier described this Patton partnership; 'Colonel Patton did not immediately make surveys of the said lands and mark out his bounds, but waited till some persons made choice of particular spots of rich land and were willing to purchase them from him; then these spots were surveyed, the rules of government complied with and patents taken out, to make a title to the purchasers.' Some surveys adjoined existing patents, while in other places lay surrounded by vast stretches of unclaimed land.

My German grandfathers eventually settled with James Patton's estate for the patent of their land surrounding Price's Fork and the Horseshoe bottoms on the New River, that they had lived on for over fifteen years. The original mill site survey issued to John Michael Price (My first generation grandfather) for my property in Clover Hollow, was most likely first executed by Colonel James Patton or his nephew William Preston.

William Preston

Born on Christmas Day, 1729, in Newtown-Limavady, Ireland, William Preston arrived in America on the ship Walpole, captained by his uncle, James Patton, on August 26, 1738, just a few days before the Winter Galley landed in Philadelphia containing my three, first generation grandfathers. William, at age nine, came over with his family, including his mother and father; John Preston and James Patton's sister, Elizabeth Patton. James Patton had encouraged John Preston to accompany him to America by securing him four thousand acres of land.

John Preston died seven years later in 1745 when William was sixteen years old. At this time, he was placed with the pastor of Tinkling Spring's congregation, by James Patton, to educate him until he turned eighteen. He was instructed by Reverend John Craig in history, mathematics, and penmanship. Because Patton directed Augusta County surveys for his land grants, and served as Colonel of the Augusta County Militia, County Sheriff, Collector of Revenues, Burgess, and general leader of county affairs, he was well positioned to make William Preston his secretary and surveyor of his land grants, and then to secure Preston's appointment as deputy surveyor for Augusta County in 1752, and as justice of the Augusta County Court in March 1755. William Preston also became the first surveyor in Montgomery County. By 1748, eighteen year old William Preston was Colonel James Patton's right hand man and nephew.

William accompanied Patton to Pennsylvania in 1752 to help negotiate the 'Treaty of Logstown' with the Iroquois, Delaware, Shawnee, and Wyandot Indians, in which Virginia asserted claims to lands south of the Ohio River. It is said that Colonel James Patton was considered very condescending towards the attending Indian chiefs and they felt forced to sign the treaty.

George Washington

George Washington was born February 22, 1732, at Popes Creek Plantation in Westmoreland County, Virginia. When his father died in 1743, eleven year old George and his mother inherited the small Ferry Farm on the Rappahannock River and his older half brother, Lawrence Washington, inherited the larger farm on the Potomac River and named it Mount Vernon. As George grew older he had little use for the meager prospects at Ferry Farm, so he concentrated his studies on geometry and surveying, using a set of surveyor's instruments from the storehouse at Ferry Farm.

At the age of sixteen, in early 1748, with as few as three practice surveys under his belt, George Washington accompanied George William Fairfax and James Genn, Surveyor of Prince William County, on a month-long trip

west across the Blue Ridge Mountains to survey land for Lord Fairfax. The trip was Washington's formal initiation that led him to pursue surveying as a profession. The trip also started a lifelong relationship between Washington and the powerful and influential Fairfax family that gave the young surveyor access to the upper echelons of Virginia society.

In the Northern Neck of Virginia, the vast region between the Rappahannock and Potomac rivers, land matters were governed by the proprietor, Lord Fairfax, and his Virginia representative and first cousin, William Fairfax. Prospective settlers in the Northern Neck were required to obtain a survey warrant from the Northern Neck Proprietor Office for a set amount of acreage in a specific location. The survey warrant issued directly to the county surveyor, instructed the surveyor to make a 'just and true' survey of the land, officially determining and limiting its boundaries.

Because they were responsible for laying out the land claims, surveyors had a unique role in Virginia Society. Their appointments guaranteed a certain social prominence since nearly all parties interested in gaining title to an area of land were required to deal with the surveyor. Surveyors were also among the best educated Virginians and were often in the best position to buy land for themselves. It was not unusual for surveyors to acquire large estates from the many opportunities that they had to patent in their own names. Additionally, their intimate knowledge of the land and official capacity as representatives of large land holders such as Lord Fairfax and William Beverly, made participation politically and practically essential to large land companies such as the Royal Land Company of Virginia, the Ohio Company, and the Mississippi Land Company.

In July, 1749, at seventeen years old and largely with the help from Lord Fairfax, George Washington secured an appointment as county surveyor for the newly created frontier county of Culpepper where he served until 1752. During his three years on the frontier, including extensive work in Frederick County, he established a reputation for fairness, honesty, and dependability, while earning a very decent living. Surveyors could earn an annual cash income that was exceeded only by the colony's finest trial lawyers. His extensive experience in the most western counties of the Northern Neck, created the opportunity to meet James Patton and William Preston, three years his senior, for the first time, in and around 1752.

It was the backcountry knowledge and map making skills he had gained from surveying that created Washington's decisive involvement in the French and Indian War in which he served as lieutenant colonel of the newly formed Virginia Regiment in 1753, one year before Lieutenant Governor Dinwiddie called for additional troops under Washington's command to defend Virginia's Ohio Valley frontier. Washington was chosen to deliver an ultimatum to the French Fort at 'Fort Le Boeuf' (present day Waterford, Pennsylvania) insisting they withdrawal from the valley. When his report on this mission 'The Journal of Major George Washington' was printed in Williamsburg and then reprinted in London, catapulted him onto the world stage. Washington's report dramatically illustrated the French threat in the Ohio Valley and contained one of the first references to the construction of a strategic French fort at the junction of the Monongahela and Allegheny Rivers, the site of present day Pittsburgh.

By the start of the 1750s, three powerful groups were competing for the lands of the Ohio Valley; the British and the British colonist in America, the French and the French colonist in Canada, and the Indians inhabiting the Ohio Valley. The British claimed the land as part of their Atlantic colonies. The western boundary of Virginia, under its royal charter of 1609, extended at least as far as the Wabash River and maybe as far as the Pacific. Pennsylvania's western boundary was ill defined and in the late 1740s and early 1750s; Pennsylvanians were extending their reach of their fur and skin trade with the Indians as far west as the Wabash River. The British interests in the Ohio Valley were not entirely uniform. Virginia and Pennsylvania had conflicting claims to land there, traders from each colony wanted as much of the fur trade as possible and Britain itself claimed ownership.

The French, competing with the British for control of North America since the late 1600s, laid claim to the Ohio Valley based on the explorations of their own pioneers, Rene-Robert Cavelier, and later Pierre-Joseph Celoron de Blainville, who left a series of metal plates up and down the Mississippi River claiming the land for France. The French wanted the fur trade in the Ohio Valley and were worried that the British westward expansion could sever trade between French Canada and French Louisiana.

The Indians in the Ohio Valley, including the Shawnee, Mingo, Miami, Delaware, and Cherokee, believed they should be able to hunt and farm there. Especially the Shawnee and the Delaware Indian tribes, who had been driven the past few decades from their ancestral lands by the pressure of British settlement first into western Pennsylvania and then into the Ohio Valley, and were very wary of British intentions to occupy their land in the Ohio Valley. The Shawnee, who had seen the onslaught of the British settlers in western Pennsylvania, are quoted as saying at the time 'where one of those people settled, like pigeons, a thousand more would settle' and after being forced into the Ohio Valley, had seen the British give land there 'to a parcel of covetous gentleman of Virginia called the Ohio Company.' They go on 'they offer to build forts among us, no doubt to make themselves master of our lands and make slaves of us.'

Delaware leaders, talking to the British, asked pointedly their 'desire to know where the Indians land lay' for that the French claimed all the land on one side of the river Ohio, and the English the other side. Other Ohio Indians exclaimed the fear 'ye Virginians and ye French intend to divide the land of Ohio between themselves.' This is a disastrous chain of events that spells doom for the very existence of the American Indian.

These clashing claims moved from all talk to actual confrontation in the 1750s as the British vied for control of the lucrative fur trade with the Ohio Valley Indians and as British colonist kept moving west, driven by the desire for cheap land. Between 1745 and 1754, the Council of Virginia issued land grants for more than two million acres in the Ohio Valley. The Ohio Company, a group of British investors that included George Washington and his half-brother Lawrence Washington, along with Virginia governor Robert Dinwiddie, in 1749, received a royal grant of a half-million acres of land west of the Alleghenies. In 1750-51, the Ohio Company sent Christopher Gist down the Ohio River to explore ways through the mountains and by the early 1750s, traders and settlers from the Ohio Company began moving into what is now western Pennsylvania. This aroused resentment on the part of the traders from Pennsylvania who had controlled trade with the Indians in much of the valley before the French expanded their presence there and the Ohio Company sent in settlers.

To bolster their own claims to the Ohio Valley and its fur trade, the French stirred up western Indians to attack Ohio Valley Indians who began to trade with the British traders instead of the French traders. Maybe one of the first acts of terrorism conceived by a foreign power in North America happened in 1752. The Ojibwas, Ottawas, and Potawatomis, under the control of the French, attacked the Miami village of Pickawillany in what is now western Ohio, killed one English trader and ate his heart, then killed, dismembered, and ate the village chief, who had broken away from an alliance with the French and was trading with the British. The Miamis in the village sensibly decided to resume trading with the French. It looked like guerrilla warfare and terrorism would be the tools of choice for the French.

By 1753, the French were building a series of forts west of the Alleghenies including Fort Presque Isle at what is now Erie, Pennsylvania, and Fort Le Boeuf, at what is now Waterford, inland from Erie. Alarmed by all this French fort building and military presence in the Ohio Valley, the Iroquois and other tribes who like to trade with the British, asked Pennsylvania and Virginia to protect them and build a fort where the Allegheny and Monongahela rivers join to form the Ohio River. This was a strategic location that was to become the site where Pittsburgh stands today. When the British colonies took their time, the Ohio Company in 1753 began on its own to build a fortified trading post there. Not until 1754 did Virginia send a few dozen militiamen to help build the fort.

The American east coast Indians had seen their numbers plummet from the ravages of European diseases, such as smallpox and measles, which caused Indian populations to drop twenty-five to ninety-five percent in the last two centuries. The Ohio Valley Indians had lost most of their lands to the east through treaties and through wars with the Iroquois and with the whites. They looked at both the French and the British as invaders seeking to dispossess them from their traditional and ancestral lands.

As the secretary to the Indians for the government of New York said, the Iroquois and their allies, or 'at least the politicians amongst them, look upon the present disputes between the English and French as a point of selfish ambition in us both and are apprehensive that whichever nation gains their point will become their masters, not their deliverers. They dread the success of either and their ablest politicians would very probably rather wish us to continue destroying each other than that either could be absolute conquerors.' One Indian leader after having something to drink asked the emissary from Pennsylvania who was trying to win the Indians over to the British side, 'why do not you and the French fight on the sea? You come only to cheat the poor Indians, and take their land from them.'

The Indians were starting to realize that they were inconsequential and meant nothing to the ambitions of Britain and France. The Indians were seen as uncivilized backwoods naked savages that were a lower form of human life, unworthy of any respect or ownership. Benjamin Franklin wrote in his autobiography in the 1750s 'If it be the design of providence to extirpate these savages to make room for cultivators of the earth, it seems not improbable that rum may be the appointed means.' The attitude Britain and their colonist had toward the Indians was the pervasive belief in British cultural and racial superiority. American Indians had long been perceived as inferior and efforts to 'civilize' them had been widespread since the days of John Smith and Miles Standish. This belief system was the predecessor to the American Manifest Destiny and the 'Trail of Tears' in the 1800s. This also spelled doom for the North American Indian.

Most of the Indians in the Ohio Valley saw the British as a greater threat than the French. The French tended to trap and trade for furs, but the British settlers, who were starting to survey land in what is now Tennessee and Kentucky, looked like incipient farmers, not just fur traders. Farming meant permanent and exclusive possession of the land and the ending of hunting and trapping by the Indians. Moreover, there were far more British than French in North America, around 1.6 million British to perhaps seventy-five thousand French. One Delaware explained the Indian's decision to join with the French against the British by saying that the Indians needed French aid to defeat the British who coveted their land because the British were 'such a numerous people' but, 'we can drive out the French when we please.' The French and Indians were now aligned with each other and they began to formulate their guerrilla war against the British and the colonies.

In March 1754, responding to the defiant French, Britain ordered the newly promoted Lt. Col. George Washington and approximately one-hundred and sixty Virginia militia to return to the Ohio country. Governor Dinwiddie wanted Washington to 'act on the defensive' but also clearly empowered Washington to 'make prisoners of or kill and destroy' all those who resisted British control of the region.

Eager to send their own diplomatic directive demanding an English withdrawal from the region, a French force of thirty-five soldiers commanded by Ensign Joseph Coulon de Villiers de Jumonville camped in a rocky ravine not far from Washington's encampment at Great Meadows (now in Fayette County) Pennsylvania. Washington was accompanied by Tanacharison, a Seneca chief (also known as the Half-King) twelve native warriors, and a party of forty militiamen on an all night march towards the French position. On May 28, 1754, Washington's party stealthily approached the French camp at dawn. Finally spotted at close range by the French, shots rang out and a vigorous firefight erupted in the wooded wilderness. Washington's forces quickly overwhelmed the surprised French force and killed thirteen soldiers and captured another twenty-one. Washington later wrote of his first military engagement with a certain amount of martial enthusiasm: 'I fortunately escaped without any wound, for the right wing, where I stood, was exposed to and received the entire enemy's fire and it was the part where the man was killed and the rest wounded. I heard the bullets whistle, and believe me, there is something charming in the sound.' Both sides claimed that the other fired first, but what neither side disputed was that this event deep in the American wilderness helped spark a war that would ultimately spread to places as far away as Europe, Africa, and India.

After learning of the attack at Jumonville Glen, Claude-Pierre Pecaudy de Contrecoeur, the veteran French commander at Fort Duquesne, ordered Captain Louis Coulon de Villiers, Ensign Jumonville's brother, to assail Washington and his force near Great Meadows. De Villiers left Fort Duquesne with nearly six-hundred French soldiers and Canadian militiamen, accompanied by one-hundred native allies.

Aware of the onset of a powerful French column, Washington busily fortified his position at Great Meadows. Despite receiving additional reinforcements, Washington's bedraggled force of around four-hundred men remained outnumbered by the approaching French. Even more concerning, the small circular wooden fort named Fort Necessity, built in the center of the meadow was poorly situated and vulnerable to fire from the nearby wooded hills that circled the position.

On July 1, 1754, the large combined French and native forces reached Great Meadows. Washington gathered his

troops and retreated into Fort Necessity, where on a rainy July 3, the French began firing on the surrounded English. Sensing the hopelessness of his situation, Washington agreed to surrender to the French. The surrender terms, written in French, poorly translated, and soaking wet, allowed Washington and his troops to return to Virginia in peace. But one clause in the document had Washington admitting that he had 'assassinated' Ensign Jumonville, something that Washington hotly contested despite his signature on the document. The Battle of Great Meadows proved to be the only time that George Washington surrendered to an enemy in battle.

The young ambitious George Washington was keenly aware that his Virginia militia rank was looked down upon by those in the British military. British regular officers, with their royal commissions, regularly dismissed provincial militia officers and sought to have even their most junior officers placed above more senior ranking militia officers. During the 1755 Braddock expedition, Washington became an unpaid, volunteer aide-de-camp to Braddock, rather than assume his militia rank and be subjected to the embarrassment of being subordinate to junior officers. Washington's interest in obtaining a royal commission became so strong that he traveled to Boston to meet with Governor William Shirley who was the acting Commander in Chief after Gen. Braddock's death. Washington was unsuccessful in obtaining a royal commission, but Shirley did issue a decree that officers in the Virginia militia would outrank British officers of lower rank.

Determined to drive the French from the Ohio Valley in February 1755, the British sent two regiments of regulars to America under Maj. Gen. Edward Braddock with the mission of capturing a series of French forts; Duquesne, Niagara, and then Frontenac in Canada. Braddock had the benefit and detriment of thirty-five years of fighting in Europe. Benjamin Franklin, helping to provide wagons and other supplies for Braddock's army on its March westward in Pennsylvania, warned Braddock that the army in its long line of march was in danger of 'ambuscades of Indians, who by constant practice, are dexterous in laying and executing them.' According to Franklin, Braddock 'smiled at my ignorance' and replied, 'these savages may indeed be a formidable enemy to your raw American militia, but, upon the King's regular and disciplined troops, sir, it is impossible they should make any impression.'

Braddock declined the assistance of Indian scouts. The Delaware chief Shingas and representatives of the Shawnee and Mingos offered to help Braddock if he would assure them that if the British won, the friendly Indians would at least 'be permitted to live and trade among the English and have hunting grounds sufficient to support themselves and families.' Braddock replied bluntly 'no savage should inherit the land.' The Delawares left and Braddock yelled after them that 'he did not need their help and had no doubt of driving the French and Indians away.' Shingas and other Delawares ended up joining the Shawnee in attacking white settlements in the western frontier country and Braddock's army ended up with only eight Indian scouts. According to one Delaware chief 'a great many of our warriors left him and would not be under his command because he looked upon us as dogs and would never hear anything what was said to him, we often endeavored to advise him and to tell him of the dangers he was in with his soldiers, but he never appeared pleased with us.'

Braddock's army headed out from Frederick, Maryland, toward western Pennsylvania in mid-May 1755. The pace was painfully slow. George Washington, serving as aid-de-camp to General Braddock, wrote to his brother that the army was 'halting to level every mole hill and erecting bridges over every brook.' Indians would often scalp stragglers and outliers from the army, which made it abundantly clear that the Indians and the French knew exactly where Braddock's men were at all times. The Indians pinned the scalps to trees and left the mutilated bodies where they would be seen by Braddock's troops as a form of psychological warfare. A Delaware Indian working with the French told a young American captive that the Indians spied on Braddock's army every day and intended to surround it, take shelter behind trees, and 'shoot um down all one pigeon.' The British, by contrast, had very few scouts ranging in front and alongside of their army.

On July 9, 1755, several hundred French and Indians, many more Indians than French, confronted in a clearing not far from Fort Duquesne, Braddock's advance party of 1,300 men which had just crossed the Monongahela. The French and Indians fanned out in the woods around the clearing flanking Braddock's troops and started firing on them from behind the trees. The American militia immediately headed for the nearest trees as they were familiar with frontier-style fighting, firing individually, behind the protection of the tree trunks. The British regulars stayed put for a while in the clearing under unrelenting crossfire. The American militiamen were shot both by the British regulars firing from the clearing and by the French and Indians firing from the woods. General Braddock, riding up to the clearing, was shot through the arm and chest.

The British, confronted with 'a manner of fighting they were very unacquainted with,' broke ranks and ran back to the Monongahela and through the supply wagons in the army's rear. Many of the troops 'threw away their arms and ammunition, and even their clothes, to escape the faster.' The wagoners in turn came under heavy fire from the French and Indians in the woods. Soon, the wagoners who were still standing, Daniel Boone among them, cut horses lose from the wagons and rode off. More of the American wagoners would have been killed if the Indians had not paused to loot the supplies from the wagons and to scalp the wounded.

With panic in the air, George Washington quickly rode into the fray and helped to reestablish some amount of order. During the ferocious fight, Washington had two horses shot out from underneath him and his coat was pierced by four musket balls. Washington's steady leadership helped many of the surviving soldiers to effectively escape the onslaught. Despite the British loss of 977 killed or wounded, Washington was lauded as the 'hero of Monongahela' by Virginia Governor Robert Dinwiddie and was given the rank of Colonel in command of the 1,200 man Virginia Regiment.

The fleeing British soldiers and American colonist could hear behind them the screams of the wounded being scalped. Twelve men taken captive by the Indians were led back to Fort Duquesne, had their faces painted black, tied naked to stakes on the banks of the Allegheny near the fort and were slowly tortured to death with red-hot irons and lighted pine splinters stuck in their bodies while the Indians danced around them.

The French and Indians reported twenty-three killed and sixteen wounded. Braddock died of his wounds three days after the battle. Washington buried him in the middle of the road and ran wagons over the site to hide the grave so that the Indians would not scalp and maim Braddock's body. Twenty years later, a British visitor to the site of the battle, reported in his journal: 'Found great numbers of bones, both men and horses...we could not find one whole skull, all of them broke to pieces in the upper part, some of them had holes broke in them about an inch diameter, suppose it to be done with a pipe tomahawk.'

These recent battles provided George Washington with many important experiences that helped shape him as a future founding father. As a young, ambitious twenty-one year old, Washington had been exposed to the realities of life at the edges of British North America and had been asked to lead and negotiate with experienced native and French commanders. As part of Braddock's command, Washington took the opportunity to read military manuals, treaties, and military histories. He practiced the art of creating clear and effective orders by transcribing orders issued by more experienced British officers around him. In more practical military terms, Washington's French and Indian War experience taught the young officer much about how to organize supplies, how to dispense military justice, how to command, how to build forts, how to manage subordinates, and how to defeat the British.

The Assassination of Colonel James Patton

On Sunday, July 8, 1755, one day before 'Braddock's Defeat' on the Monongahela, and on Colonel Patton's sixty-third birthday, twenty Shawnee warriors attacked a small cluster of cabins called Drapers Meadow and either kidnapped or killed everyone there that day.

The original 7,500 acre tract that became known as Draper's Meadow was granted sometime before 1747 by Governor Robert Dinwiddie to Colonel James Patton, the Irish sea-captain turned land speculator. This land was

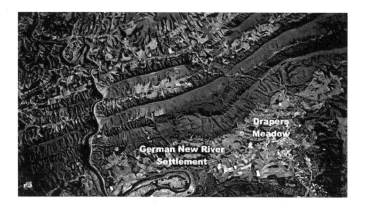

bordered by Tom's Creek on the north, Stroubles Creek on the south, and the Mississippi watershed (modern-day U.S. Route 460) on the east, and it approached the New River on the west. The settlement was situated near the present day campus of Virginia Tech in Blacksburg, Virginia on one side and next to the German New River Settlement on the other. Drapers Meadow was located about seven miles down the Indian trail from the property I now own.

Drapers Meadow was situated adjacent to the New River German Settlement which included Michael Price's fort and homestead. Drapers Meadow was mostly settled by the Scotch-Irish brought in from Pattonsburg, Virginia, by James Patton around 1748. These families included the Ingles and the Drapers who had previously settled on the James River. The Draper family originally consisted of George Draper, his wife, and two children, John and Mary. While living in Pattonsburg, George Draper went out hunting one day and was never seen again. The family then picked up stakes at the urging of Patton and along with the Ingles, Henry Leonard, the Lybrook's, Harman's and others, settled near the present-day town of Blacksburg. Casper Barger, one of the original Germans who came over on the Winter Galley in 1738 bought four-hundred acres beside the William Ingles tract. The Drapers and Ingles built their cabins closely together for protection but never had much trouble until that hot summer day in July.

William Ingles and Mary Draper were married in 1750, John Draper and Bettie Robertson in 1754. These were some of the first recorded marriages west of the Blue Ridge

Mountains. In 1755, word of Indian uprisings up north was known but Drapers Meadow seemed so far away from there at the time. The only problems the Scotch-Irish or the Germans had with the Indians were that the Indians would sometimes help themselves to food, supplies, and even furs. The Indians did not look on this as stealing, but thought they had the right to these things because they came from their sacred hunting grounds. The German settlers did not seem to mind too much if it kept the peace and they got along well with the peaceful Cherokee to the south.

In July 1755, Colonel Patton went to Draper's Meadow on business and was accompanied by his nephew, William Preston. Patton was resting from the fatigue of his journey, and was also recovering from sickness at the home of William Ingles and the Drapers. The most pressing business at the time for this settlement was to harvest the fields. They were very dependent on the crops that they could produce and on Sunday, July 8, 1755, most of the men at the settlement headed off early to the fields, unarmed, with no immediate sense of danger in the air.

That morning, Colonel Patton sent his nephew William Preston, to go fetch Phillip Lybrook up on Sinking Creek to help with the harvest. This would place young William Preston directly on my property in Clover Hollow. Early that summer morning, Colonel Patton sat down at a table to write a letter, some believe a letter to George Washington updating the security situation in the valleys of western Virginia. The first sound of alarm came from the direction of the garden when he heard John Draper's wife, Betty, scream in terror. She rushed into the house loaded with fear to warn that Indians were near. She quickly grabbed her sleeping baby and fled through a side door. A bullet from an Indian gun shattered her right arm, but still grasping the baby in her left hand, she continued to run. Her baby was then seized by the Indians and cruelly killed on the spot by bashing his head into a log.

When Mary Ingles, husband of William Ingles, rushed into the house with her two children, George and Thomas, followed by the Indians, Colonel Patton seized his broadsword from a nearby table and forcibly placed himself in front of the defenseless women and children.

It is said, that six foot two inch Patton nearly sliced in two the first two warriors that rushed through the door before a musket ball caught him in the temple. The women and children, now defenseless, were made captives. The warriors quickly grabbed everything of value they could carry on horses and set fire to all the cabins before they left with their captives.

Killed were Colonel James Patton - shot and probably scalped. Casper Barger - scalped, Betty Draper's baby-head bashed against a log, and Eleanor Draper - stabbed and scalped. The men in the fields had to restrain William Ingles from running unarmed back into the fray to come to the aid of his family. Captured were Mary Ingles and her two sons, George and Thomas, Betty Draper and Henry Leonard.

The Indians quickly made their retreat by taking the Sinking Creek trail back towards the New River as they made their way back to the Ohio River Valley. This places the Indians and their captives also on my property that fateful day. Escaping from Drapers Meadow, they stopped at Phillip Barger's cabin, brother of Casper Barger, and when he came outside to see what was going on, the Indians proceeded to cut off his head with Colonel Patton's broadsword and placed it in a burlap sack. The story goes that when they got to Phillip Lybrooks cabin at the mouth of Sinking Creek, they presented the sack with Barger's head to Mrs. Lybrook. The Indians mentioned to Mrs. Lybrook that she might recognize the contents of the sack. Mrs. Lybrook was sure it was her husband's head as the Indians would have had to run right into William Preston and her husband Phillip Lybrook who were on their way back to Drapers Meadow. Both the Indians and their captives, plus William Preston and Phillip Lybrook, must have crossed my property on Sinking Creek that day.

If these events are true, it spotlights my particular and specific piece of land deep in the Appalachian Mountains. The property lies directly on top of the entrance to the ancient Sinking Creek Indian trail which is only one of two mountain passages west through the Appalachian Mountains anywhere around the area. The Sinking Creek trail is a branch off the 'Great Indian War Path' that travels past Drapers Meadow, and the German settlements in the New River Valley.

This site, very early on, was picked out by my first-generation grandfather, Michael Price, for a future mill site. He would arrange before his death for his oldest son, David Price, to become owner of the mill site survey. Without a doubt, Michael Price must have recognized the strategic importance of this little spot. Only God could have created something so beautiful and brought him here to paradise he must have thought.

It has been determined that William Preston crossed over my property that morning on his way to fetch Phillip Lybrook who lived downstream on Sinking Creek. On the way back to Drapers Meadow, the two young men decided to take a shortcut directly over the mountain, thus missing the Shawnee warriors escaping with their hostages. The other visitors to cross over my yard that day were the Shawnee Indian war party as they made their escape with their captives and the sack that held the head of Phillip Barger. The only piece of the original Sinking Creek Trail that is left today is about ten yards from my front porch.

Most people think of the Drapers Meadow Massacre as a random act of violence, perpetrated by a group of uncivilized naked savages. However, I have seen evidence that suggest this was a pre-planned secret mission to assassinate Colonel Patton and scare the white settlers out of the New River Valley.

As the turmoil between the British and the French and Indians heated up, the focus of battle seemed to be contained within Braddock's army and their attempt to conquer the French forts. The British were going to do it the British way, with brute force, overwhelming numbers, marching in the open in clusters and firing in unison. It always worked before. The French and especially the Indians were very skilled in guerrilla warfare; the Indians even had developed a sophisticated and extensive spy network with many scouts to transfer communications relatively quickly.

Records show that the Shawnee targeted Colonel Patton soon after the 'Treaty of Logstown' was signed in 1752, in which Patton was one of the commissioners who negotiated with the Iroquois, Delaware, and Shawnee.

Patton was said to have distinguished himself to the Indians by the inept way in which he had spoken in the preliminaries to the Logstown treaty meeting. His request for a council was taken as a threat and the Indians were 'generally affronted.' By 1755, Patton owned 17,007 acres in his own name as well as being a Colonel in the Militia, a leading negotiator with the Indians and the Lieutenant of Augusta County. He was a good first target in the Indians strategy to kill British settlers and force them from their land.

When the Indians attacked that day they seemed to know that all the men were in the fields and James Patton was left unprotected with the women and children back in the small cluster of cabins. The Indians must have been surveilling the settlement from the mountains overlooking the valley for a number of days waiting for the right moment to attack. We know now that Colonel Patton had armed Drapers Meadow with a wagon load of ammunition and it was being stored in William Ingles cabin. This was some information that probably did not escape the Indians scout's attention. All the cabins were set afire afterward and the smoke could be seen for miles around. This could have been the ammunition that could not be carried away from the site by the Indian attackers. It also is noteworthy that the Indians did not attack the Germans that day, suggesting that Drapers Meadow was their sole target.

The attack on Drapers Meadow and the killing of Colonel Patton was a complete success and chased out most of the settlers in the New River Valley for almost twenty years, accept for some of the Germans including my grandfather, Michael Price.

Colonel Patton was buried near the Drapers Meadow settlement along with Eleanor Draper, Casper Barger, and the little Draper baby. Most of the settlers decided to pack up their belongings and pull back to Dunkard's Bottom where they were building a fort and where they could hunker down and formulate their next moves. This attack came as a total shock to everybody in the New River Valley and most decided to leave, except for a handful of Germans and their families. Luckily, Michael Price and his family were secure at Price's Fort.

It took four days for Captain John Buchanan, Colonel Patton's brother-in-law and Virginia militia member who lived upriver, to muster thirty armed horsemen to pursue the Shawnee kidnappers. William Ingles and his two sons, John and Matthew, with John Draper, led the mass rush back down Sinking Creek hoping to pick up the trail and rescue their family, pretty much hopeless since so much time had passed since the tragic event. But again, they would have to cross my property on Sinking Creek near the entrance to Clover Hollow.

Reluctantly they had to turn back after a few days when they permanently lost the Shawnee trail. With heavy hearts, William Ingles and John Draper would go back to Drapers Meadow, harvest as much as they could, and move back to Dunkard's Bottom. While there they would contact the Cherokee and see if they could arrange a ransom with the Shawnee in the Ohio River Valley to get their loved ones back if they were still alive.

Miraculously, twenty-five year old Mary Ingles escaped her captors after two and a half months and traveled hundreds of miles back across the Appalachians. The Indians and their captives had traveled for a month to Lower Shawneetown on the banks of the Scioto and Ohio Rivers. As a prisoner, Mary sewed shirts and due to her skill with medicinal herbs acted as a healer and a nurse. On two occasions, she was taken to the Big Bone salt lick to make salt for the Indians by boiling brine.

On the second trip to Big Bone Lick in late October, 1755, Mary persuaded another captive woman referred to as the 'old Dutch woman' who may actually have been German, to escape with her. The next day, probably October 19, they set off retracing the same route that the Indians had taken when they were abducted. They wore moccasins and carried with them only a tomahawk and a knife (both of which were eventually lost) and two blankets. As they were leaving the camp they met three French traders from Detroit who were harvesting walnuts and Mary traded her old dull tomahawk for a new one.

During their journey they crossed at least 145 creeks and rivers, remarkable in that neither woman could swim. On at least one occasion they 'tied logs together with a grapevine and made a raft to cross a major river' according to James Alexander Thom's 'Follow the River.' They may have traveled as much as five to six hundred miles, averaging between eleven and twenty-one miles a day.

Once the corn ran out they were able to subsist on black walnuts, wild grapes, pawpaws, sassafras leaves, blackberries and frogs, but as the weather grew cold they were forced to eat dead animals that they found along the way. By now the temperature had dropped, it was starting to snow and the two women were weak from starvation. Mary feared that the Old Dutch woman had become psychotic and would kill her in her sleep. So one night, Mary went off alone and finding a canoe, crossed the New River at its junction with the East River, near what is now Glen Lynn, Virginia. Mary continued southeast along the riverbank, passing through present-day Pembroke, Virginia and arrived at the home of her friend Adam Harmon on or about December 1, 1755, forty-two days after leaving Big Bone salt lick. The old Dutch woman was found shortly afterwards and Adam Harman took her to the fort at Dunkard's Bottom where she was able to join a party traveling to Pennsylvania by wagon.

After recovering from her journey and reuniting with her husband, Mary went on to have four more children; Mary, Susan, Rhoda, and John. In 1762, William and Mary established the Ingles Ferry across the New River, the Ingles Ferry Hill Tavern and a blacksmith shop, and she died there in 1815 at the age of eighty-three. The site of her log cabin with a stable and a family cemetery constitute part of the Ingles Bottom archeological sites.

Mary's son George died in Indian captivity, but Thomas was ransomed and returned to Virginia in 1768 at the age of seventeen. By then he had become fully assimilated and spoke only Shawnee. He underwent several years of rehabilitation and education under Dr. Thomas Walker at Castle Hill, Virginia. He later served as a lieutenant under Colonel William Christian in Lord Dunmore's War (1773-1774) against the Shawnee. He married Eleanor Grills in 1775 and settled in Burke's Garden, Virginia, where in 1782; his wife and three children were kidnapped by Indians who killed Eleanor and the two older children. The youngest daughter was rescued by her father.

In 1761, Mary Ingles' brother, John Draper, attended a gathering of Cherokee chiefs at which a treaty to end the Anglo-Cherokee War was prepared. He found a man who knew of his wife, Bettie Robertson Draper, who was then living with the family of a widowed Cherokee chief. She was ransomed and John took her back to the New River Valley.

Chapter 5 The Feud

Although quite bitter over his uncle's death, William Preston had acquired experience, maturity, and standing, and by 1755, after his uncle James Patton was killed, became a key leader in southwest Virginia. Through such offices as Vestry Clerk, and Assistant Surveyor, he began developing political leadership skills and important contacts for even greater influence. He also possessed a modest amount of land from inheritance and purchases which formed the basis for him to become a major landholder. As a recently appointed militia captain, he was also developing crucial military experience in fighting Indians, which would give him even greater status as a regional leader, although with some sense of revenge built into the mix.

During the next ten years through 1764, Preston experienced further maturation in all of these critical areas. He would receive appointment to additional offices, gain more land, marry, and begin a family, develop commercial contacts, and lead Augusta militiamen and rangers into important engagements with the Indians. During this period, he came out from under the shadow of his powerful uncle and matured into a leader and member of the elite in his own right.

The conflict between the French and English over who would control territory in the Ohio Valley, dominated the lives of Preston and his fellow colonists in southwestern Virginia as they sought to buy, develop, and sell lands on the frontier. Ultimately, the efforts of both sides to enlist Indian allies posed the greatest disruptions to the daily life of those families that settled on the frontier. This war, later known as the French and Indian War, the Seven Year's War, or the Great War for Empire, ultimately became part of a larger world war. But, for Preston's fellow settlers on the frontier in Augusta County, the war constituted a local struggle by families to stay on their frontier lands in safety, rather than a desire to help Great Britain add further territory or protect its empire. On the other hand, a few frontier leaders who worked as surveyors for the Ohio Company had a business stake in seeing that their land company's claims to lands in the Ohio territory be maintained in English hands. Even though Preston served as one of those surveyors, local motivations revolving around a desire to live in peace on the frontier represented his major motivation for taking a leadership role in the upcoming war.

What began as a very optimistic July in 1755 for Governor Dinwiddie with hopes for a quick British victory over the French, ended with an emergency call for a special session of the Virginia legislature to deal with the problems left as a result of Braddock's defeat and the growing threat of Indian attacks on the frontier. The withdrawal of British regular troops left Virginia's borders completely exposed to attack which created great dismay in Dinwiddie. The Governor's language in his opening address to the House of Burgesses on August 5 was clear: 'As the road from Fort Cumberland to the Ohio is now opened and our enemies possessed of great part of our artillery, y's colony is extremely laid open and exposed to the insults of a barbarous and inhuman enemy flushed and elated with their late success. This lays you, gentleman, under an indispensable necessity of doing ever that may conduce to dislodge those murderers and preserve our fellow subjects from the base and horrid butcheries, they have already given us so many exasperating specimens of, and are impatient to repeat the brutal savages who are lurking and prowling about our habitations to perpetrate the most cruel outrages have justly subjected themselves to be considered rather as devouring beasts of prey than hostile men.'

In Dinwiddie's view, Virginia faced a fight to preserve its religious and civil liberty. Within three days after giving this speech the undeclared war came even closer as the burgesses received word of the death by Indians of one of its own members, James Patton. Sometime during this session, William Preston also arrived in Williamsburg with direct news of his uncle's death.

These dramatic reports brought from the frontline by such individuals as Preston moved the legislature from its lethargy and it adopted four measures they thought would confront the grave threat faced in Augusta County. A poll and land tax would support money for 'raising, maintaining, arming, and providing' for twelve-hundred men to protect the frontier. As an incentive for joining the military, volunteers would receive a bonus and an exemption from most taxes. If not enough men could be raised from these incentives, the law also provided for a draft from the militia. However, a provision allowing a person to get out of military service by finding someone else to serve in his place or pay a fine somewhat weakened the law. Still, the law represented the strongest effort yet for raising an adequate military force to defend Virginia's frontier areas.

The law aided militia captains such as Preston, who faced major problems of discipline, by providing for a thorough accounting of all available men, better supplying of the militiamen, more regular musters, and stronger penalties for those who refused to cooperate. Further, another law provided for quick response to potential threats by allowing militia officers to call out their militia before notifying the county lieutenant upon the report of any invasion or insurrection.

To provide an even greater incentive for frontiersmen to look for Indians, they would receive a scalp fee for any Indian above the age of twelve, taken prisoner or killed. Of course, problems developed with this kind of incentive when whites killed members of Indian tribes allied with the English and colonists such as the Cherokee, just to get the scalping fee. Even with their Indian allies a tendency existed among Virginians to lump all Indians together, even though at this time they had strong allies among the Cherokee. The Shawnee of the Six Nations posed the greatest threat until 1759 when the Cherokee switched sides. This barbaric scalping fee seemed so contradictory to the idea of religious freedom that this new world was based on.

Even the preamble to the scalping act reveals this colonial attitude that made no differentiation between the Indians; 'Whereas cruel and barbarous murders have been lately committed in the upper part of this colony by Indians, supposed to be in the interest of the French, without any provocation from us and contrary to the laws of nature and nations, they still continue in skulking parties, to perpetrate their barbarous and savage cruelties, in the most base and treacherous manner, torturing, killing and scalping, not only our men, who live dispersedly in the frontiers, but also their helpless wives and children, sparing neither age nor sex; for prevention of which shocking inhumanities and for repelling such malicious and detestable enemies.'

It is important to note that the Germans in the New River Valley that stayed behind during the Indian wars would have nothing to do with the white militias and would not raise arms against any Indian unless it was for self defense. Their unwillingness to serve may have been attributed to the fact that they could not or would not learn the King's English. However, they didn't have any problem trading and dealing with their Cherokee blood brothers.

Virginians had seen too many years of shifting alliances with Indian tribes who understandably sought agreements most advantageous to their own interests. In the view of many colonists, all Indians, even their allies, represented a slightly subhuman and untrustworthy category of people. They had little sympathy for the genuine needs of the American Indian who feared further encroachments on their lands.

Governor Dinwiddie in a further attempt to defend the frontier gave George Washington the commission of Colonel to serve as Commander-in-Chief of the Virginia forces being raised to fight the French and Indians. The governor hoped that in the spring of 1756, this force would be effective enough to regain control of the forts in Ohio.

And, it was hoped that local county leaders such as William Preston with the support of the previously mentioned laws, would be able to better defend their communities.

Preston probably received orders while still in Williamsburg to join his recently recruited company of rangers with those of Major John Smith to 'scour the woods' for the enemy, urge people to return to their homes, and begin the process of building a series of forts along the Augusta County border as an encouragement for colonists to feel protected. With continuing Indian attacks taking place throughout the frontier, many settlers fearing their wholesale destruction, moved to more populated areas. Through these measures, Governor Dinwiddie hoped to avoid calling out the nearly useless militia and instead to rely upon ranger companies headed by captains like Preston until the colony could strengthen the regular regimental army.

By the end of August 1755, rumors continued to mount that the French and Indians would very soon launch an attack on the Augusta borders where Preston now patrolled with his rangers, thus taking advantage of the absence of regular troops on the border. Meanwhile, the desertion rate among the militia and even officers reached alarming numbers. Obviously the new militia laws did not work. These rumors came to fruition in September in the Greenbrier area (now Monroe County, West Virginia) when Indians killed twelve colonists and took another ten as prisoners including eight children. Throughout the frontier area of Virginia, Dinwiddie reported 'flying parties robbed our frontier settlements, murdered and carried off above one-hundred of our people and burnt all their houses.' This reality caused even further desertions and families fleeing from their farms, a fact that bothered Dinwiddie greatly. The governor became so upset that he requested a list of names of all who left their homesteads. It was not easy for him to sense the true feelings of danger on the frontier from the governor's palace in Williamsburg.

To counteract this problem, Dinwiddie agreed with Preston's request that he 'range the woods' urging him not to stay in one place, but to go wherever he thought the Indians might annoy the settlers. He asked Preston to stay on duty with his rangers until Christmas when cold

weather would diminish the threat of Indian attacks. The arrival of Cherokee allies was also expected who would remain through the winter to help guard the frontier, good news for the beleaguered colony.

The governor gave permission for Preston to persuade local inhabitants to build forts located at strategic places where frontiersmen could come when threatened by Indian attacks. Not a great deal is known about the first fort built by Preston during the fall, but later records refer to it as Fort William or Fort Preston, named after its young builder. Preston took a very personal view of this fort, continually referring to it as 'my fort.' Part of a series of forts, Preston's fort was located on the South Branch of Catawba Creek guarding Catawba Valley and Stone Coal Gap's opening to the Greenbrier. At least sixteen rangers helped in the task of building the fort and later received a reward of six gallons of whiskey for their efforts.

With a fort being built that served like a local tourist attraction, the Cherokee who visited Preston and his men also had to be kept happy. Virginians did not want to lose their valuable allies and tried to keep them satisfied with various gifts. In September, Preston bought for their Indian visitors four gallons of rum, ten pounds of tobacco, a shirt for a 'Cherokee Indian going to the Catawba Nation' three dozen pipes and an 'extraordinary fine tomahawk for a Cherokee warrior.' A month later, Indians visited the fort while Preston was absent and his friend and subordinate, David Robinson, reported that they had endeavored to pay them all 'difference' imaginable. 'We were obliged to send for rum in the night that we might answer their expectations and accommodate them to their satisfaction.'

During the fall of 1755, Preston's men spent much of their time 'ranging the woods' looking for the French and Shawnee. It was difficult work and to prevent them from becoming too tired he divided them into two detachments. No evidence exists that any more settlers were killed by Indians in 1755, but the possibility of Indian attack was always present and they lived in a constant state of tension.

Dinwiddie appointed Preston's second cousin, Major Andrew Lewis, to command an expedition against the Shawnee. He, along with two-hundred and twenty rangers and volunteers, and one-hundred and thirty Cherokee, were ordered to attack the Shawnee in their towns and 'to punish them for insults and great barbarities.' But, Washington's reservations and predictions that the expedition would 'prove abortive' because the Shawnee had moved further up the river to Fort Duquesne were rejected by Dinwiddie.

Major Lewis began the process of carrying out his directives with the first order going to his cousin, William Preston, informing him, pending the governor's approval; that he would probably be needed on the expedition. The governor responded by leaving the decision to Lewis, but urged him use all possible 'frugality.' With this permission, Lewis then ordered Preston to rendezvous with the Cherokee and other assembled troops at Fort Frederick on the New River, with an officer, two sergeants, two corporals, and thirty men, along with whatever horses were necessary for baggage and provisions, including two-thousand pounds of beef. Before Preston's men would march they insisted on their pay which he provided out of his own pocket.

Preston was joined by four other officers in Lewis's command, and Richard Pearls, a Cherokee trader and major contact with the Indians who Dinwiddie hoped in vain would 'behave well and keeps sober.' He also expressed great concern that Outacite, the Cherokee chief, be shown 'proper regard and respect' and hoped 'everything will prove easy and agreeable.'

The Sandy Creek Expedition had little effect on the ultimate outcome of the war but because of three eyewitness reports, it serves as one of the most dramatic accounts of any colonial military expedition. Preston's report is the most detailed, but ends early. However, it provides information concerning the problems met with and illustrates why it was so difficult to get men to volunteer and why desertion rates soared so high during wars of this period.

As the expedition ended, Preston's home county, Augusta, sent a desperate petition to the House of Burgesses requesting immediate help 'against the incursions and depredations of the savages.' They asked for the erection of a chain of forts across the frontier and for a treaty of 'trade and friendship' with confederate Indians to help serve as a barrier against the French. The Burgesses responded favorably with a law that allowed for raising funds to provide two-thousand more men for the regular regimental army in Virginia. In addition, a chain of forts would be erected across the frontier 'to put a stop to those violent outrages of the enemy and to protect the inhabitants in their lives and properties.'

But, there were problems. George Washington told Dinwiddie that forts without an adequate number of men supporting them would never answer the expectations of the frontier. He anticipated needing a regular army with strong discipline to counteract the tactics of the Indians who 'prowl about like wolves and like them, do their mischief by stealth.' The murders then being committed in the Winchester area and the daring attacks by Indians on their forts during the middle of the day constituted a more immediate problem. Further, Washington predicted 'unless a stop is put to the depredations of the Indians, the Blue Ridge will soon become our frontier.' He suggested the possibility of having frontiersmen live in towns and then work each other's farms on a shared basis which would prevent them being cut off by small parties of Indians. Although the suggestion was impractical when one considers the independent minds of men living on the frontier and the nature of frontier farming, the idea illustrates the desperate feelings of many who dealt with the grave threat to Virginia.

To help Washington, Dinwiddie ordered Preston and other captains on April 24, to summon all of their militiamen immediately for the purpose of drafting one-third of the 'most chosen men' to defend the Augusta frontier. He also asked that they be kept in readiness to march towards Winchester when needed while the remaining militia would patrol during their absence. When the militia officers of Augusta County met as a 'Council of War' on May 20 to carry out the drafting order, they quickly determined that most of their able bodied single men were already on duty on the frontier to protect the inhabitants. Until forces from elsewhere relieved these men they requested a postponement of the draft.

Efforts now focused on getting forts built along the frontier with twenty to thirty mile intervals between each one. Both Dinwiddie and Washington expressed reservations about having such a large number of small forts. Washington preferred having three or four 'large, strong forts built at convenient distances' and garrisoned with a large number of soldiers. He envisioned problems of providing provisions to ranging parties sent out from small forts which then left only a few men to guard the fort. Dinwiddie agreed, but argued that the House of Burgesses was so 'fond' of the forts that he could not alter their position. The problem became further complicated with the poor quality of militiamen in Augusta County being used to garrison the forts. Dinwiddie called them a 'dastardly set of people' who had 'neither courage, spirits, or conduct.' These questions about the forts and militia led to George Washington's first trip to Augusta County as commander and to his first meeting with Preston. On September 28, 1756, Washington left his Winchester headquarters for southern Virginia. Upon leaving, he received word of Indian 'depredations' and so attempted to raise a party of militia to 'scour the woods' around Jacksons River. Washington got a firsthand illustration of the recruiting difficulties on the frontier. After waiting five days for Colonel Stewart to raise the militia, only five men showed up. Preston, who was also present, was subsequently 'kind enough to conduct' Washington on the sixty mile journey to Luney's Ferry on the James River to get help from Colonel John Buchanan, then the leader of the Augusta Militia. On the journey, Preston and Washington engaged in intensive conversations about the manpower problems on the frontier and undoubtedly many other topics of mutual concern.

William Preston was appointed as a justice to the Virginia courts on June 20, 1757. The court, on which Preston now sat, represented the highest level of county government with responsibilities for wills, estates, taverns, liquor prices, water mills, ferries, levies, and legal document notarization. It was the 'fountainhead' of justice in Virginia.

At the same time he became Justice, Preston became deputy to Wallace Estill, the sheriff for Augusta County. The first evidence of his work in this capacity came as he carried out court orders such as seizing goods. A year later, he became Sheriff, a post he would hold several years fulfilling the many duties connected with it including tax collection. Rounding out his appointments in 1759, he also was appointed as Escheator and Coroner for Augusta County.

Obviously Preston's growing maturity as a military leader had become evident through his assignments. He had already received major political appointments as a justice of the peace and sheriff and now he would also begin to receive military promotions. The new governor, Francis Fauquier, appointed him to the rank of major in the Virginia Militia in September of 1758 and a year later he was made lieutenant colonel in the Augusta County Militia as the Indian attacks continued.

By 1759 the war was beginning to wind down. The English captured Fort Niagara in Quebec, thus removing any direct threat by the French against the Ohio area. But, the Cherokee now turned against their former English allies as a result of skirmishes with aggressive Virginia frontiersmen who had always hated all Indians. Since the Cherokee did not live in Virginia, only using the colony as a pathway home, Virginia did not face the same kind of threat experienced by fellow colonists in North and South Carolina.

Despite the lessened threat, Augusta County residents still felt under pressure. Shawnee attacks continued resulting in deaths and capture. Preston apparently wrote Fauquier on behalf of his fellow citizens requesting that additional militia be stationed in their area. But, the governor, following the example of his predecessor, replied that no militiamen would be forthcoming to help quiet the 'ill-grounded fears of a few people.' The Indians were already fighting a war in their own territory he said, which would help protect Virginians from any possible Indian threat.

With the war coming to an end, William Preston found himself having accomplished much, but he was thirty-years old and he did not have a wife or children. Preston married Susanna Smith, daughter of Francis Smith who was educated by Reverend Patrick Henry, on January 17, 1761. By 1763, they had settled in their new home, an estate approximately five miles west of Fincastle and one mile from Amsterdam, later to be known as Greenfield, which would eventually be the first real home for him and his wife. Greenfield stood on the 'Great Road' also known as the 'Indian Road' which led to the Alleghenies. They had plenty of visitors to keep their social life active. Greenfield was described by a neighbor: 'a block-house or fort surrounded by a stockade.' The original portion, for defense against Indian attack, was of heavy log construction and according to tradition, 'loop-holed.' Later, this original log construction was covered over with hand sawed clapboarding outside and finished inside with plaster and wood paneling. During an eight year period up to 1772, Greenfield would be the birthplace for half of William and Susanna Preston's twelve children. The house remained in the Preston family until 1959, when it burned. While the demands for the services of surveyors increased with peace, a greater threat came from the accompanying 'Proclamation of 1763.' For several years during the war, questions arose about the advisability of allowing colonists to settle on lands claimed by the Indians on the frontier. To avoid problems, Colonel Henry Bouquet, a British officer of Swiss nationality in charge of Fort Pitt, gave an order in October 1761 outlawing settlements west of the Appalachian divide which ran along the ridge of the Allegheny Mountains. Permission for such settlements could only come with Bouquet's permission or from a colonial governor. Two months later the British government ordered the governors not to grant any land which conflicted with Indian claims which in effect transferred the right to buy Indian lands from the colonies to the British imperial government. Initially, Virginians who constantly opposed these new policies viewed them as temporary until more permanent arrangements could be made after the war ended. But, on October 7, 1763, the King signed the Proclamation of 1763 confirming the earlier actions but now ordering settlers in the forbidden areas to leave. A major problem with this decision involved the lands promised to soldiers during the war in exchange for their military service.

Much of the disputed land lay in Preston's surveying territory and he had already surveyed lands in the forbidden area. John Buchanan, one of his uncle's executors, even talked of going to London in an attempt to lay out the case for his continued ownership of lands in the disputed area. In later years, Preston as an executor of Patton's estate, appealed to the North Carolina and Virginia legislatures to receive the lands they felt had been wrongfully deprived them because of this proclamation. Even though the British never officially changed their policy, the colonists resisted by refusing to move and even continued their surveying efforts. In the next ten years leading up to the American Revolution, this action by the British formed one of the grievances used to show how unfair the British had been. Yet, the British were merely trying to gain time to work out more official agreements with the Indians so the frontier could be settled on a peaceful basis. They feared the opposite approach would result in continuing skirmishes between Indians and colonists which would require a large expense to maintain an army to protect the settlers. If strictly enforced, the British proclamation represented a real threat to Preston's ability to earn income through surveying in the disputed territory and through his own personal land purchases. Unbeknownst to Preston and his fellow Virginians at the time was their own responsibility and involvement in the precursor and establishment of attitudes that led to the 'Trail of Tears' and the end of the east coast American Indian.

While Preston's business, civic, and personal life continued with more normalcies, the threat of further Indian attacks continued in spite of the recent peace treaty with the French. Settlers began to return to their homes which made necessary the Augusta County Court to ask Preston to 'apportion the tithables' in the frontier district as far as Fort Lewis. Now, a new challenge developed. Pontiac, Chief of the Ottawas, organized a full-blown attack by many Indian tribes later known as 'Pontiac's Conspiracy' against British forts and settlers along much of the frontier in May 1763.

With the threat of Indian attacks again revived, Preston sent an express in June 1763 to Governor Fauquier requesting help. To assist the frontier counties, the governor ordered out the militia from the neighboring Bedford County and sent ten barrels of powder and some lead for Preston's usage. Again he reiterated a common attitude among Virginia's governors that the Augusta frontiersmen should be inspired with courage so they would not run away anytime twenty or thirty Indians showed up. In private correspondence to the Board of Trade, Governor Fauquier placed major blame on the colonists for agitating the Indians as a result of their illegal settlements in the New River area. He feared that the English would never be able to 'live upon the same terms with the Indians, as the French did, unless the enthusiasm of running backwards to hunt for fresh lands can be stopped.'

The few remaining families in the Roanoke River area now began to gather around the various forts. Preston also built a little fort which protected a total of eighty-seven people, including his own family and two of his sisters with their families. Although no Indians had yet appeared, Preston reported 'their guns are frequently heard and their footing observed which makes us believe they will pay us a visit.'

During the middle of these threats, Preston received another major promotion in August when Fauquier appointed him as a Colonel of the Militia for Augusta County, four years after his last promotion. No attacks came in his area during that summer and fall. William Ingles, one of his subordinates, did report in September about a skirmish between his militiamen who 'all behaved like good soldiers' and a group of Indians who were 'loath to give way.' The ensuing battle resulted in several Indians being killed and the colonists taking plunder of thirty horses. As a token of appreciation, Ingles sent his leader Preston, a shot pouch taken from one of the Indian captains as a 'small trophee of our victory.' Although short of powder and lead, Ingles asked Preston for permission to continue serving on the frontier since they could help protect settlers in both Augusta and Halifax Counties.

The year 1764 did bring trauma to the young Preston family. In late winter or early spring, Preston left Susanna and his young family to transact some business in Staunton, Virginia. Many years later their daughter, Leticia, reported that early one morning her mother was startled by hearing two guns fired in 'quick succession.' Shortly thereafter, Joseph Cloyd, a neighbor, arrived on his 'plough horse with gears on' with word that Indians had just killed his brother John and had shot at him but missed 'although his shirt was powder burnt' and had then gone to his house where they probably killed his mother. Susanna, in complete control, immediately wrote a letter 'free from tremor or trepidation' to Captain Francis Smith who commanded a small nearby fort on Craig's Creek, for help in pursuing the attackers. Next, she sent a white man and two black men to the Cloyd's house where they found the mother tomahawked in three places, the whole house destroyed and the money carried off (Mr. Cloyd had a large sum of gold stowed away). Mrs. Cloyd was perfectly in her senses, told all the circumstances of the savage revelry in getting drunk, ripping up the feather beds and one of them taking a corn cob and wiping off the blood of her temples exclaiming 'poor old woman.' She died the next morning.

All of these threats and loss of lives over the years caused frontiersmen to do some soul searching about why God would permit such tragedies to take place. Preston may have shared the theological explanation of his brother-in-law, Reverend John Brown, who blamed community sin as the cause of all calamity, but denied that the suffering by a few could 'expiate the sins of many, or even their own sins.' He also rejected the idea that individuals 'do not suffer only for the sins of the nation to whom they belong, but more especially for the particular sins that they themselves have committed.' For instance 'none have suffered equivalent to the demerit of their sins.' Such thoughts would be expected from a clergyman, but one wonders whether such views had an impact on the way people practiced their religion. Did it cause them to lead more moral and upright lives? If others 'acted up' did the community come down on those individuals for bringing potential calamity on the whole community as a result of the sins of a few? Maybe an early example of good energy versus evil energy and maybe 'you reap what you sew.'

The attacks against Augusta County residents represented only a small part of Chief Pontiac's effort. After initial success by the Indians against virtually every fort except for Detroit and Fort Pitt, the British managed to relieve the threatened Fort Pitt under the leadership of Colonel Bouquet in August 1763. Two regiments from Augusta County aided him in this relief effort, a main goal being to retrieve prisoners taken by the Indians in recent raids. Bouquet's peace negotiations with the Indians resulted in a peace treaty with the Ohio Indians in November 1764 causing a marked reduction of tension and the discharge of most militiamen. To guarantee the treaty, Lewis reported that hostages were being given by each Indian nation to guarantee the peace. While always wondering about the validity of Indian claims, they expected to find out their true intentions by the manner in which they treated the few prisoners still held in Indian captivity. Illustrating the more peaceful atmosphere, Lewis ordered Preston to discharge all but nine of his men.

The time now came for Augusta County to begin the process of restoring itself from the ravages of the war, a war that had clearly delayed the county's growth. In 1754 the county contained 10,560 inhabitants, which went to a low of 5,496 in 1758 at the peak of the struggle. With the end of the war in 1763, the county's population came to 10,160 inhabitants, still under its high point ten years earlier.

William Preston stood poised to take advantage of the upcoming years of expansion on the frontier. The last ten years up to 1764 had been years of great maturation for William Preston as he furthered his experience in personal, business, and civic affairs. He was now on the verge of becoming the most significant founder and leader in three new counties which would prepare him for the pivotal role of leadership he carried into the American Revolution.

Preston had visited Williamsburg, the capital of Virginia, in May 1765. The reasons for going are not clear but shortly after his arrival, news came from his cousin, Andrew Lewis, who was Colonel of the Augusta County militia, that five Cherokee Indians, part of a group of ten on their way to the Ohio, had been killed near Staunton by a gang of 'villainous bloody minded rascals' who would later be called the 'Augusta Boys.' Lewis, after warning the Indians of frontiersmen who hated them, had granted a pass for safe travel. Unfortunately among those killed was Choconantee, son of 'The Standing Turkey' Emperor of the Cherokee. Absolutely certain that the remaining Indians who escaped would return home with the bad news, Lewis quickly wrote the Cherokee chiefs of the Overhill Towns confirming the murders and informing them that two of the perpetrators had already been imprisoned. He assured them that the governor abhorred the 'spilling of blood in so detestable a manner' and pledged that the 'Chain of Friendship Treaty' would continue.

In Williamsburg, government leaders must have consulted Preston and the action was quickly condemned with a reward offered for the apprehension of the murderers. In addition, Fauquier wrote a personal letter to the Cherokee chiefs blaming the murders on 'some hot headed inconsiderate young men, whom yourselves own you cannot sometimes restrain from mischief.' Fauquier told Lewis 'I wish your county were made sensible of the risk they run of losing their property, if not their lives, by permitting these atrocious practices.' Lewis probably did not have time to reflect on this because one hundred armed men had broken into the jail of Augusta County and freed one of the arrested men. These 'Augusta Boys' declared that no one should ever be brought to trial for the 'killin of savages' and in fact, the perpetrators were never brought to justice.

During Preston's visit to Williamsburg, Virginia's opposition to the new Stamp Act came to a head when new House of Burgesses' member, Patrick Henry, introduced seven resolutions against the act, five of which were ultimately passed on May 29. Williamsburg was a very small town and Preston certainly discussed and perhaps witnessed Patrick Henry's 'sublime eloquence' as well as the resolutions which argued that Virginians received all the liberties of English citizens, including the right to be governed in their internal affairs by their own elected representatives. William Preston must have at this early point, eleven years before the Declaration of Independence, begun to form initial attitudes toward the burgeoning movement of the Patriots, or Whigs as they became known.

Beginning in 1772, Preston began to piece together a new plantation through the careful purchase of lands in the Draper's Meadows area near modern-day Blacksburg and today sits on the Virginia Tech campus, not far from where his uncle, James Patton was killed in 1755, and next to his old friend, Michael Price, my first generation grandfather. He named the new plantation 'Smithfield' in honor of his wife, Susanna Smith, even before they moved from Greenfield in March 1774. Although he never indicated why he moved, he probably wanted to be closer to where his own personal land empire was developing and to where he could more easily direct the surveying of lands as County Surveyor. Greenfield was located just at the edge of Fincastle County, whereas Smithfield placed him nearer the center of the county where future growth would take place. This was just seven miles down the mountain from my property in Clover Hollow.

Being closer to these lands also would enable potential settlers to use his plantation as a center from which to leave for their new lands. Just like his neighbor and friend Michael Price, who never had left this land, opened his doors to future settlers. Or, maybe he had a special connection to this land where he had buried his uncle, seventeen years ago. A further consideration for the move may have been the rich farmlands in that area located on a plateau 2,200 to 2,300 feet above sea level with an average growing season of 161 days, average precipitation of thirty-eight inches per year, and an average snowfall of only twenty inches. The house he built there, now beautifully restored, represents a remarkable achievement for a frontier family. The house clearly conveyed Preston's commitment to being among the elite living on the frontier. The home he built showed the civility and sophistication that might be expected from a Williamsburg home or a Tidewater plantation he had seen on his trips to the east. This L-shaped frame structure with a stone and brick foundation and three chimneys consists of ten rooms including a drawing room with a handsome mantle over the fireplace, a great bed chamber, dining room, kitchen, and two bedrooms. This home still stands just a few miles east of Clover Hollow.

Beginning in the spring of 1774, many of Preston's business activities were threatened by the increasing danger of Indian attacks. During the remainder of 1774, Preston became the pivotal leader in orchestrating and coordinating the frontier response to these challenges which became known as Dunmore's War. In many ways the experience gained here was to prepare him for the larger responsibilities that emerged when the American Revolution began in a few months. The borders between Virginia and the Indians which resulted from the Proclamation of 1763, constituted a major issue. And, the border between Pennsylvania and Virginia was similarly disputed with both colonies claiming the lands around Fort Pitt. The stakes were high since Virginia still claimed Kentucky and Ohio as their territory with surveyors from Virginia continuing their efforts to lay out lands for claims from Virginians.

Through Dunmore's War conflict, Preston showed his full development as a frontier leader. Although he could not be present for the expedition he effectively coordinated the effort to raise troops and provisions. He also provided a sense of security for his frontier neighborhood through his personal presence and coordination of defense efforts on Virginia's frontier. Mature and experienced, William Preston now represented the full embodiment of the frontier leader as a public servant, politician, family man, surveyor, businessman, and Colonel. He was fully prepared for the larger conflict that was now to take place.

The Fincastle Resolutions was a statement adopted on January 20, 1775, by thirteen elected representatives of Fincastle County, Colony of Virginia, which included signers William Preston and William Ingles. Part of the political movement that became the American Revolution, the resolutions were addressed to Virginia's delegation at the First Continental Congress and expressed support for Congress' resistance to the Intolerable Acts issued in 1774 by the British Parliament. Other counties in Virginia had passed similar resolutions in 1774, such as the Fairfax Resolves, but the Fincastle Resolutions were the first adopted statement by the colonists which promised resistance to the death and to the British Crown to preserve political liberties. It was the predecessor to the Declaration of Independence.

New River Tories

During the spring of 1775, Virginia committed herself to the cause of American Independence. In June, Lord Dunmore, the Tory governor, fled to a British war vessel and from the safety of its deck still made a pretense of asserting his authority. During the summer, he gathered a few ships and with a force of British and Tories, began to patrol the shores of the Chesapeake. His style of warfare consisted of plundering plantation houses, maltreating women and children, stealing slaves and burning seaports. In October, he was repulsed from Hampton and in December was defeated near Norfolk. But, on New Year's Day, 1776, he bombarded Norfolk with canon and burned it down. General Andrew Lewis took command of the Virginia forces and drove Dunmore from his stronghold on Gwin's Island in the Chesapeake. The late governor sailed for England and for three years the British had no foothold on Virginia soil. Yet, their navy enabled them to dominate the sea and the counties lying on navigable waters were thus kept in frequent alarm.

The first phase of the Revolution, as it relates to Virginia, was the contest with Dunmore on the tidal waters. It was fought with militia who came in part from the counties toward the Blue Ridge. The militia of the Tidewater continued to be called out, here and there, to repel the parties which landed from ships for the purpose of plunder.

The second phase consisted of trouble from the Indians on the western frontier. They had been stunned by their defeat at Point Pleasant in 1774, but being urged on by

British emissaries and white renegades, they at length began to harass the weak settlements in Kentucky, along the Holston, and toward the Ohio. To quell the Cherokee in the Southwest, a large force of militia was sent to the Holston early on in the war. This army was in part made up of men from east of the Blue Ridge. But, the militias of the Shenandoah Valley were able to stand off the Indians who threatened them from the northwest. The war parties of the Indians scarcely ventured east of the Alleghany divide, yet the scattered settlements beyond were subjected to much distress. The deliberate murder of Chief Cornstalk, at Point Pleasant, was the immediate cause of the Indian raid into the Greenbrier in 1778. The Indian depredations continued throughout the war and garrisons had to be maintained in the frontier forts throughout the threatened area.

In the summer of 1777, the Patriot government issued a law requiring all white males over age sixteen to take an oath of allegiance to the Revolutionary cause. The conflicting responses incited by the Revolution became even more pronounced. Many valley settlers flatly refused to swear the oath, including all but a few of William Preston's neighbors, including Michael Price, who pledged allegiance to the King when he landed in the colonies in 1738. By early 1778, the Tory movement began to turn violent with reports of Loyalists 'stealing horses and robbing Whig sympathizers.' The county courts tried to control the Tories but to little effect. Efforts to subdue them by revoking their rights fell flat because, as Preston wrote, the Loyalists 'bring no suits, they never elect, they don't attend court, they can dispose of their arms, and they don't want to purchase land.' At the height of the movement, Montgomery County was home to Virginia's largest group of Tories. The extent was such that another valley Patriot leader wrote to Preston 'we seem but a handful in the middle, and surrounded by a multitude.'

As the Tory movement gathered force, another era of the New River Valley's history was shaped by the tensions arising from the events of the time. Loyalist recruiters roamed the valley and the dangers faced by the Patriot leaders grew even greater. Preston wrote that he anticipated 'a general mutiny which I am really and not without foundation, apprehensive of.' Only three miles from Smithfield, settlers began administering oaths of loyalty to the King. Preston's daughter, Leticia Preston Floyd, later remembered 'Colonel Preston found himself surrounded by a neighborhood of Tories who kept him continually on the alert to prevent them from murdering himself and family, as well as every other Whig in the county.' Indeed, plots began to surface to kill Preston and capture the Montgomery County munitions kept at Smithfield and even to take Preston's scalp.

The climax of the conflict transpired in spring of 1779 when Montgomery County became the scene of a conspiracy, which had it been successful, might have caused the Revolution to take a very different turn. John Cox, a Patriot taken prisoner by a group of Loyalists, learned of a 'diabolical plot' being formed to murder the valley's Patriot leaders. Soon afterwards, Preston received the 'disagreeable intelligence' of another plot not only to kill valley leaders, but also to join with the English and Indians to destroy the local lead mines and to sweep through the backcountry destroying the settlements before meeting up with British troops in South Carolina. Upon learning of these plans, Patriot leaders hastily infiltrated spies into the Tory ring and put down the rebellion. The Valley had narrowly missed being caught up in a path of destruction that had originated from disagreements over political involvement.

On July 20, 1779, William Preston wrote a letter to my great grandfather Michael Price, his German neighbor in the New River Valley, informing him of the popular feeling against the Tories and proposed a conference the next Saturday at Michael Price's fort and home. His concerns lay with the Tory outrages and the threats against his life.

On July 22, Michael Price responded to William Preston by letter concerning the destruction of his property, avows his innocence of any offense, that his and his neighbors 'are desirous of peace' refuses to take the oath of loyalty for noble reasons and ask compassion for his wife and family.

On July 28, 1783, Colonel William Preston fell ill while on a regimental muster at Michael Price's home and fort and died shortly afterward in my grandfather's bed at the age of 54. At the time of his death in 1783, Preston was the wealthiest man in Montgomery County with seven-thousand acres of land, thirty-four slaves, thirty-six horses, and eighty-six cattle. The Preston's were arguably southwestern Virginia's most prominent and powerful family from the mid-18th century until the period following the Civil War.

Many prominent Americans descended from Colonel William Preston and his wife Susanna. They were the parents or grandparents to governors, senators, presidential cabinet members, university founders and presidents, and military leaders. Most notably among them is Preston's son, James Patton Preston, who was governor of Virginia from 1816 to 1819, and helped charter the University of Virginia, and their grandson William Ballard Preston, who was a congressman, Secretary of the Navy under Zachary Taylor, and later a Senator from the Confederates States of America. William Ballard Preston also offered the Ordinance of Succession to the Virginia Legislature, which resulted in Virginia joining the Confederacy, and also was the cofounder of a small Methodist college, the Preston and Olin Institute, which became what is today Virginia Tech in Blacksburg, Virginia. The legacy of leadership and patriotism left by William Preston is very long and storied and makes him a true American hero. He surely would have been known as an American founding father had he lived a little longer.

Chapter 6 Price's Mill

Johan David Preisch said goodbye to this world on July 11, 1735, in Offenbach, Germany. Preisch is a German spelling for the American name Price. On June 27, 1713, he married Agnes Hoffman, who was the daughter of Henrich and Anna Elizabetha Hoffman. After they both had passed, all of their surviving children traveled to America on the ship 'Winter Galley' arriving in Philadelphia on September 5, 1738. I am the ninth generation grandson of John David Price. The Price children who came to America on the Winter Galley together were:

John Michael Price (first-generation grandfather) baptized October 9, 1718, in Offenbach, Germany.
Anna Margaretha Price (older sister of Michael Price) baptized September 21, 1713 in Offenbach, Germany. On February 17, 1738, she married *John Phillip Harless* (first-generation grandfather) and they came together to America on the Winter Galley.
Augustine Price: baptized May 31, 1722
Daniel Price: baptized April 10, 1724
Henry Price: baptized September 8, 1726

It was common to baptize children in Germany within a week of their birth. Michael Price was the oldest son and his older sister was married to Phillip Harless, another direct ancestor of mine on the Winter Galley. These two families stayed closely together until the Indian wars on the Virginia frontier forced them apart.

Only men over the age of sixteen had to sign the 'Oaths of Fidelity and Abjuration' which was declaring allegiance to the King of England upon debarkation in Philadelphia and the women and children under sixteen were not recorded. Philip Harless, Michael Price, and John Sibold were of age and signed the oath.

Family friend and fellow traveler with the Price family was John Phillip Sibold, he was the third great-grandfather of mine on the same boat. I'm his eighth generation grandson. It is believed he traveled to Rockingham County with the Price and Harless family, but remained there until John Sibold Jr. (second-generation grandfather) settled near Michael Price's homestead on upper Thom's Creek on property that is now owned by Virginia Tech.

It's not known how long it took for the young Germans to get to the Shenandoah Valley, presumably by horse and wagon down the 'Great Warrior Path' which is now known as the 81 Corridor. Upon arrival on the Shenandoah River they settled near what is now McGaheysville, Virginia, near Peaked Mountain Church.

Almost immediately, Phillip Harless and Michael Price continued on to the furthest part of the western frontier. They put down stakes around the 'horseshoe bottom' on the New River by 1741. In July, 1748, Israel Norton, agent for the Wood's River Company, sold to Michael Price and Philip Harless four-hundred acres at the mouth of Jones and Thom's Creek, and four-hundred acres to Augustine, Henry and Daniel Price, also on the horseshoe bottom. This German New River Settlement became the first European settlement beyond the Alleghenies. Augustine, Daniel, and Henry Price followed their brother and brother-in-law to the horseshoe bottom and settled there around 1745 on land next to their older brother, Michael Price.

The Initial boundaries of the first colonists to the New River Valley were soon filled up from Sinking Creek to

Reed Creek where the settlers there were mostly Scotch-Irish and a few more of the same scattered here and there between the two creek valleys. It can be said that the center and beginning of the 'Middle New River Settlement' was on the 'horseshoe bottoms' and immediate contiguous bottoms. This horseshoe and its contiguous bottoms included the bottoms at the mouth of Thoms, Stroubles, and Back creeks. This was not only the center and beginning of the 'Middle New River Settlements' but was for a time, a unit, and would become the 'German Settlement of the New River.' From this common center, settlements and movements were made including all creeks and valleys between Sinking and Reed Creeks, and especially extending up the valleys of Thom and Strouble's Creeks including the plateau between them. The German New River Settlement had become a frontier colony within a colony.

There is no record of settlers on Sinking Creek before 1749 while there were settlers on Reed Creek by 1745. As the contiguous bottoms of the horseshoe filled up, they settled next in order; the plateau, and then around the site of Old St Michael's-St Peter's Lutheran Church, which includes the surroundings of Prices's Fork. This German New River Settlement was regarded in the Virginia Historical Magazine by a Lutheran writer as being a *lost* settlement.

Not a lot is known about these early German settlers and none were of known or renown, either for the colony or nation, probably for a few reasons. It's partly accounted for by the remoteness of the settlement from the more fully and permanently settled conditions of the Valleys of Virginia. But, even more is the fact that my German forefathers conversed only in the German dialect. Literature left by them were bibles and hymn books, all in German. Church services were conducted in the German language in Old St. Peter's Church until 1840. This fact alone disqualified the German people for leadership of any kind. The leaders of the community came naturally of the English speaking people. They were the conceded leaders in civic and national affairs by all the Germans.

The Germans had a religious background of Pietism that caused them to be opposed to war. They had a natural aversion to it. They had traveled far from the confines of civilization with the purpose to make treaties with the Indians, as did their mentor, William Penn. For a number of years the Germans were at peace with their Indian neighbors. Their homes were built near the Indian path leading from the settlements of the Northern Indians (Mohawks, Algonquin's, Shawnee and Iroquois) to the settlements of the southern Indians, the Cherokee and others, and that trail was called the 'Great Warriors Path.' The northern Indians who were warlike, like to travel down the trail to attack the Cherokee, plunder, and then return. When white settlers moved into the area, the Indians raided them instead. They stole horses, kidnapped able bodied men and women, killed whole families and otherwise terrorized the settlers. This would occur all along the western border.

It was 1749 when the New River settlements suffered its first Indian depredation when Adam Harman's cabin was raided by marauding Indians and his furs and skins in the hundreds were stolen. In those times, furs and skins were more important than money. Adam Harman had settled in Gunpowder Springs near the mouth of Sinking Creek, now known as Eggleston Springs on the New River. Harman came with the Ingles, Drapers and others from Pattonsburg, in the Virginia valley in the spring of 1749. He had settled up from Phillip Lybrooks place near the mouth of Sinking Creek.

The story goes that Harman suspected a man named Castle as being in league with and prompting the Indians to steal his furs. Harman obtained a warrant from a magistrate of Augusta County for the arrest of Castle, and with a posse, among them a large, stout, athletic man named Clinche, met serious resistance from Castle and the Indians and forced them to beat a hasty retreat. Clinche was thrown from his horse in crossing the river. The Indians saw him as lame, and disabled from the fall, when one warrior dashed into the river and seized him, the bigger, stronger Clinche was an overmatch for his Indian enemy and succeeded in drowning him, hence the name 'Clinche River' was given.

The New River settlements went unscathed from Indian attacks until that fateful day on July 8, 1755, one day before

'Braddock's Defeat' and on Colonel James Patton's sixty-third birthday, when Drapers Meadow was attacked. The Indians did not disturb the families of Adam Harman and Phillip Lybrook, not to mention any of the German settlers whose settlements were immediately on the river and along the path. The Shawnee Indians bypassing the Germans might have been an indication James Patton was their sole target. This emphasizes my assertion that the attack on Drapers Meadow was a pre-planned preemptive attack to kill the head of the militia and to scare the settlers out of the valley. It was frightening and completely successful.

Most all the settlers, including some of the Germans, decided it was too dangerous to be so close to the frontier and started to pull back to Dunkards Bottom and Vaux's fort on the Roanoke, nearby where Shawsville now stands. After Mrs. Ingles escape and return from captivity, she went directly to Vaux's Fort to be with her husband, but was not willing to stay there for very long. She was well aware that the Indians would repeat their visit to the settlements and that she and her friends would again be exposed to danger of death or capture. Her fears were well grounded and on the next day after the departure of herself and family from Vaux's fort in the summer of 1756, the fort was attacked by the Indians and the inmates were killed or captured and carried away, but two or three afterwards escaped.

About 1748, *John Phillip Harless* (first generation grandfather) acquired land patents with Michael Price on Thom's Creek around the horseshoe bottoms and by 1762, John Harless had a patent to land on Cow Pasture River, four miles from Natural Bridge where he moved his family to safety after the Drapers Meadow Massacre. This land was southeast of what is now Lexington, Virginia. John Phillip Harless and his wife, Anna Margaretha Price, had seven children that survived to adulthood. They had five sons and two daughters: Martin, *John Phillip Harless Jr* (second-generation grandfather) David, Henry, Emanuel, Mary, and Dorothy.

John Phillip Harless Jr and his wife Hannah Boscher Harless are buried in the Harless Cemetery near Longshop, outside Prices Fork. It's not clear when the Harless's returned to the New River Valley, but it is known that John

Phillip Harless Sr. (first-generation grandfather) was buried in the Harless Cemetery near Price's Fork after he died in 1772.

Martin Harless (second-generation uncle) the first child of John Phillip Harless and Anna Margaretha Price was born on July 25, 1738, at sea, when his parents were coming to the New World on the Winter Galley. Martin was baptized in the Holy Trinity Church in Lancaster, Lancaster County, Pennsylvania, on March 11, 1739. He grew up on the frontiers of Southwest Virginia, where life was not easy. When Martin was eleven years old, the first 'depredation by Indians west of the Blue Ridge' took place on his neighbor, Harman's farm. From then on, except for the few years they took refuge in Rockingham County, the family never felt safe from Indian attacks.

Undoubtedly, these Germans were known for their sharpshooting and game-hunting, and never went to the fields to work without carrying their guns. Supposedly, today's custom of keeping one's hand in his lap while eating with the other came from the founding fathers having to eat with one hand while holding a gun in the lap with the other. During the Indian Wars, Martin served in the Virginia Militia under Captain Looney while his brothers served in the Company of Captain John Taylor. Martin also served in the Virginia Militia during the Revolutionary War, as did his teen-age sons. It was common practice to will the homestead to the oldest son and divide the remaining property between the other siblings. That's why the oldest son usually stayed with the homestead and the other family members would have to find land further west.

At the time of the French and Indian War, 1755-63, when Indians were raiding, killing, and taking prisoners on the frontier, Henry, Daniel, and Augustine Price (first-generation uncles) left the New River and went to a safer location in Rockingham County, Virginia. Records can be found in the Peaked Mountain Church of marriages, baptisms, and burials. However, Michael Price remained on Thom's Creek and built a stone fort for his family and friends for protection. It was to become completely sustainable. Price built the stone fort around a spring in case there were Indian attacks and they could not get out.

On the property he built a grist mill beside Thom's Creek. They had their own tannery, springhouse, and gunpowder production, with plenty of food and fiber available on nearby farms. For the next 30 years his farm and fort was used as a mustering place for the militia, for parties going in pursuit of marauding Indians and as a staging area for other families trying to get a start. It is where William Preston died, presumably by heat stroke while attending a military muster in 1783.

The children of *John Michael Price*:

John Michael Price Jr (second-generation grandfather) b. 1746, Augusta County, Virginia
John David Price b. 1744, Augusta County, Virginia, first owner of record for my property
Alexander Price b. 1748, Augusta County, Virginia
Elizabeth Price b. 1761, Augusta County, Virginia
Margaret E. Price b. 1750, Augusta County, Virginia
George Price b. 1752, Augusta County, Virginia
John Price b. 1757, Augusta County, Virginia
Agnes Price b. 1759, Augusta County, Virginia
Jacob Price b. 1760, Augusta County, Virginia
Christian Price b: 1769, Augusta County, Virginia
Henry Price b. 1766, Augusta County, Virginia

WILL: His will, on record at the Montgomery County, Virginia court house, is here quoted in its entirety: "I, J. Michael Price of the county of Montgomery and State of Virginia being of sound and perfect mind and memory, do make and ordain this my last will and testament, in form following, I will and bequeath my soul to God, and my body to the earth to be buried in a decent and Christian like manner at the direction of my executors herein named, an as to such worldly estate wherewith I have been blessed in this life. I will and dispose of the same as follows, vis. It is my will and desire that all my just debts and funeral expenses be first paid out of my personal estate or so much thereof as may be necessary for that purpose and I order the same accordingly. I give to my son David one Negro Woman Slave, Nell, he paying therefore to my executors the sum of Two hundred dollars, I give to my son Michael, a small Negro girl Lindsey, he paying therefore to my executors the sum of fifty dollars, and to my son Lewis (Lewis is believed to be a twin to John) my big Bible. I give to my son Jacob a Negro Boy Slave, Will, he paying therefore to my executors the sum of one hundred and thirty-three dollars, thirty-three cents. Also my house clock, still and slitting utensils, including a large copper kettle, he paying therefore to my executors the sum of one hundred dollars, likewise my blacksmith's tools he paying to my son Christian in lieu thereof the sum of sixteen pounds. I give to my son Henry a Negro Woman Slave Clary and her increase now in his possession also my iron stove. He paying therefore to my executors the sum of two hundred and seventy dollars. I give to my son George the Big Wagon and Jack Screw, without the harness or _____, he paying therefore to my executors the sum of sixteen pounds to them severally and their heirs forever and should it happen that any of the Negroes aforesaid should die, be emancipated or kept out of the estate, then and in that case, I will and order that the price of such slaves or slaves be re-willed to such of my said sons or sons as by chance he lose the gain. It is my will and desire that in case my wife Margaret should survive me that she have and enjoy her bed and bedding, spinning wheel and other household furniture during her natural life also one full and equal third part in addition to the aforesaid bequest of all my estate, that I may die seized of her comfort and support but should she marry after my decease, she is to have and receive from my estate no more than a child's part, and I will and devise the same accordingly and whereas there may be some of my real estate not disposed of and personal estate not herein before devised. I order that such part or parcel of any such remain, and the money in the hands of my executors, and all moneys which may come into their hands, by virtue of this my will, be equally divided among all my children and their legal representative alone (my son Alexander excepted) and I devise the same accordingly. And or the due exception of this my will I appoint my worthy friend and Neighbor James Patton Preston and my sons David and Henry my whole and sole executors. Hereby revoking and making void all former wills by me made, declaring this only to be my last will and testament. In witness whereof I here unto set my hand and seal this 11th day of June in the year of our Lord 1802." The will was Signed, Sealed and acknowledged before Abram Trigg and John Gardner. "A codicle to my last will and testament above written made and subscribed this ninth day of July eighteen hundred and two. Whereas from my present infirmity I am impressed with the opinion that I shall not recover, I have thought proper, in justice to my wife Margaret to alter the devise to my son Michael, be it therefore understood that it is my will and thereby my devise that my wife shall have during her natural life, my Negro Girl named Lizzie, and she shall afterwards as is here fore devised. But my executors shall not demand from my son Michael the sum which by my will he is to pay until the same Negro Slave Lizzie shall be delivered to him by some one of my executors. In testimony wherewith I have herewith set my hand and seal this day and date above mentioned in the presence of John Gardiner and James P. Preston." (Signed) J. Michael Price. This will was probated by Charles Taylor at Montgomery October Court 1802.

Note: The will was witnessed by *James Patton Preston*, neighbor and the son of *Colonel William Preston's,* and future governor of Virginia. Also, John Michael Price had seven sons who are named in his will, but no daughters are mentioned. According to records, Michael Price deeded out much of his land to his sons before his will was written in 1802.

It is also believed that Michael Price assisted his son David Price in obtaining the mill site on Sinking Creek in Clover Hollow. This would include the property I now own and what this book is all about. It is thought that Michael Price picked out the Sinking Creek mill site very early on because of its features and location. It was located just over the mountain from the Michael Price homestead.

Lewis Price (third-generation grandfather) in 1801, bought six-hundred and ninety acres on Sinking Creek, and David Price, in 1803, bought two parcels of one-hundred and fifty acres and one parcel of 1167 acres on Sinking Creek, and in 1809, bought another one-hundred and twenty acres on Sinking Creek. Most of the land that John David Price acquired on Sinking Creek lay on the borders of Clover Hollow. We do know that most of the first settlers to come to Clover Hollow, starting around 1800 were the Germans. David Price was the largest land owner on Sinking Creek and the very first legal owner of my property and the Price Mill site in Clover Hollow.

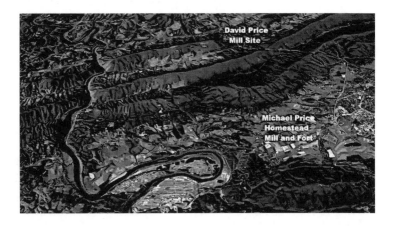

From almost the first moment my ancestors reached the horseshoe bottoms of the New River in 1740 they built a long-lasting relationship and friendship with the Cherokee, and humbly shared and lived on their neighbor's sacred hunting grounds. The German New River Settlement was located adjacent to the Great Warriors Path that traveled north and south near where the 81 Corridor runs today. The western path, known as the 'New River Trail' crossed over my property and then led to the Ohio River Valley and the warring Indian tribes such as the Shawnee. Although the Germans had to be on their guard from marauding factions
of hostile Indians from the north and west, they became blood brothers with the Cherokee to the south. To live in harmony with the Cherokee, was to live with them like family and to share everything that you had.

Between 1790 and 1830 the population of Georgia increased six-fold. The western push of the settlers created a problem. Georgians continued to take American Indian lands and force both the Cherokee and the Creek Indians into the frontier. By 1825, the Lower Creek had been completely removed from the state under provisions of the Treaty of Indian Springs. By 1827, the Creek were gone.

White resentment of the Cherokee had been building and reached a pinnacle following the discovery of gold in northern Georgia. This discovery was made just after the creation and passage of the original Cherokee Nation constitution and establishment of a Cherokee Supreme Court. Possessed by 'gold fever' and a thirst for expansion, many white communities turned on their Cherokee neighbors. The U.S. government ultimately decided it was time for the Cherokee to be 'removed' leaving behind their farms, their land, and their homes.

President Andrew Jackson's military command and almost certainly his life were saved thanks to the aid of five-hundred Cherokee allies at the Battle of Horseshoe Bend in 1814. Unbelievably, it was Jackson who authorized the Indian Removal Act of 1830 following the recommendation of President James Monroe in his final address to Congress in 1825. Jackson, as president, sanctioned an attitude that had persisted for many years among many white immigrants. Even Thomas Jefferson, who often cited the Great Law of Peace of the Iroquois Confederacy as the model for the U.S. Constitution, supported Indian Removal as early as 1802.

The Cherokee in 1828 were not nomadic savages. In fact, they had assimilated many European-style customs including the wearing of gowns by Cherokee women. They built roads, schools and churches, had a system of representational government, and were farmers and cattle ranchers. A Cherokee alphabet called the 'Talking Leaves' was created.

In 1830, the Congress of the United States passed the 'Indian Removal Act.' Although many Americans were against the act, most notably Tennessee Congressman Davy Crockett, it passed anyway. President Andrew Jackson quickly signed the bill into law. The Cherokee attempted to fight removal legally by challenging the removal laws in the Supreme Court and by establishing an independent Cherokee Nation. At first the court seemed to rule against the Indians. In Cherokee Nation v. Georgia, the Court refused to hear a case extending Georgia's laws on the Cherokee because they did not represent a sovereign nation.

But in 1832, the U.S. Supreme Court ruled in favor of the Cherokee on the same issue in Worcester v. Cherokee. In this case, Chief Justice John Marshall ruled that the Cherokee Nation was sovereign, making the removal laws invalid. The Cherokee would have to agree to removal in a treaty. The treaty then would have to be ratified by the Senate.

Worcester vs. Georgia, 1832, and Cherokee Nation vs. Georgia, 1831, are considered the two most influential legal decisions in Indian law. The U.S. Supreme Court ruled for Georgia in the 1831 case, but in Worcester vs. Georgia, the court affirmed Cherokee sovereignty. President Andrew Jackson arrogantly defied the decision of the court and ordered the removal an act that established the U.S. government's precedent for the future removal of many Native Americans from their ancestral homelands. This was a sin for our nation.

The U.S. government used the Treaty of New Echota in 1835 to justify the removal. The treaty, signed by about one-hundred Cherokee known as the Treaty Party, relinquished all lands east of the Mississippi River in exchange for land in Indian Territory and the promise of money, livestock, various provisions, tools and other benefits.

When these pro-removal Cherokee leaders signed the Treaty of New Echota, they also signed their own death warrants since the Cherokee Nation Council had earlier passed a law calling for the death of anyone agreeing to give up tribal land. The signing and the removal led to bitter factionalism and ultimately to the deaths of most of the Treaty Party leaders once the Cherokee arrived in Indian Territory.

Opposition to the removal was led by Chief John Ross, a mixed-blood of Scottish and one-eighth Cherokee descent. The Ross party and most Cherokee opposed the New Echota Treaty but Georgia and the U.S. government prevailed and used it as justification to force almost all of the seventeen-thousand Cherokee from their southeastern homeland.

Under orders from President Jackson, the U.S. Army began enforcement of the Removal Act. The Cherokee were rounded up in the summer of 1838 and loaded onto boats that traveled the Tennessee, Ohio, Mississippi and Arkansas Rivers into Indian Territory. Many were held in prison camps awaiting their fate. An estimated four-thousand died from hunger, exposure and disease. The journey became a cultural memory called the 'trail where they cried' for the Cherokee and other removed tribes. Today it is widely remembered by the general public as the 'Trail of Tears.'

In his book *Don't Know Much About History*, Kenneth C. Davis writes:

'Hollywood has left the impression that the great Indian wars came in the Old West during the late 1800's, a period that many think of simplistically as the 'cowboy and Indian' days. But in fact that was a 'mopping up' effort. By that time the Indians were nearly finished, their subjugation complete, their numbers decimated. The killing, enslavement, and land theft had begun with the arrival of the Europeans. But it may have reached its nadir when it became federal policy under President Andrew Jackson.'

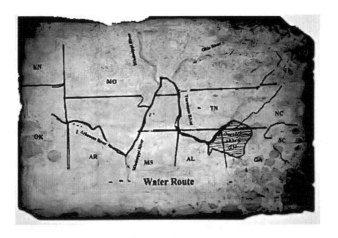

How heartsick my ancestors must have been as they settled Clover Hollow, knowing their Cherokee neighbors, friends, and blood brothers to the south, were being forcibly removed from their ancestral lands.

~~~~~~

John David Price and his family settled in Clover Hollow in the early 1800s, but it was his son John David

Price's Mill 1957   Same Spot 2012

Price Jr that completed building the dam and mill on
Sinking Creek in Clover Hollow by 1840. It is known that
slaves were used to build the concrete dam and that there
is a slave graveyard just up from the house on Sinking

Creek Mountain. My property today overlooks the dam on Sinking Creek as the mill burned down in the 1960s.

During these early times, log cabins were built first and then gradually switched over to frame as resources permitted. We know that the mill on Sinking Creek in Clover Hollow, built by David Price Jr. was frame and eventually had three stories and the capability to perform a different function on each floor. It could operate as a grist mill or a saw mill and at one time produced electricity. It was made from white oak grown in the area and probably sawn onsite.

The dam was thirty yards wide and ten feet high, producing more than enough power using a turbine that passed thru the dam instead of using a water wheel. It was a great example of man finding that perfect balance between nature and technology and produced sustainable power without harm to the environment, and they thanked God for all that they have received.

After the Civil War, Robert Price, the great-grandson of David Price, built a large home near the mill using architects brought in from Richmond sometime between 1870 and 1880. Soon after Robert Price built their house, the country went into a depression. Robert had financial difficulties and had to sell his house. His uncle, Charles H. Payne bought the house and later sold it to William Echols, who also bought the mill that was built by Robert's grandfather, David, in 1840.

Ben Kendrick ran the mill for Mr. Echols; he lived in a nearby house until his house could be built on Echols land. This miller's house is now the house I own in Clover Hollow. It was originally built with two rooms on top of two rooms using plank construction of white oak from local trees. The house has changed a lot over 125 years but you can still see the large planks of white oak up in the rafters. The rafters were most likely rough sawn at the mill that this house overlooked. The mill burned down in the early 1960s and only the dam remains. My property and house overlooks the dam, Sinking Creek, and Clover Hollow Mountain, where many of my ancestors are buried.

Between 1791 and 1800, a few settlers, most of which came from the German settlement located on the New River near Price's Fork, settled along Sinking Creek on the

Clover Hollow

other side of Brush Mountain from the New River Settlement. They built homes and a mill or two and named it Clover Hollow. On the north side of Sinking Creek lay Clover Hollow and to the south was the town of Chapman's Mill, later to be called the Village of Newport.

Clover Hollow is a carved out bowl of bottom land surrounded on both sides by two mountain chains, Clover Hollow Mountain and John's Creek Mountain. These mountains have numerous ridges and valleys cut between the mountain fingers that were ideal locations for farms along the many springs and creeks.

Most of the early settlers were farmers in search of fertile land, mill sites, and other activities that came along with a permanent settlement. This area consists of fine springs, mountain streams and fertile land, which made it very appealing to farmers and millers. Farmers let their cattle range in the mountains and would drive them to the pond on Salt Pond Mountain, now known as Mountain Lake, the location where 'Dirty Dancing' was filmed.

It is believed that Mountain Lake was discovered by *Christopher Gist*, a surveyor for the Ohio Land Company who surveyed the lake on Salt Pond Mountain in 1751 and is now known as Mountain Lake. He was likely one of the first white men to cross over my property on record. Christopher Gist (1706–1759) was an accomplished colonial British explorer, surveyor, and frontiersman. He was one of the first white explorers of the Ohio country (the present-day states of Ohio, eastern Indiana, western Pennsylvania, and northwestern West Virginia). He is credited with providing the first detailed description of the Ohio country to Great Britain and her colonists. At the outset of the French and Indian War in 1754, Gist accompanied Colonel George Washington on missions into the wilderness and saved Washington's life on two separate occasions. He was also with George Washington when they accompanied General Braddock on that fateful day on July 9, 1755.

My property is seven miles away from Mountain Lake with a direct view of Salt Pond Mountain, now known as John's Creek Mountain and overlooks the old Price Mill site and dam on Sinking Creek. As mentioned before, Sinking Creek gets its name because it disappears into the ground at times only to reappear above ground further downstream. It is a main tributary of, and running west into, the New River.

Clover Hollow was perfect for homesteading because the settlers could locate their homes between the mountain fingers coming off Clover Hollow Mountain which offered them rich bottom land and protection from the mountains.

Sibold

The Sibold's are probably my biggest connection to Clover Hollow. You see, I have a double dose of Sibold blood, a very unique genetic marker which may be a contributing factor in my ancestors ability to connect with me and somehow bring me to Clover Hollow. It gets a little tricky and complicated explaining how this all unfolded.

My Sibold research included family stories and traditional folk lore, but most importantly, information from the Lucy Lee Lancaster Collection archived at Virginia Tech. As mentioned earlier, she was one of the first five women to graduate from Virginia Tech in 1925. After graduation, she became the librarian at Virginia Tech for the next fifty-two years. Her hobbies included travel and genealogy, and now, forty-one boxes of her papers, letters, and research, are archived at the Virginia Tech library. She kept detailed records and correspondence which included information on the Price, Harless, and Sibold families, among many others. Lucy Lee and I share the same fourth-generation grandfather, Jacob Franz Sibold, who passed away in Clover Hollow.

Another one of those five women graduates of Virginia Tech in 1925 was Carrie Taylor Sibold, she was also a cousin of mine. Carrie and I share the same third-generation grandfather, John Phillip Sibold III. She grew up on the old Sibold farm in Blacksburg and her doll collection is also archived at the Virginia Tech Library.

One of the reasons it is so hard to research the Sibold name is that it has been spelled many different ways over the years. On one copy of the Winter Galley manifest the name was spelled Seibolt, here are a few more examples as compiled by Lucy Lee:

Saybold	Schripole	Scibold	Scipold	Seibels
Seebolt	Sebolltt	Seibolt	Seyboldt	Seepole
Seboldt	Sebolt	Seible	Seibold	Seibel
Seibell	Seipel	Seapole	Seabald	Seabold
Seybolt	Sebold	Seybold	Seybel	Seypell
Sibel	Sible	Sibole	Siple	Siples
Sibbald	Sipole	Siebold	Sibold	Sybel
Syble	Syple	Sypole	Zebolt	Ziebold

Lucy Lee Lancaster

Carrie Sibold

John Phillip Sibold, 26, arrived in Philadelphia along with the Harless and Prices aboard the Winter Galley, September 5, 1738. He also signed the Oath of Allegiance to the King of England. I have not found any records of the Sibold's in Germany; however I do have the Sibold coat of arms. Again, all three men, John Phillip Harless, John Michael Price, and John Phillip Sibold are my first-generation grandfathers and I am their eighth-generation grandson.

The senior Sibold traveled with the other Germans from the Palatinate State of Germany on the Winter Galley and as far as the Shenandoah Valley in Virginia, where he first settled and started a family. His son, John Phillip Sibold Jr (second-generation grandfather) traveled down to the German New River Settlement when he was of age and settled next to the Prices on upper Thoms Creek, and some of this land today is owned by Virginia Tech. The Sibold farm and home was located near where Route 460 passes Virginia Tech today. The Sibold family graveyard, where John Phillip Sibold Jr and John Phillip Sibold III are buried, can still be found overlooking the old Sibold property.

John Phillip Sibold Jr had two children, John Phillip Sibold III (third-generation grandfather), born in 1790, and Mary Sibold, born in 1798. John Sibold Jr bought what became the Sibold farm from Michael Surface in 1807.

John Phillip Sibold III (third-generation grandfather) died prematurely on the Sibold farm when he was killed by his pet bull in 1845. He had two boys and four girls:

Jacob Franz (fourth-generation grandfather) b. 1821
John Henry b. 1829
Hattie Elizabeth
Marie Catherine b. 1831
Susan b. 1823   Sallie

Jacob Franz Sibold was born 1821 and died 1903 (fourth-generation grandfather). He was nineteen years old when he left the Sibold farm and with his wife, Margaret Evelina Surface, settled in Clover Hollow around 1840. They lived in a small log house until their larger house was built nearby. I'm sorry to report that their beautiful house that lasted 175 years succumbed to fire less than a year ago.

Jacob and Evelina acquired a total of 633 acres in Clover Hollow on Clover Hollow Mountain. Jacob Franz Sibold took an active part in the life of his county. He was a Mason, a Lutheran, and served in various public offices, including being a justice of the piece and supervisor for his district.

Evelina and Jacob had thirteen children, seven boys and six girls. All but Jacob Franz Jr lived to maturity and had families having more than fifty offspring in the next generation. Their children were:

Harriet Francis b. 1843 d. 1875
Martin Luther Sibold b. 1844 d. 1914
When Martin Luther was sixteen years old he enlisted August 30, 1961, in CO. F. 24th Regiment, Virginia Infantry, Confederate States Army in order to take his father's place. He was wounded in his left shoulder in May 1864 and was hospitalized at Chimborazo Hospital in Richmond where he was furloughed for sixty days. He suffered injury to one lung at this time and on April 1, 1865 was taken prisoner at Five Forks, Virginia and then imprisoned at Point Lookout, Maryland, from which he was released on June 19, 1865. Martin Luther Sibold was *Lucy Lee Lancaster's* grandfather.

John Michael b. 1846 d. 1920
Hannah Katherine b. 1848 d. 1907
Elizabeth Jane b. 1850 d. 1884
Sarah Ann b. 1852 d. 1932
George Washington Sibold (fifth-generation grandfather) b. 1853 d. 1917 He settled in Monroe County, West Virginia.

James William Sibold (fifth-generation grandfather) b. 1855 d. 1934. He also settled in Monroe County, West Virginia. What's the deal with two, fifth-generation, Sibold grandfathers?

Mary Susan b. 1856 d. 1928
Jacob Franz b. 1858 d. 1860
Jefferson Davis Sibold b.1861 d. 1921
Thomas Jackson Sibold b. 1864 d. 1932
Thomas remained in Clover Hollow, and his son, Frank W. Sibold, owned my property on Sinking Creek for many years.

Margaret Lee b. 1866 d. 1927

One thing I can say about my ancestors is that they certainly handled death well. Their cemeteries and graves would generally be situated on the highest hill in their communities with breathtaking eternal views of the countryside.

Jacob and Evelina lived long and happy lives. I wanted to publish each of their obituaries for they tell their story far better than I could express. These were copied from clippings lent to Lucy Lee Lancaster by Mrs. Frank Sibold of Clover Hollow:

Obituary of Margaret Evelina Sibold

At her home in Giles County, Va. Mrs. Margaret E. Sibold, wife of Jacob Sibold, fell asleep in death on the evening of April 10, 1891, in the 67th year of her age. Mrs. Sibold had been in a declining state of health for a number of years, but only for a few weeks before death came and laid his cold grip upon her was she confined to the house and to her bed. During this time of absolute confinement she suffered without murmuring, manifesting all the while meekness, gentleness and patience. She lived a true and exemplary Christian since the days of her early youth, and had been for a long time a member of Clover Hollow Evangelical Lutheran Church. Her love for her church was great because her love for the Lord was intense. Her life, it may be said, was one of success. She tried as best she could to fulfill the true object of her creation. She had walked with her husband in joy and sorrow, identifying her life with his, imparting to him sweet Christian counsel, ministering to his wants, and sharing his labors and trails through a series of 48 years, thus filling well the sphere of a wife. She also filled successfully her sphere as a mother, and was permitted to live to enjoy the reward of her labors in seeing all of her children, and some of her grandchildren, embrace religion and become active members of the church. For such a wife and mother tears should be freely shed, and he who wept over the body of his friend Lazarus would not stay them. As might have been expected, her Christian walk brought a triumphant, calm, hopeful Christian death. With her mind perfectly clear to the last and her faith firm as a rock, she quietly "fell asleep in Jesus" and now the day has dawned, the glory has been revealed, and she has awaked "satisfied with his likeness." From her grave, which may be found in the beautiful "Hollow of Clover", comes a sound of warning, "Be ye also ready, for in such an hour as ye think not, the Son of Man Cometh." Newport, Va., April 30, 1891.

Obituary of Jacob Franz Sibold

Jacob Franz Sibold, was born near Blacksburg, Va., Nov. 10, 1821 and died at the home of his son T. J. Sibold, in Clover Hollow, Giles Co., Va., Nov. 2nd, 1903, aged 82 years. He married Evelina Surface of Giles Co., and by this happy union raised a large family who are honored citizens of the community in which they live, she having passed before him to the spirit world. Just before the end came he said to his son, let me die. When asked if he wished to die, he said yes. He was then asked if he was prepared for death, his answer was yes, the last words he ever spoke. He folded his arms and passed away without a struggle. He joined the Lutheran church when but a youth, and was always faithful to his vows. He was an honest and industrious man, always in sympathy with the less fortunate then himself. He was a kind father and husband, and was held in high esteem as a citizen of his county, having been honored with the office of Justice, and being Supervisor of his district for many years. His body was taken from home to the church where the funeral service was conducted by Rev. J. E. Bushnell, according to the form of the Lutheran church, after which his body was taken charge of the Masonic Brethren, he being an honored member of Simmonsville Lodge of Craig Co., they being present together with Sinking Lodge of Newport, joined in paying the last tribute of respect to their departed brother, and together with many other friends proceeded to the family graveyard nearby, and there while the beautiful and impressive service of the Masonic Fraternity was read the body was lowered in the grave, and with the emblems of the order and the grand honor by the brethren, earth to earth and dust to dust, the grave closed over the mortal remains of J. F. Sibold, there to remain until the craft is called from labor to refreshment, and join the great architect of the universe, where parting is no more. He has served his purpose here on earth, and we trust he has entered upon the enjoyment of that rest that remains for the people of God. So dear mourners, you have reason to believe that the departed is now free from toil and suffering, and is happy in the mansions above. Let this thought comfort your hearts, but as you so live, labor and trust that when death summons you hence it will be to join your loved ones who are happy in the Paradise of God. L.M.S.

No discussion of Clover Hollow would be complete without mentioning the Village of Newport, Virginia. Near Clover Hollow, Newport is located between Gap Mountain, Salt Pond Mountain, and Spruce Run Mountain, and is the community center for Spruce Run, Mountain Lake, Clover Hollow and Sinking Creek. Archaeologists have determined that Indians did live there and there is evidence that Paleoindians also inhabited the area.

In 1832, the Fincastle-Cumberland Turnpike going from Fincastle through Newport, Eggleston, and Bland, increased trade in Newport by stagecoach tremendously.

From 1832 to 1850 the population grew as many more moved there. The name Chapman's Mill changed to Newport and it was commonly thought that the people named it after Captain Newport who sailed across the Atlantic a few times for England to Jamestown bringing emigrants to settle in the Americas. Old records however, state that Newport was the crossroads village, thus making it a 'new port' to the old western frontier.

In 1858, the railroad from Petersburg came as far as Dublin and regularly operated stagecoach routes along the Wilderness Trail. Records show that Newport became a resort town with many people staying overnight at the Newport hotels before continuing on with their travels. They often used Newport as a stopover on the way to the many hot spring resorts a little further west. Some stayed and settled because of the beauty.

All this came to a halt during the Civil War when 123 soldiers from Newport left to join the confederacy including Martin Luther Sibold who enlisted to take his father's place. There was a Civil War skirmish in Newport with Union troops on top of Newport Hill and Confederate troops on top of Parsonage Hill. As the Union troops retreated, they looted the town of Newport before heading north over Salt Pond Mountain. To get the wagons across the mountain they had to throw all of their ammunition over a cliff, that cliff was named Minnie-ball Hill. After the war, the men came home and rebuilt the community. They restocked their farms, ran mills, and merchants opened businesses. Cabinetmakers started making furniture, hotels reopened, and stagecoaches came through just like they had before. Newport was incorporated in 1872 and a smelting furnace was put into operation. Remains of the old iron furnace still stand on the old furnace road that can still be found on the north-side of Gap Mountain.

In 1895, Falls Manufacturing Company came to Newport and made farm equipment, guns, wagons, buggies, and certain types of kitchen utensils. Like old western stagecoach towns, Newport had four distilleries and three saloons. On Saturday night, men came to town to drink which led to many fights. It was once said that Newport was referred to as 'Hells Half-Acre.' Even so, on Sunday morning the church bells would always still ring.

Years later, the distilleries and saloons were voted out and Newport became the largest town in Giles County by the late 1800s. The town's growth came to a sudden halt on April 1, 1902, when the center of the town burned to the ground. Five store buildings, two hotels, a longhouse, tannery, jail, two dwellings and a Masonic hall, all went up in smoke. Only one store and one hotel were rebuilt. After the fire, any remaining businesses soon left due to the introduction of the automobile along with the construction of good roads for them to travel. This was the end of the stagecoach in this part of the country.

Sketch by Lewis Miller of the village of Newport in the 1850's

Chapter 7 Greenville

Monroe County, West Virginia, the land of sinkholes and hollows, is one of sixteen counties named in honor of the fifth president of the United States. The bordering counties are Greenbrier, Summers, Mercer, Alleghany, Craig, and Giles. The first three lie in West Virginia, and the last three in Virginia. Before the Civil War, this land was all part of Virginia and lay in the Ridge and Valley Region of the Appalachian Mountains. Clover Hollow is in Giles County, Virginia, thirty miles as the crow flies southeast of Greenville, West Virginia.

No other county in the state send its waters partly toward the Atlantic and partly toward the Gulf of Mexico. It is within these borders that the watershed between these two drainage areas leaves the Alleghany Front and passes from mountain to mountain by a succession of saddle-ridges, until it joins the eastern arm of the Blue Ridge in Floyd County. It is because Monroe lies astride the Alleghany Front that the valleys and ridges of its eastern portion display the symmetry which is so characteristic of the main Alleghany and all the mountain ranges farther east. But, the contour of the western portion shows the irregularity which is almost universal throughout that part of West Virginia that drains into the Ohio. In the deep

119

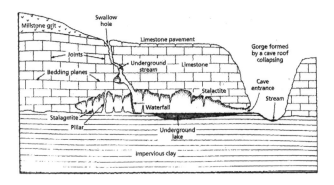

valleys of Monroe are some very bold springs. These mark the reappearance of the waters that fall on the limestone belts. The surface drainage sinks into the underground channels with which the limestone strata are honeycombed. Several of the streams lose themselves in the ground and reappear some distance away. But in places, a creek bed will be dry except in wet weather, although there may be running waters above as well as below.

A thick formation of blue, massive limestone, covers much of the county, as may be observed from the frequent outcrops and the very numerous sinkholes. The limestone under Monroe County was laid down in two periods when the eastern United States was covered by tropical shallow seas. Limestone near Peter's Mountain, was laid down between 570 and 450 million years ago. The Greenbriar group was formed between 350 and 335 million years ago. Calcium-rich shells and skeletons collected and solidified into limestone. This meaning that limestone was once living organisms, which may explain some of their electromagnetic properties and the belief that a spiritual essence still radiates from the ancient limestone. Additional sediment accumulated and turned to rock on top of the limestone. As tectonic plates collided, creating the Appalachian Mountains 260 million years ago, the limestone was alternatively buried, uplifted, faulted, folded, and fractured.

Limestone is relatively impermeable. Water cannot flow through it like it flows through sandstone. Over millions of years, groundwater, slightly acidified by organic material in the soil, seeped onto cracks in the limestone, dissolving it and carving caves, conduits, pipes and channels. Highly eroded limestone is called karst. Water flowing through dissolved openings in the rocks and energy manifest into low grade radiation, geomagnetic induced current, and chemical off-gassing can be released even to this day.

Anticlines (structural hills) and synclines (structural hollows) are formed when the limestone is wrinkled during tectonic plate collisions. They are structures in the underlying rock that effect how the water flows through it but are not always visible from the surface.

Springs occur when underground water resurfaces. Caves carved by acidic, moving water, often forms at seams in the rocks. Contact caves that form where the limestone meets a shale layer below it are often quite large. Sinkholes form over time as water seeping into cracks dissolves the limestone. Cave entrances and direct conduits into the karst aquifer are often found in sinkholes. Elsewhere, the rock formation is usually of a sandstone nature. Some of the limestone is of so fine a grain as to resemble marble. Even the existence of lithographic stone has been reported. The geology of Monroe County is very ancient.

~~~~~~

The political divisions of Monroe County are the magisterial districts of Red Sulphur, Second Creek, Springfield, Sweet Springs, Wolf Creek, and Union. Union lies in the center, Red Sulphur is in the extreme south and Springfield is between. Springfield is composed of Greenville, Lillydale, and Rock Camp.

When the country beyond the Alleghenies became known to the English speaking whites of the seacoast, there were probably fewer than a half dozen small villages of Indians in what is now West Virginia. And yet, it does not follow that this has always been a vacant land.

A great number of arrowheads, hatchets, scrapers and other tools of stone have been frequently picked up in Monroe County and are not sufficiently accounted for by assuming they have been dropped by visiting hunters.

Arrowheads are tedious to manufacture. The quarries, from which the raw material was taken were of so great consequence in the eyes of the Indians that they were sometimes neutral ground, even in the case of tribes that were at war with each other. It is seen that the arrowheads would not have been used wastefully.

Indian burial mounds containing skeletons does not by any means signify that the remains are warriors slain in battle, but entire village burial grounds and the mound growing in size as internments were added. The village might leave only faint signs of its existence because the huts were of perishable materials.

Village sites have been found within and near the borders of Monroe usually on rich bottom land. The choice of the left bank is seemingly because of the westerly winds. It can't be determined if the villages found were occupied by only one or more tribes. Between the oldest and youngest of the village sites in and around this county, several, perhaps many centuries may have elapsed and tribe may have succeeded tribe. Also, evidence of Paleolithic Indians older than ten-thousand years have been found in the county.

There was a flint quarry at the mouth of Stinking Lick and another a few miles east of Peterstown. On the Dunlap farm near the mouth of Hans Creek was once a burial mound. It was sixty feet across and contained many relics. Among these were sheets of mica that seem to have been used to cover the faces of the dead. Mica is known to have special electromagnetic properties and often electromagnetic properties are thought to have a strong spiritual meaning as well. This mica must have been obtained from the mountains of North Carolina. An excavation in Union in 1889 for the foundation of the new Methodist church revealed fourteen skulls and at least one complete skeleton. With these bones were found relics as the Indians were accustomed to deposit in their graves.

Monroe County is the first transalleghany county of West Virginia to be trodden by the feet of European explorers. The visit took place only sixty-four years after the founding of Jamestown and at least seventy years before any white person attempted to make his home here. Philadelphia had not yet established itself and where now stands the city of Petersburg, Virginia, was Fort Henry. And, in command of the fort was Major Abraham Wood. He had come to Virginia in 1620 when he was only ten years old. It was his duty to carry out the wishes of the House of Burgesses in the matter of promoting trade with the natives. English traders from Wood's post had already traveled four-hundred miles toward the southwest on what was known as the Occoneechee path.

Major Wood knew of the discovery of the New River thirty years earlier and understood that it must be significant that so large a river should be flowing in a direction contrary to those of Tidewater, Virginia. In 1671, Major Wood commissioned Thomas Batt, Robert Fullam, and Thomas Wood, to find out about 'the ebbing and flowing of the waters on the other side of the mountains in order to the discovery of the south sea.' There were added to the party, Jack Neasom, a servant to Major Wood and Perecute, an Appomattox Indian. A few days later the explorers were joined by seven more of the same tribe to serve as guides and scouts. The start from Fort Henry was made September 1, 1671, and in six days the Blue Ridge was sighted.

It was current opinion when under Indian occupancy; the Atlantic states was an unbroken forest. A map of 1719 shows a 'large savannah' laying a little east of the Blue Ridge and parallel with it. By a savannah was meant a prairie, the latter word not yet having come into the English language. Five years later, Colonel William Byrd, in speaking of the Roanoke Valley says 'there is scarce a shrub in view to intercept your prospect, but grass as high as a man on horseback.' These savannah's were seen by the Woods party in the Roanoke Valley and then in the New River Valley.

The New River was first touched by the Woods expedition about three and one-half miles north of Radford, Virginia. Maintaining a northerly course, Peters Mountain was crossed by using one of the Indian paths. The journal kept by the party speaks of valleys tending westward and adds 'it was a pleasing though dreadful sight to see the mountains and hills as if piled upon one another.' An easy descent of three miles brought them about noon to two trees, on one of which were marked with a coal, the letters *MAN*. The other was cut in with the letters M A, and several other 'scrabblemonts.' These trees were close by a run coursing sometimes westerly, sometimes northerly, with 'curious meadows' on each side. Pressing forward, the party found stony hills, but rich soil, and meadows with grass above a man's height. They also found 'many streams running west-northwest and several from the mountains looking southerly, all running northerly into the Great River.'

This Great River (the New River) was referred to as 'Woods River' in many of the old maps. In seven miles, they came to a steep descent with a great run in it 'their course by the path being west southwest.' They turned west and again meeting the river, they made quarters for the night. The farther they went that day the richer they found the soil. It was 'stony but full of brave meadows and old fields.' The encampment near the site of Union, West Virginia was September 13, old style, equivalent to September 24, new style. The change in the calendar did not take place until 1752.

After again reaching the New River, the explorers kept down the stream and found cornstalks in the bottoms. They were told the Mohicans had once lived here. More marked trees were found. From the upland, they went down to the river over ground where the natives had once lived and the old fields were found so encumbered with weeds and locusts that they could hardly get through. When they came to a quiet pool they imagined they were at the head of the tide. From a river-hill they thought they saw a tidal estuary in the distance. They were now far below Hinton and in reality were viewing a fog in the river canyon. The sunlight glimmering upon the fog gave it the appearance of an inlet from the sea. When the party had been out sixteen days the Indians said bad weather would soon be coming on and they wished to return. Grapes, haws, and gooseberries were found but their provisions were used up and not only was the game scarce, it was hard to get at.

The Wood expedition was absent from Fort Henry just one month. As an exploit, it is undoubtedly genuine and it was much relied upon by the British government in its controversy with France as to the ownership of the

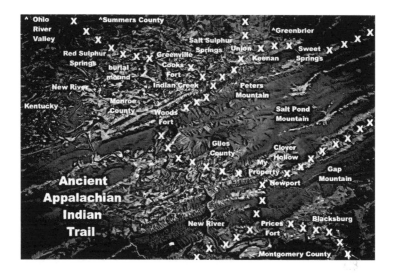

Mississippi Valley. Notwithstanding the energy of the French explorers, the actual priority of claim is on the side of the English. But, the idea of the explorers that they were and almost within sight of the Pacific shows a strange ignorance of American geography, even for that day and age. They seem to have been unaware of the extensive travel of De Soto, Coronado, and other Spanish explorers in the preceding century.

It is absolutely clear to me by studying the Wood expedition journals that they followed an ancient Indian trail starting near the horseshoe bottom on the New River near Price's Fork, and running all the way to the end of the expedition just past Hinton. By studying topographical maps and researching my family history, I have been able to map out this ancient Indian trail where my ancestors had settled, lived, and are buried along this great Indian path crossing through the Appalachians.

The entire Alleghany region was threaded by Indian trails. Some of these were through lines of travel. Others were only of local importance. In some and perhaps many instances, these paths were doubtless first opened by the herds of buffalo as these animals journeyed from one feeding ground to another. When the white man came on the scene, he found it very convenient to use the Indian trails as a bridlepath. Here and there it was accepted as a public highway and given into the care of road overseers. Such converted thoroughfares were termed Indian roads.

Elsewhere the trail lapsed into disuse and after a century of tillage, it is only now and then, especially in the woods, recognized. In Monroe, as in other mountain counties, the Indian paths were the ones first used by the early settlers. It is true that the Gap Mills Valley and the basin of Indian Creek were favored points of settlement and it was largely because of the trail that came up Dunlap and down Second, and Indian Creek, to the New River. Near Gap Mills, it was joined by a path crossing Peters Mountain. The trail then took the general direction of Indian Creek to its mouth, passing south of Thorny Hollow and intersecting the present road from Union to Willow Bend and was near the Alexander farm. From Ellison's Ridge, a side-path crossed Indian Creek below Greenville and went up Indian Draft reaching the Greenbrier near Lowell. From the mouth of Indian, another path came up Stinking Lick to the vicinity of Ballard and then ran eastward, crossing Peters Mountain at Simms Gap. Near Ballard, this path has been traced a considerable distance, while on Little Mountain, a section of the Dunlap path is still perfectly observable. The last named path was used by the many immigrants from the Cowpasture, Calfpasture, and Bullpasture valleys. Other settlers came direct from the upper James, the Roanoke, and the New, by means of the trails crossing Peters Mountain, or penetrating the narrows of the New River.

The enterprise shown in the Woods expedition was not promptly followed up. The accomplishment of 1671 seems to have become half forgotten, although, when prospectors were examining the valley of the New some seventy years later, the stream was commonly known as Wood's River. It was not until 1716, that Governor Spottswood undertook his celebrated junketing trip to the South Fork of the Shenandoah. Even yet, the dwellers in Tidewater had hazy and very unfavorable ideas of the country beyond the Blue Ridge. But, the veil was now permanently lifted and exploration became active.

In 1732, John Lewis and his Irish followers, along with the Germans flowing in from Philadelphia, started to settle Augusta County. So rapid was this immigration from Ulster and Germany that the new county, authorized in 1738, was definitely organized by 1745. By this time, venturesome land-seekers like my grandfathers Michael Price and John Harless were building cabins on the New River.

In 1749, we find a definite beginning of settlement on the lower course of the Greenbrier. Virginia had the Headright Law, permitting each adult male immigrant, who had paid his way to Virginia, to take up fifty acres of the public domain. This was a wise policy and it was similar to the homestead law of the federal government. It tended to fill the colony with a class of thrifty immigrants and at no more than a reasonable speed. But, the operation of the Headright Law was largely neutralized by what is known as the 'Order of Council.' So far as this other method was followed, the public lands were parceled out in immense blocks to associations of influential men who stood in line with the government. In theory, these companies were immigration agencies. They were supposed to solicit bona-fide settlers and bring them to the land in question. The company was supposed to see that its lands were settled within a definite limit of time. But, the colonial government was very lenient in enforcing its conditions against its own favorites. The practical working of this system was to enable a syndicate to corner the desirable land over a very large area and to extort a price from the settler which was seemingly low yet relatively high. The settler therefore had to pay this price or move farther on. Often, he did move on. One result was to push forward too rapidly a thin fringe of settlement and expose it unduly to raids by hostile Indians. By giving little service in return, the members of these syndicates were permitted to line their pockets at the expense of the public.

In pursuance of this policy of favoritism, the Greenbrier Land Company was organized in 1749. Its president was John Robinson, Treasurer of Virginia and Speaker of the House of Burgesses. The other members were William Beverly, Beverly Robinson, Thomas Nelson, Jr., John Craig, John Wilson, and four Lewis's, Robert, John, William and Charles. Of these, all but Wilson, John, William, and Charles Lewis were planters from Tidewater. They were little else than silent partners whose names were supposed to lend dignity and prestige to the enterprise.

The active partners were John Lewis and his sons, Thomas and Andrew, both of whom were surveyors. By Order of Council, the company was granted one-hundred thousand acres lying in the present counties of Pocahontas, Greenbrier, and Monroe. It was allowed four years in which to make surveys and pay for settlement rights. The grant was not in one solid block, the company being allowed to pick out the choice parcels and leave the adjacent cull lands to take care of themselves.

There is not much early mention about surveys in the fertile tableland of the sinks. It was the bottoms and the coves with running water that always had the strongest appeal to the immigrants. My ancestors sought out the fertile bottom land (sinks) for farming and along streams so they could build their mills, in particularly, the mill on Sinking Creek in Clover Hollow.

After the shocking rout of the army under Braddock took place on July 9, 1755, the Indians immediately undertook to push back the encroaching settlements. During this year and the next, the Greenbrier was visited by the storm. In a letter to Andrew Lewis, Governor Dinwiddie says he is 'sorry for the death of thirteen of our subjects at Greenbrier, victims of the barbarous Indians.' Writing twelve days later to Lieutenant John McNeill, a resident of the Greenbrier Valley, he is surprised that the 'fifty-nine people in Fort Greenbrier at the time of Indian attack did not resist.' He thinks they could not have been properly armed. The raid into the Greenbrier was a thorough piece of work. The infant settlements west of the Alleghany Front were utterly wiped out and the wilderness resumed its reign. The same effect the Draper's Meadow Massacre had on the New River Valley settlements.

With respect to Virginia, the war for independence presents three phases; first, the campaign against Dunmore, ending with the expulsion of the Tory governor early in 1776; second, a war with the Indians, beginning about two years after the battle of Point Pleasant and not ending until several years after the treaty with Britain; third, a campaign east of the Blue Ridge, beginning near the close of 1780 and terminating with the capture of Cornwallis in October 1781.

The inhabitants of Monroe and Greenbrier saw little of the war except for the trouble with the Indians, which was the result of British emissaries. Their settlements included little more than two-thousand people. It was nearly as much as they could do to stand off the Indians. The only actual forts within the present limits of Monroe were Wood's Fort on Rich Creek and Cook's Fort on Indian Creek, near Greenville. But, while such defenses were very serviceable against the Indians, they were not regarded as government posts.

The outbreak of Dunmore's war in the summer of 1774 found a chain of settlements all die away from Sweet Springs to Gap Mills and to the head of Indian Creek, and then down Indian to its mouth on the New.

The Lost Settlement of Springfield

In parallel with the New River German Settlement's founding families, the Price, Harless, and Sibold's, the Mann and Miller families came to the Port of Philadelphia on September 21, 1732 aboard the ship 'Pink Plaisance.' The Mann and Miller families were neighbors in Germany and traveled together down the Great Valley Road until they reached the frontier woodlands a couple of miles up Indian Creek from where Greenville, West Virginia stands today.

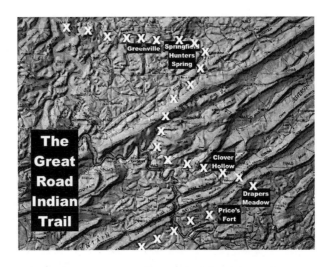

Jacob Mann Sr. was born in Germany in 1724 and emigrated to the Colonies with his parents, first settling in Lancaster, Pennsylvania and then moving to Virginia. He married Barbara 'Barbary' Miller from Augusta County, Virginia. Their son, Jacob Mann Jr., was born in Augusta County in 1745. Between 1770 and 1775, Jacob Jr, came to the area that was later called Springfield, along with his father, mother, and brother Adam. By 1785, Jacob Jr. owned nine-hundred acres of land and in addition to farming, had built a blacksmith shop and a powder mill. Jacob was married in 1779 to Mary Kessinger and they had ten children. An energetic leader in the community from the time of their arrival, Jacob died in 1815 and Mary in 1851.

John Miller Sr, brother of Barbara Miller and uncle and friend of Jacob Mann Jr, also crossed over the mountains and settled on Indian Creek around 1775. John Miller was married to Barbara Mauzy in Rockingham County, Virginia, and raised nine children. In 1785, the year that his youngest was born, John Miller acquired 395 acres adjacent to Jacob Mann's holding. He and his wife Barbara are buried in the Miller-Halstead Cemetery, which is located on the original land grant.

The growth of the Miller and Mann families, the gradual addition to of others to the neighborhood, their marriages, births, deaths, and complex land transactions, formed the

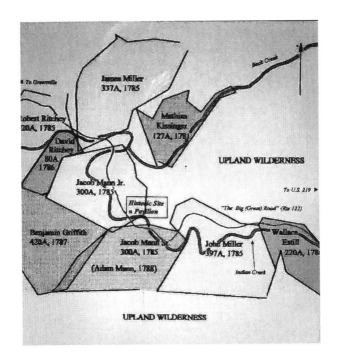

James Miller
337A, 1785

Rock Creek

To Greenville

Robert Ritchey
220A, 1785

Mathias
Kissinger
127A, 178?

David
Ritchey
80A
1786

UPLAND WILDERNESS

Jacob Mann Jr.
300A, 1785

To U.S. 219 ▶

Historic Site
a Pavilion

"The Big (Great) Road" (Rte 122)

Benjamin Griffith
420A, 1787

Jacob Mann Sr.
300A, 1785

John Miller
197A, 1785

Wallace
Estill
220A, 178?

(Adam Mann, 1788)

Indian Creek

UPLAND WILDERNESS

131

basis of the Springfield community. Their blood runs in my blood. The next generation after Jacob Mann Jr. and John Miller Sr. began to cross the formidable barrier of the Alleghany Mountains and settle in the drainage of the Ohio River. Most of these plots were occupied by the 1770s, but the surveying process was delayed until after the American Revolution. Moreover, the grants were formalized with warrants following the 1780s. In some cases, like the Jacob Mann Sr. tract, the land was 'assigned' to a family member or friend after the survey but before the legal process took place. 'The Big Road' also known as 'The Great Road' roughly followed the course of Route 122 today. Indian Creek crosses the map from east to west and Back Creek comes in from the Northeast - both are shown in the map on the next page. The ancient Indian trail that crosses through Clover Hollow is the same Indian trail that followed along Indian Creek here which later evolved into 'The Great Road' used by these settlers.

So, the land changed hands with time as a number of the initial settlers moved on to Kentucky. Those who remained on Indian Creek expanded their holdings so that most of the land labeled 'Upper Wilderness' was occupied during the 1790s. From the early 1800s to the early 1900s this spot was the site of an active community. It was the core of the Village of Springfield, later known as Hunters Springs.

Most likely, combinations of forces were responsible for the disappearance of this community. Stricken by an epidemic of diphtheria fever in the mid 1800s and typhoid fever in the early 1900s, the village never recovered. By the late 1940s, there was little evidence of this once thriving community. All that remains to this day is the remaining stones of the village mill dam just upstream on Indian Creek.

Cook's Fort

In building a palisade, a trench was dug to a depth of some four feet and in it was planted a double row of logs set in a vertical position and projecting about ten feet above the general level of the ground. The row was doubled to leave no crevices for bullets to pass through. The Cook

stockade is said to have been enclosed in an oblong space of an acre and a half. Three hundred people found refuge there in 1778. The enclosure at Woods' Fort was probably much smaller. Within the stockades of Cook's Fort were cabins, the palisade forming one of the walls, and the cabin roof serving as a parapet to shoot from. The people who assembled in these forts for protection rendered them crowded, uncomfortable, and insanitary. They would sometimes take too great of risks to escape for a time the stuffiness of their quarters. Yet it required a great deal of hard labor to enclose even one acre. For this reason, the stockade was much less common than the unenclosed blockhouse.

The latter was a dwelling built to make the wall ball-proof. The door was very thick, sometimes studded with broad-headed nails and was so firmly secured as to withstand a shock by a log used as a battering ram. The windows were too narrow for a person to crawl through. Where there was an upper story, it sometimes projected over the lower to enable the defenders to shoot an enemy coming close to the lower wall. These fortified houses could sometimes hold out against a formidable attack. The greatest danger was a blazing arrow directed at the roof. Hence, it was important that the foe should not find cover within arrow-shot.

It appears that about the year 1770, Valentine and his wife Susanna Cook, along with his brother Jacob, came to the farm located one-fourth mile west of Greenville. With the help of other families whose names would have included John Miller Sr., Jacob Mann Jr., Campbell,

Ellison, Bradshaw, Henderson, Thompson, and Bland, they constructed a fort known as Cook's Fort.

Cook's fort stood about midway in the Indian Creek bottom on the south side of the stream and perhaps two-hundred yards west of the road crossing at the ford just below Greenville. The swale close by may then have furnished water. The position was such as to command the trail from Ellison's Ridge that crossed Indian Creek nearby and ran up Indian Draft.

Among the many skirmishes the settlers had with the Indians, those of Valentine Cook are best known. At one time he was captured by the Indians, taken up on Indian Draft and there forced to trade his good rifle with the Indians for a very poor one, after which he was permitted to return home unharmed. Between 1773 and 1781, Cook's Fort at times would be attacked by Indians every day. Where the fort once stood, relics like arrowheads can still be found when the field is turned up during the spring planting.

Jacob Mann, the great grandfather of S.M. Mann of Greenville, was born in Albemarle County, Virginia, near where the city of Charlottesville now stands. When about thirty years of age, he moved to this community and assisted in the construction of Cook's Fort. He was one of the most outstanding Indian fighters of the community. On one occasion, the Indians killed an entire family who lived nearby. Jacob Mann in command of five others started in pursuit of the Indians. After following them for five days they came upon them at the close of day camped on the banks of the Ohio River. It was decided, after holding a 'Council of War' to wait until morning before attacking the Indians who were seven in number.

Jacob Mann's instructions to his men were that each one should select his Indian, so that no two would shoot at the same one. At the first fire, six Indians fell dead. The seventh dropped his gun and jumped into the Ohio River. Jacob Mann, being a great swimmer and possessed unusual physical strength leaped in after him, catching the Indian about midway of the river and killed him with his hunting knife.

At another time when the food supply at the fort became exhausted, Jacob Mann started up Cook's Run and across

Cook's Fort
original location

the flat woods on a deer hunt. He succeeded in getting a deer and had begun his return with the carcass on his back when he met with Indians. He started on the run for the fort. But, within three-fourths of a mile from the fort he saw it was both throw away the venison and let those at the fort suffer, or be captured himself as the Indians were consistently gaining on him. About that time he saw a depression in the ground, which turned out to be a small cave. Throwing the deer into the hole he immediately crawled in after it. His dog followed, and hearing the bark of the dog, Jacob Mann held its mouth shut tight while the Indians prowled around so close at times that the muzzles of their long rifles brushed the weeds about the mouth of the cave. After a time the Indians departed and he was successful in reaching the fort with the precious venison before daylight.

The first marriage in the stockade is said to have been that of Philip Hammond to Christiana, a daughter of Valentine Cook, in 1778. Hammond distinguished himself as one of the two messengers sent from Fort Randolph at Point Pleasant to warn the settlers around Donally's Fort of the impending Indian attack in retribution for the murder of their Shawnee chief, Cornstalk. They outran the Indian army by several hours. Both men had been disguised to look like Indians by an Indian woman who had come with her cattle to take refuge at the fort. It is believed that she was a sister to Cornstalk. By the whites, she was known as the 'Grenadier Squaw' as a result of her 'commanding stature.'

Cook's Mill

We know from Valentine Cook's will of 1797 that a gristmill had been established upstream from Cook's Fort. During the early to mid-1800s, the mill remained in the ownership of the Cook family spanning three generations. Late in 1857, the Cook family contracted with James Humphrey's to build a new mill, apparently on the site of the original one that may have been small and outdated. It is now an example of the Gothic Revival style as indicated by the ornamental verge boards along the eaves and the board-and-batten siding on the facade.

According to the current owners of the mill, Fred and Barbara Ziegler, Valentine Cook had carved out a 650 acre tract by the time of a 1774 survey. They surmise that the mill was built soon after because much of the tillable farmland along Indian Creek had already been claimed and was presumably being cleared and farmed to some degree. So, there would have been a real need to grind corn and wheat in an area so remote from other facilities. The mill would have been small and powered by a waterwheel connected to at least one 'run of grindstones' by wooden shafts and gears. More elaborate mills existed at the time, with elevators, sifters, etc., but a mill on the frontier would have been more basic. Valentine Cook also had a gunpowder mill by 1797 using saltpeter from local caves, but whether this was on this site is unknown.

They explain that the present mill must have been built in 1858, to judge by a contract signed late in 1857 by Jacob A. Cook, Riley B. Cook, and the builder, James Humphreys. The contract specifies a waterwheel driven mill and implies that the machinery was to be constructed on site, rather than factory built. At least two runs of stones were included, together with a range of hoppers, screen chests, bolting chests, etc., all to be connected with elevators and conveyors.

Clearly, this large mill was fully equipped to take advantage of all four levels and could produce a large volume of flour and feed. A wooden dam was used at the time, and remnants are still visible when the pond is drained.

By about 1870, the waterwheel succumbed to a double turbine system and the grindstones were replaced by roller mills about 1893, a technology still current. The concrete dam was built about 1906. The water supply for the millpond emerges from a large spring just one quarter of a mile upstream. In fact, the dam causes the water to 'pond' all the way to these springs. Perhaps half the water comes from the Laurel Creek watershed which lies to the north of the main Indian Creek drainage. A cave system over three miles long is the source that brings the Laurel Creek waters to the Cooks Mill, millpond.

Saltpeter Caves, Greenville, West Virginia

This cave system has five entrances and 3.8 miles of surveyed passages. The southern entrance is above the mill pond and is the place where Laurel Creek, which sinks about one mile north of Greenville, reemerges from the ground. The three northern entrances to the cave are in a small valley about a third of a mile north of the mill pond entrance. They were about a quarter-mile hike through a couple hollows, behind my grandparent's farm. One of these, the northeastern entrance, is called the water entrance and is situated where a portion of the underground route of Laurel Creek is exposed to the surface. The cave was owned by John Maddy in 1804 and then sold to Jacob and John Mann who manufactured saltpeter (potassium nitrate) at the site for several years. Saltpeter was used in the manufacture of gunpowder. The cave was again mined for saltpeter during the Civil War. Unfortunately, the saltpeter section of the cave has been vandalized and few traces of mining or the old leaching hoppers remain. The cave has several large rooms but few calcite formations. The passages intertwine and form a maze. The majority of all my summers as a kid were spent exploring these caves. It was my first real taste for adventure.

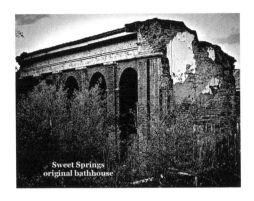

Sweet Springs
original bathhouse

Sweet Springs is the oldest, most permanent, and most interesting of the watering places of Monroe County, West Virginia. James Moss, said to have been the first settler on the upper course of Dunlap, reared his cabin about 1760 near the mineral spring. He did not acquire title and disposed of his interest to William Lewis. A land patent was issued in 1774. Like his more famous brothers, William Lewis was a determined land prospector and secured choice tracts in several localities but Sweet Springs was the spot he selected for a home. The Lewis brothers often conducted their land operations in partnership. So, Thomas Lewis deeded to William in 1786 his interest in 1220 acres on 'Sweet Springs Branch' the consideration being one-thousand pounds.

After the restoration of peace, William Lewis began to develop Sweet Springs as a health resort. As a related step in his own interest, he offered to provide a home for the court of the circuit that embraced the counties of Botetourt, Greenbrier, Kanawha, and Montgomery. The inducements included a courthouse and a jail.

Sweet Springs has been that of a well known summer resort and very small social and commercial center. Next to Berkeley Springs and the resorts of Warm Springs Valley, it is the oldest watering place in the Virginias. Sweet Springs, located on State Route 3 in eastern Monroe County is the site of a historic mineral spring resort in use since the late 1700s. The spring water, which emerges from the ground at 73 degrees F, contains a concentration of iron and carbon dioxide and has been credited with medicinal properties. The first hotel was erected in 1792 by William Lewis, who developed the resort around the spring of that year. From 1795 to 1807, a Virginia district court representing the counties of Botetourt, Greenbrier, Kanawha, and Montgomery, met at the facility.

The heyday of the resort was from 1820 until the Civil War. In the 1830s, the present large brick hotel was constructed with columned porticos. Its design was long attributed to Thomas Jefferson but more recently has been accredited to a Jefferson associate. A second large building and five cottages were erected in 1857. Sweet Springs, during this period, was a day's carriage drive from eight other mineral spring resorts in what was termed the 'Springs Region' of pre-Civil War Virginia. Guests would frequently make a circuit of several mineral springs' resorts during the busy summer season sampling the water and social life at each. Famous visitors to Sweet Springs included George and Martha Washington, General Lafayette, Chief Justice John Marshall, Jerome Bonaparte, Napoleon Bonaparte's brother, Patrick Henry, James and Dolly Madison, and Robert E. Lee. Presidents Pierce and Fillmore also visited the resort.

In June 1864, the resort was visited by Union forces under the command of General David Hunter. His troops camped nearby the resort but there is no record that the buildings were harmed. Sweet Springs continued to attract guests after the Civil War but many potential visitors preferred to go to resorts that were more convenient to the rail lines.

The resort continued to operate under a succession of owners until it went into receivership in 1930. In 1945 the state of West Virginia purchased the property and established the Andrew S. Rowan Memorial Home for the Aged in the old resort's buildings. A major renovation was undertaken from 1972 to 1975. The Rowan Home was closed in 1991 and the state turned the facility over to Monroe County to establish a rehabilitation center for drug addicts. This project failed and in 1996 the former resort was sold into private hands but now lays vacant and abandoned. The paranormal community considers this complex of old buildings to be haunted.

Salt Sulfur Springs

On Indian Creek, where it is yet a small stream, in-between Union and Greenville and three miles from the county seat is Salt Sulphur Springs. The fine lawn of eleven acres is a cross-section of the narrow creek bottom and it lies between lofty bluffs. On this lawn are the two mineral springs, the waters being chalybeate and sweetly sulfurous, and containing iodine.

The land was once held by the Benson family and two daughters thereof married William Erskine and Isaac Caruthers. As the firm of Erskine and Caruthers, these men conducted a summer resort in 1823 and they continued the business for many years later. The largest building is of stone, 45 by 206 feet in size, contains seventy-two rooms and cost thirty-thousand dollars to build. It overlooks the lawn and the other buildings standing along the brink of the stream. For several decades before the war of 1861, Salt Sulphur Springs was a famous watering place and was numerously frequented by people from the lower south, especially South Carolina. Many Virginians from the tidewater counties also came here. The high water mark came in 1860 and the old time patronage was interrupted by the Civil War, and never recovered.

Red Sulphur Springs lies in a deep hollow near the mouth of a small tributary of Indian Creek. It is where my father was born and raised. The elevation is sixteen-hundred feet. The waters, which have a temperature of 54 degrees all year round, derive their name from a peculiar sulphur compound which is held in solution. It is separated, in the form of a jelly, by atmospheric air and by acids. Mixed with a small quantity of common water and raised to a temperature of 80 degrees, this compound decomposes and gives off a powerful odor. But, the spring water itself is colorless and transparent.

These waters have long been known to have a 'quieting effect' on the circulatory and nervous systems, reducing the pulse and promoting sleep. It can have a positive effect on diabetes, chronic diarrhea and other affections of the secretory organs, and in functional 'derangements' of the heart and liver, but, their greatest 'repute is in the treatment of pulmonary consumption.' The water appears to combat the 'great white plague' whatever that is, by building up in the system and enabling nature to rid itself of the germ that causes the disease. As a resort, Red Sulphur Springs was opened in 1832 by a Harvey. In the spring of 1837, a company was incorporated with William Burk as proprietor. Next year, the Assembly authorized it to increase its capital stock by fifty-thousand dollars. In 1844 the license paid was thirty-five dollars, showing that the patronage was not as large as at Sweet Springs or Salt

Sulphur Springs. During the Civil War, the buildings were used as a military hospital.

Not one of the three historic resorts of Monroe were near any railroads, which after the war caused their demise. A few other mineral springs occurred in Monroe County; Gray Sulphur, a mile east of Peterstown has been closed a long time and about midway between it and Sweet Springs, is Crimson Springs, which was never developed into a watering place. And, on Hans Creek is the Laurel Spring, the sulphur waters of which at one time attracted summer guests.

Road to Greenville

Winter Galley

Debarkation- Philadelphia, Pa.
September 5, 1738
Passengers

1st Gen.	John Phillip Sibold	John Michael Price	John Phillip Harless
2nd Gen.	John Phillip Sibold Jr	Michael Price Jr	Phillip Harless Jr
3rd Gen.	John Phillip Sibold III	Lewis Price married	Peggy Harless
4th Gen.	Jacob Franz Sibold	John Price	

5th Gen.   James William Sibold   married   Mary Elizabeth Price
5th Gen.   (James William Sibold's brother)   George Washington Sibold
6th Gen.   John Franz Sibold
7th Gen.   Annie May Sibold
6th Gen.   John Arlington Sibold   married   7th Gen.   Annie May Sibold
        (son of James William Sibold, 5th Gen.)   (daughter of John Franz Sibold, 6th Gen.)
7th and 8th Gen. Sibold   Ann Lorraine Sibold

8th and 9th Gen. Sibold   John David Miller

George Washington Sibold (fifth-generation grandfather)
James William Sibold (fifth-generation grandfather)

Okay, here goes, George Washington Sibold and James William Sibold were brothers. They were the sons of Jacob and Evelina Sibold and were born and raised in Clover Hollow. George was born in 1853 and James was born in 1855. George was my great-great grandfather, and James was my great-grandfather. This double dose of Sibold blood could only have happened because of a few specific events.

This would be the fact that George Washington Sibold had a son named John Franz Sibold who became my great-grandfather when he had a daughter named Annie May Sibold, who became my grandmother when she had a daughter named Ann Loraine Sibold, who is my mother. Also the fact that James William Sibold had a son named John Arlington Sibold who became my grandfather when he married Annie May Sibold, daughter of John Franz Sibold, and they became my grandparents on my mother's side.

In other words, my mother's great-grandfather on her mother's side was George Washington Sibold and her grandfather on her father's side was James William Sibold, and George and James Sibold were brothers. Or, my great-great grandfather on my mother's mother side, George Washington Sibold, and my great grandfather on my mother's father side, James William Sibold, were brothers and that George and James's father was Jacob Franz Sibold, my fourth-generation grandfather.

Please note that my direct connection to my two other first generation grandfathers on the Winter Galley, Michael Price and John Harless, was only possible when James William Sibold married Mary Elizabeth Price. There is no blood connection to the Harless or Price families through George Washington Sibold.

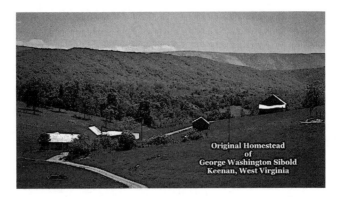

Original Homestead
of
George Washington Sibold
Keenan, West Virginia

John Franz Sibold?

Anna Harvey Sibold?

George Washington Sibold?

George Washington Sibold (great-great-grandfather) was born October 6, 1853, and died in 1917. He married Anna Harvey in 1877. He then settled in Monroe County in the little town of Keenan. Keenan was located near the old Indian trail, right outside of present day Union. He built a home near Peters Mountain and raised seven children to maturity, one, William Dale Sibold, died when he was four years old. George Washington Sibold's children were:

John Franz Sibold (great-grandfather) b. 1878
Charles Thomas Sibold (Tom) b. 1880
William Dale Sibold b. 1886 d, 1890
Lucy May Sibold b.1891
George Sibold
Frank D. Sibold b. 1898
Fred Sibold b. 1900
Elizabeth (Lizzie) b. 1888
Carl Sibold b. 1893
John Franz Sibold (great-grandfather) married Berdie
Loraine Hoover in 1899.
They raised eleven children:
Annie May Sibold (grandmother) b. 1902 d.1972
Cecil Bryan Sibold
Eva Faye
Osbie Sibold
Joe Duane Sibold
Charles Russell Sibold
John Otis Sibold

Edith Lorraine Sibold
Dennis Sibold
Jessie Sibold
Roy Sibold

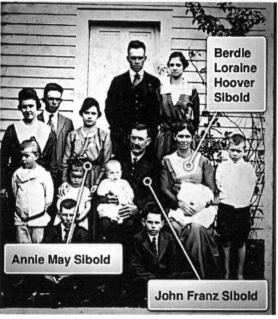

James William Sibold (great-grandfather) George Washington Sibold's younger brother, was born in 1855 and grew up in Clover Hollow. He married Mary Elizabeth

Price. He also settled in Monroe County, just north of Greenville. James William and Mary Elizabeth had five children:

John Arlington Sibold (grandfather) b.1892 d.1962
May Sibold
George Gibson Sibold
Hubbard Sibold
Pearl Sibold

Greenville lies on top of the old Indian trail that followed Indian Creek as it cut through the mountains flowing west towards its mouth on the New River. This natural passage through the mountains has been in existence long before man entered the area. However, when they did come here, they found a very special place with a very special hidden energy.

A family by the name of Meeks lived near the mouth of Indian Creek some ten miles west of the house built by Mr. Ellison. They were attacked by Indians and the entire family except for Mr. Meeks were captured and carried away. The oldest and the youngest in the group, Mr. Meek's mother and his baby were killed by the Indians. Mr. Meek's mother, who was a very large woman, had on a homespun dress at the time. The chief of the Indians appropriated it for his own personal costume. We are told that it reached about to his knees. John Ellison was the nearest neighbor

147

of the family and a runner was immediately sent to notify him of the capture. Ellison in command of five men, three of them, his sons, and two others by the name of Paul, set out in pursuit of the Indians whom they overtook on the Kanawha River. Mrs. Meeks seemed to realize that help was near. She quietly got her children together at a place as far removed from the Indians as possible. The rescuers fired into the six Indians and killed them all. Ellison afterwards returned the Meeks family to their home.

Among the early settlers of the Greenville Community was a Mrs. Anne Maddy. Her husband, who had been a soldier in the Revolutionary War, was accidentally drowned in the Shenandoah River. Mrs. Maddy came with her children to Monroe County and settled on the land now known as the Charles Maddy Farm near the Saltpeter Caves. At this place, she brought up her family. Being the owner of considerable property in Virginia, she was compelled at one time to go back east to dispose of her holdings there. She rode alone all the way on horseback through the mountains and wilderness country. After transacting her business and receiving the money for her land, she started on her way home. She stopped over night in the wilderness with a settler. During her stay there, she happened to disclose the fact that she had considerable funds with her. The settler suggested to her that she take a short cut across the mountain on her way home. In addition, he offered to pilot her part of the way. He took her to the top of a very high cliff and told her that he wanted her money, and that he intended to push her over the bluff and kill her. She told him that her money was sewed up in her clothes and that she would have to take off her dress to get it. She asked him to turn his back while she removed her dress. He turned his back facing the cliff and she immediately pushed him over, killing him and saving her own life. Mrs. William Comer, Frank and Luther Maddy, all of Greenville, were direct descendants of this Mrs. Anne Maddy.

What is now Greenville was once known as Centerville. During a lot sale in the town, John Houchins bought two lots, one opposite the Presbyterian Church, where he constructed a building that ran a carding machine run by horsepower. The Methodist parsonage was built at a very early date. About the same time a dwelling house was put up by Jim Lawrence, in which Dr. Shannon Butt lived. Dr. Butt was the father of Dr. Henry Butt who had for years the largest country practice that any physician ever had in Monroe County. Not far from this time, Anderson McNeer put up a tobacco factory, and his brother, John, a tannery.

Tom Miller, who had been a captain in the war of 1812, came to Greenville in April 1851. He was the father of A. P. Miller, who made an unusual and distinguished record in the Civil War. He fought in Stonewall Jackson's Brigade and took part in every engagement but one. He missed that battle only because he was severely wounded at the time. He was wounded three times, and on one occasion lay on the battle field for three days and nights without food or water. Despite his wounds, he lived to the age of 93, and died in Greenville in the year 1924.

John Arlington Sibold 'Arlie' son of James William Sibold, my great-grandfather, was my mother's father and my grandfather. He was born in 1892 and grew up just outside Greenville in a hollow off Lillydale Road. He served in the Tank Corp, Third Army, in Germany during World War I. He married Annie May Sibold, my grandmother and daughter of John Franz Sibold (great-grandfather) whose father was George Washington Sibold, James William Sibold's older brother.

When my grandfather, Arlie Sibold, married my grandmother, *Annie Sibold*, they moved to Greenville.

149

'Granny' suffered two miscarriages before my mother, *Ann Loraine Sibold*, was born in 1932. My mom grew up in the center of Greenville. My grandfather, Arlie Sibold, became a school teacher and delivered the mail. He started to be effected by Rheumatoid Arthritis which made him confined to home in his later years. It was suggested that he may have come into contact with poison gas used in the war.

My grandmother became a mail carrier from Greenville to Union when my grandfather could no longer do it. She later became a guard at the Federal Prison for Women in Alderson, West Virginia, where Tokyo Rose had been incarcerated. The Sibold's lived just up from the Greenville High School. Later on they moved a few houses away and across from the general store. There were two churches built in Greenville, one a Methodist church and the other a Presbyterian. There were eventually a couple other stores, plus a bank and a post office. Cooks Mill is still there today.

The Sibold's lived in the center of town and in no way were considered wealthy; however, they were much better off than many folks who lived in and around Greenville, as this was the heart of Appalachia which was very poor. My mom was somewhat of a tomboy, even playing in the saltpeter caves nearby. At one point, she and a friend who lived directly across the street, rigged a pulley and rope attached between their bedroom windows so they could

My mother and father

pass messages back and forth. Texting old school if you will.

A few miles west of Greenville in the community of Red Sulphur Springs, Henry and Lilly Miller raised two sons, Glen and Don Miller. *Donald Gene Miller* was my father. Henry and Lilly Miller were my grandparents, and they came from a long line of farmers. They were also of German descent but I have no documentation on their genealogy before their generation.

My mother and father met each other for the first time in first grade. The grade school was located right beside the high school. Actually, grades one through six, shared the same classroom. Even in first grade, my father was known to always be dressed well and cute as a button. My mother and father did not start dating until their senior year at Greenville High School. Their yearbook tells us a lot about those times. My mother was a cheerleader, and my father was voted most popular, best dressed, and played all sports. Evidently my sense of humor came from my father, as he willed his 'corny jokes' to Price Mann. After my mother and father graduated high school, they married and moved to Fort Belvoir, Virginia, where my father was stationed after he joined the army. After he served and was discharged, my parents moved to Richmond, where I was born in 1956.

Chapter 8 Summer of Love

Everything I am today and will be tomorrow can be traced back to my childhood in the little town of Greenville, West Virginia. Although I was born and raised in Richmond, I spent all my summers in Greenville as a kid. I even got married at the Methodist Church where my grandparents on my father's side, Henry and Lilly Miller are buried. My first introduction to organized religion came from alternating visits to the Methodist and Presbyterian churches located in this tiny town. When I was very young, Henry and Lilly Miller moved to a farm right across the street from my grandparent's house on my mother's side, the Sibold's.

How great a setup is this I thought. The Miller's house was located on a small farm with a barn, smokehouse, garden, chickens, cows, and an occasional pig. Henry and Lilly Miller came from a long line of farmers and I knew them as Pawpaw and Mawmaw. Of the two families, the Millers and the Sibold's, I always thought of the Sibold's as being on the revenuer side and the Millers were on the moonshiner side of the family, especially after finding the

The Miller's   The Sibold's

picture of my great-grandfather, John Franz Sibold, as the sheriff of Monroe County, standing beside a collection of still confiscations.

My brother and I would alternate back and forth between spending the night at the Miller's and the Sibold's. We would mostly play at Pawpaw and Mawmaw's since they had the farm and access to the Saltpeter Caves a short distance behind their property.

There are specific memories of the Miller's which had a strong effect on my early childhood. Pawpaw and Mawmaw were true country farmers. Pawpaw was always in his dungarees, up at dawn and in bed at dusk. He would start off his day with fresh milk poured over cornbread. Warm milk right from the cow really grossed me out as a kid; I think it was that brown crust floating on top. They did get a pasteurizer eventually, but the cream on top still didn't sit well with me. Maybe it was because I was use to city milk back in Richmond.

Mawmaw kept the wood stove in the kitchen stoked all day and it contributed to the warmth of the home during the winter. Dinner was the big meal of the day and was served around 1 pm. There were many dishes to choose from including two or three types of meats and a variety of beans and potatoes. Once dinner was finished, Mawmaw would cover the table full of food with a table cloth until supper time came around and you could have any leftovers from dinner that you wanted. The Miller farm was mostly sustainable and they produced much of what they needed. They seemed very much at piece with God and nature.

Overnights in the winter were great because we slept upstairs in a soft feather bed loaded with handmade quilts that Mawmaw had made on her loom. There wasn't much heat upstairs but it didn't matter because you were weighted down in the bed by what seemed like dozens of those fluffy quilts. Mawmaw also placed a bedpan under the bed just in case you needed it because the one bathroom was downstairs.

My very earliest memory of Pawpaw, who was missing his right index finger due to being run over by a wagon when he was young, was him plucking at his banjo. It was my very first introduction to a string instrument for which I had a strong passion for from then on. I still have that banjo that Pawpaw played. He was a quiet man, yet overflowing with wisdom and experience. He would often tell us stories about the Indians that used to inhabit the area and how they attacked Cook's Fort every day at times. I still have a few of the Indian arrowheads that Pawpaw had found as a kid growing up in the area. You can still find

arrowheads and hatchets in the field where Cook's Fort once stood after a good rain on a recently plowed field. It was the Indian stories that Pawpaw talked about that made such a profound impression on me for some unknown reason. Playing around the farm and exploring nearby caves at a very early age ingrained in me a lifelong passion for adventure.

On the white collar side of the street were the Sibold's. My grandfather, John Arlington Sibold, passed away when I was six years old. I do remember him and that it was my first experience with an open casket viewing at the house, all set up in the parlor. Not the fondest of memories, but it did prepare me for more to come and the dreaded visits to the nursing homes around Greenville. There were lots of elderly Sibold's and Miller's throughout the area.

My grandfather on my mother's side, John Arlington Sibold, was married to Annie May Sibold and we called her Granny. Granny took over delivering the mail from my grandfather when he was no longer able to do it because of his rheumatoid arthritis. Later, she became a guard at the Federal Reformatory for Women in Alderson, West Virginia, where 'Tokyo Rose' Iva Toguri, had been an inmate. Tokyo Rose served six years and two months of her ten year sentence for one count of high treason before being released on good behavior in 1956 and later pardoned.

Granny took me to the prison for some reason one day when I was very little. She was always befriending the inmates and other people less fortunate than herself. I went to one of the 'jail cells' with her and I could hardly believe my eyes. There were no locks on the doors, nor bars on the windows. It was like a very nice hotel and the rooms were decorated with the inmate's belongings and furnishings, very comfortable indeed. Somehow, I figured the men's prison wouldn't be quite this pleasant.

The Sibold's were on the more modern side of the family and Granny would even make pizza and tacos on occasion. She was always busy helping out someone and on one occasion we visited a family that literally had no shoes to wear. It was the heart of Appalachia, arguably one of the poorest parts of the United States at the time. I clearly remember looking through cracks in the bare wood floor at the dirt below. Lesson learned, there are many people a whole lot worse off than you.

The Saltpeter Caves

I cannot over emphasize the importance and effect that exploring the Saltpeter Caves in Greenville, West Virginia had on me during my childhood and my entire life. To me, it was like having full access to another world or dimension that no one else had access to. Early on I felt that these caves had their own energy or spirit and were trying to impart wisdom of some sort. If only I knew what they were trying to say? It was the first time that I noticed an association between spiritualism and nature.

There were five entrances to these caves that I knew of and they were spread around the hollows surrounding Greenville. We would start off going out the back of Mawmaw and Pawpaw's house, through the barn, over a fence and up and down a couple hollows before we would come to one of the entrances. It was the closest one to the Miller farm and we would always enter the cave system from there.

The Saltpeter Caves in Greenville had been explored since the late 1700s and were marked by chalk arrows providing some bearings on where to go. The Maddy brothers were the first owners of these caves and would mine saltpeter which would be used for gunpowder. This practice continued through the Civil War when confederate soldiers gathered up the saltpeter and left behind their wooden troughs and hoppers plus the tracks they created.

The basics of exploring the caves were learned early on. The caves always stayed a constant temperature all year round, about fifty-four degrees as I remember. This was the first indication that you were entering a completely different ecosystem than anything you would experience above ground. The caves were divided into three zones, the light zone, which was near the entrance and had direct light from outside, the black zone, which received no light, and the twilight zone, the zone in between which only receives some indirect light from the entrance. The twilight zone was recognized by the bluish tone to the darkness.

Cows would gather at the cave entrance to get relief from the heat during the summer and would make it a mine field you had to cross to be able to enter. Fences had to be erected in the entrances to keep the cows from entering and hurting themselves. We sometimes would camp out by the entrance which would keep us cool in the summer and warm in the winter. If we camped out in the caves, we would have to make sure the fire was always between us and the entrance, because the flow of air was always toward the outside.

When entering the caves, the first thing we would do was get to at least the twilight zone, sit down and turn off the lights for at least fifteen minutes to let our eyes get accustom to the dark. This made it a lot easier to see with less light when you did turn your lights back on. We would explore every nook and cranny that we could find. You could go in the main entrance and travel a mile or so before coming out a different entrance. One part of the cave system would be dry and in other parts a passing stream might be flowing through some of the corridors. The water that traveled through this cave system was part of Laurel Creek, which is the source of water for Cook's Mill and millpond, about a quarter mile away down the mountain. The millpond by the way was the only place that I was afraid to go, probably because my grandparents told me at an early age that the pond was bottomless. Just trying to keep me safe for sure. I was afraid to go anywhere near it.

In the dark zone part of the caves we would often find salamanders or other strange life forms that would have no eyes because they didn't need them. There were a couple different species of endangered bats that inhabited the caves. We would often find ourselves with our flashlights pointed at the ceiling as opposed to the floor because we didn't want to get bats entangled in our hair. We would often play hide-and-seek or flashlight war, sometimes all day long in these caves. There was a special energy that emanated from deep within the heart of these caves.

This cave system was set up as a natural maze with two or three different pathways to get to the same spot. There was the 'Round Room' which was a large cavern that appeared to be completely round with no entrance or exit. You had to explore the whole room before you would go over a particular mound to find the only way out. One large stalagmite was called the 'Strawberry' because that's what it looked like. I was told that with the right equipment and expertise, you could climb over the Strawberry and enter another part of the cave system. This apparently was pretty dangerous and people had been injured trying to scale the wet surface.

My favorite spot was located a few hundred yards down a long round tunnel that would get progressively smaller and smaller to the point where you had to crawl on your hands and knees. At the far end of this tunnel was a horizontal flat rock, about three or four inches thick that would divide the tunnel down the middle horizontally. This rock was called the 'Devil's Writing Table' and you could continue on no further. I would see the symbol of a *circle, divided by a horizontal line* as a representation of this energetic spot. Interestingly, through out my life, I've had a strange fascination with round and circular symbols and the energy emanating from them. I didn't know why, but I felt closer to God when I was in these caves.. Spending every summer of my childhood in the Saltpeter caves provided me with many life lessons I would find invaluable for the rest of my life.

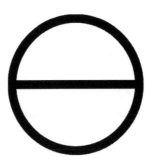

Life lessons Learned:

Always be aware of your surroundings at all times
Ability to assess any situation you might find yourself in
Always knowing your direction
Navigation skills
Problem solving skills
Curiosity for the unknown
Reliance on intuition for guidance
Confidence in the decision making process
Always question the authorities
Plan your dive and dive your plan
Fundamental desire for adventure

Fundamental desire for travel
Ability to investigate and research
There are no coincidences
Everything happens for a reason
Everything is connected
Energy emanates from natural surroundings

~ ~ ~ ~ ~ ~

Exploring these caves gave me my first indication that supernatural events may be real. There were many instances where I would detect severe energy spikes, seemingly to be coming from natural sources like caves, mountains, rocks, water, and animals. The energy would manifest itself in me as chill bumps that would pulse up and down my spine. Certain locations would produce goosebumps every time I would visit. It happened so regularly that I gained a confidence that I could rely on. I began to trust my intuition.

Chariots of the Gods

When I was twelve years old I read the book *Chariots of the Gods* by Erich von Daniken and it changed everything I knew about everything. I sensed there was much that we as humans did not know or understood about things and this book verified it for me. It made reasonable sense to me at the time that extraterrestrials, UFO's, and other inhabited planets would have to exist. Seeing the photograph of an astronaut carved into a Peruvian mountainside completely fascinated me. I made a promise to myself that one day I would go and explore places just like the Plains of Nazca. It looked to me as proof that ancient extraterrestrials had visited Earth and maybe they still do. From crystal skulls to elongated skulls, from the Egyptian pyramids to the Mayan and Aztec ruins, there was an insatiable compulsion to investigate and research mystical places like these and I just couldn't get enough. It only made sense to me that extraterrestrial life would have to exist.

I found a diagram in a UFO magazine at the time that illustrated how to make a UFO detector out of some wire, battery, magnet, and an electric bell. It appeared to me to be very clever and was based on scientific fact using the electromagnetic field generated by the UFO. It was just a magnet hanging on a wire through the center of a wire ring that was attached to a battery. The theory was that all UFO's have a magnetic field and if they fly by your window at night, the magnetic field would move the magnet so it touched the wire causing the bell to ring. I thought it was ingenious. It only went off once, while it was sitting in my brother's bedroom window late one night. I'm highly skeptical. I also learned to never use an Ouija board with your older brother.

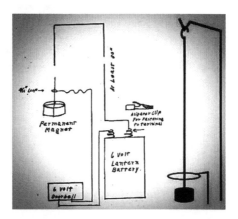

Other than Erich von Daniken books, Robert Heinlein's science fiction, David Hagberg aka Sean Flannery's spy novels, Wilbur Smith and Clive Cussler adventure novels, and of course every Hardy Boys book ever written have made a lasting impression on me. As for philosophy, the works by Carlos Castaneda and teachings of Shamanism held a particular interest to me, it was my first introduction to altered consciousness. I was rebellious by nature and torn between what I was taught to believe and what I actually did.

Introduction to the Arts

As I mentioned earlier, my first introduction to music was Pawpaw's banjo, but soon thereafter I remember my father playing his hollow body guitar with F holes he got from Sears and Roebuck when he was young. He tried to refinish it a few times but the neck became way too warped to make it playable anymore. He switched up and played electrics from Sears from then on. There has been this strong connection to music ever since.

Bluegrass music in particular was my favorite right from the get go. There was something about that bluegrass sound that I seem to really resonate with. It was genuine and you could hear the expression and emotion radiating from the acoustic instruments. It was the energy emanating from the instruments that I seemed to noticed the most. My interest in playing an instrument started to build along with a desire to experience live music whenever I could.

Ralph Stanley with Keith Whitely and Ricky Scaggs

My first road trip to see live music was a visit to Ralph Stanley's Bluegrass Festival on Clinch Mountain in Southwest Virginia. It was a traditional bluegrass festival with the likes of Ralph Stanley and the Clinch Mountain Boys, Bill Monroe and the Bluegrass Boys, The Country Gentleman, Earl Scruggs and Lester Flat, and Jim and Jesse. Carter Stanley of the Stanley Brothers was buried up on the hill overlooking the old home-place. These trips also took me back to the mountains that I adored.

I moved to Bon Air, a suburb of Richmond, Virginia, when I was eight years old. When I was not growing up in Bon Air, all my time was spent in Greenville. Greenville was about ten years behind the times of New York or even Richmond. The music that was popular at the time in New York took many years to filter its way towards Greenville. Bon Air was different and my friend's older brothers turned me on to a whole new way of life.

In 1964, there was a complete change of culture in America taking place. All my friend's older brothers in the neighborhood were of age and were on the forefront of the anti-war movement and participated in the 'May Day' protest in Washington, DC. The killings at Kent State provided a very surreal nature to it all. Who could possibly believe that the government would shoot unarmed college students? To rebel against authority was my only option. I started to associate authority with organized religion and although I still believed in God, but it was more spiritual and way counter to the mainstream religious community.

Although I was just a little too young to make it to Woodstock or the Watkins Glen music festivals, I knew many people who did. This was the kind of music I wanted to listen to. To me, there was always a close relationship between folk, bluegrass, and electric rock and roll. I liked the Beatles and the Rolling Stones, but there was only one band that I thought was one of a kind and I had never heard anything like it before. I was hooked for life the first time I heard American Beauty by the Grateful Dead. Older brothers in Bon Air were the only reason we would have ever even heard about this band as they were opposite of popular. It was all about the music. This way of life attitude is the reason the Grateful Dead amassed such a huge following, which is still thriving today. It was the closest thing to a religious moment I had ever experienced up to that point.

The Bon Air Banner

My first chance to see the Grateful Dead live came in the summer of 1973 at RFK Stadium in Washington, DC. The Grateful Dead and The Allman Brothers were playing two days in row, perfect. My friend, David Eccleston, who is no longer with us, did most of the work coloring in chalk a four-foot by six-foot cloth banner we were going to take to the show. We based it on the *Skull and Roses* design the Grateful Dead made famous. Across the top of the banner where it would normally read 'Grateful' we fit in the following line; *'BON AIR RICHMOND VA IS HERE'* It looked very professional and Dave did a great job. I don't think any of us knew exactly what we were really going to do with it when we got it there but we did want the Grateful Dead to know where their fans were from.

About eight of us arranged to stay at a condo belonging to one of the fathers of the bunch who worked at the Pentagon. The two days were on a Saturday and Sunday and we had tickets for both days. We showed up on that miserably hot Saturday around noon with our tickets in hand. I had never been to a concert so big. I continued to look for someone to take my ticket and by the time I was all the way inside the stadium I realized they decided not to collect the tickets that day. Below is that ticket that was never collected, seven dollars for admission wasn't too shabby.

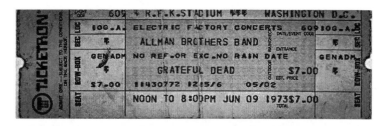

It was the first time I had seen fifty-thousand people in one spot, all for one reason, the music. As I was down on the field crammed within the masses, I noticed my friend, David Eccleston, carrying the rolled-up Bon Air Banner up to the immense stage and then heaving it up to the top of the platform. We all figured that would be the last time we would ever see it again, but it was still worth it.

Everything I was ever told about a Grateful Dead concert came true that day. What they said about Jerry Garcia was true. He could communicate with every single person on an individual bases as well as on a whole. It was the most magnificent sound I had ever heard and I was now hooked for life. At one point in the heat of the day, when the band started playing 'Looks like Rain,' a single dark cloud drifted over the crowd and let loose a quick downpour over the crowd. Now, that's fifty-thousand people using positive thinking. That's the power of the people I thought at the time. You can still hear this recording at archive.org and about twenty seconds into 'Looks Like Rain' you can hear the ahh's and ohh's as that single black cloud burst over RFK Stadium. Nature spirits synching with the Dead I was thinking.

The Dead played first that day with the Allman Brothers closing out the show. Most of us got split up during the show and when we all met up afterwards, we were all under the influence of some illegal substances that was given out free during the show.

They did collect tickets on Sunday and they didn't let you bring in the coolers of beer like you could the day before. It was just as hot as Saturday and The Allman Brothers were scheduled to come on first. Life is good, I am happy, all is well.

As I settled in, nestled with minions on the field, I looked up at the massive stage and low and behold, there was the Bon Air Banner attached to the back wall on the right side behind some of the sound equipment. Bon Air is on the map! The Grateful Dead came on at six pm that day and played until the wee hours of the morning with the likes of Dickie Betts and Butch Trucks of the Allman Brothers, and Merl Saunders. I can now absolutely verify 'there is nothing like a Grateful Dead concert.'

On a whim a couple of years ago I got a notion to do an internet image search of the Dead playing at RFK in 1973, just on the slim chance I might get a glance of the Bon Air Banner. It really didn't take all that long to find this image. You can definitely find anything you want on the internet. My understanding is that Bill Kreutzmann, the drummer for the Grateful Dead, now has the Bon Air Banner but I'm not really sure. I would see the Grateful Dead many more times throughout the years and no two shows were ever alike. I have seen them play large stadiums down to the front row in a small theater. They played Richmond a few times but the most memorable time was when they played the Mosque, May 25, 1977.

167

Jerry Garcia inspired me to learn and play the guitar. I am inspired by the music as much today as I was forty-five years ago. It was at a 1975 'Legion of Mary' show at the Kennedy Center in DC, featuring Jerry Garcia and Merl Saunders that hooked me on photography forever. I managed to get up front against the chest high stage and it felt like I was sitting in Jerry's basement as he rehearsed for a show. Luckily, I brought my Pocket Ten Instamatic Camera in with me and was able to capture the moment Jerry Garcia and I had a mind meld.

You could pick out Jerry's playing in the midst of a thousand other guitar players because of his tone and emotion in every note. He inspired me to study music. This introduced me to the phenomenon of resonance which I would understand later was the mathematical relationship of sympathetic natural vibrations of one object being influenced by the natural vibrations of a neighboring object, and it may be one of the keys to the universe.

One of the most pleasurable things I still do today is take road trips to see good live music. As cameras and technology got better, You were able to capture better images. To me, a good photograph is one that captures that special moment-in-time but also tells a story.

Chapter 9 The Search

It became apparent to me at an early age that there may be a guardian angel attached and it has already stepped in to help me on numerous occasions. I couldn't see it or touch it, but I was sure it was there. Rule number one was to pay special attention to those subtle messages that may be directed at me, like intuition, dreams, signs and symbols. As confidence grew in the ability to recognize these seemingly random pieces of information, more risk could be taken on.

One of my earliest memories was playing in the barn loft on the Miller farm in Greenville and not paying attention to my surroundings. I stepped backwards and plunged through the loft landing on top of a hard and sharp half licked salt lick. There was absolutely no pain and I could not remember the exact moment of impact. It was like a hand reached out and caught me and laid me gently on the ground. I did recognize the importance of this moment and the effect it has had on me ever since.

Traveling back and forth from Richmond to Greenville as a kid initially generated my desire for adventure travel. Every trip was different and every time I came home I became a slightly different person. It was if I was searching for something in particular but didn't have any idea what it was. I was always much more comfortable deep in a cave or hiking some trail, or having a close encounter with some wild animal than interacting with other people. Strange and unique experiences seem to follow me where ever I would venture.

One rainy night while driving up to Greenville with a friend in my new 1973 Toyota Corolla, before the use of radial tires, my destiny would take another turn. We were only thirty minutes outside Greenville when we were winding around a mountain in the pouring rain. When I bore left on a curve, the car tires hydroplaned and we went straight off the mountain. Luckily we had our seat belts on when we hit a cutoff telephone pole head on and the pole ended up halfway up the engine compartment. Upon impact, my head snapped forward, my jaw shut, and I nearly bit my tongue in two.

There was someone right behind us at the time and fortunately stopped to help. The next thing I remember I was sitting in his passenger seat on the way to the hospital in Lewisburg, West Virginia and I remember bleeding profusely all over a roll of paper towels that was in my hands. When the driver looked over at me and told me his name was David Miller and that he was taking me to the hospital, I thought he was putting me on and somehow had hold of my driver's license. There was no pain at the time, but a day after twenty stitches were put in my tongue, it swelled up like a baseball. I still have a scar in the shape of a circle on the end of my tongue. Just another weird experience that I associated with my guardian angel.

Mexico 1972

When I was sixteen years old, I took my first plane ride and left the country for the very first time. A friend and neighbor in Bon Air whose father owned a produce company in Nogales, Arizona, invited me to come along for a visit. Chuck's father lived in Nogales, Arizona, which was just on the American side of the border with Mexico. The border goes through the center of town. Nogales, Arizona is on one side of the border and Nogales Sonora, Mexico, is on the other. The first night there, Chuck's family and I walked through the border checkpoint to go have dinner at a restaurant called the Cavern which was built in a cave along some cliffs in the middle of town. Oh, it just happened to be the fifth of May, Mexican Independence Day, Cinco de Mayo.

After we got back from the Cavern and it was still early, Chuck's dad let him have the keys to his car so we could go back to the border to experience it on our own. Yee Ha! Back to Mexico on our own! The first thing I noticed after crossing the border for the second time that day was the smell. It smelled completely different on the other side of the fence. Not necessarily horrible, but more like the lack of refrigeration, or maybe it was the cooked animal carcasses hanging upside down along the road that had something to do with it.

Just as it was getting dark and cooling down all hell seemed to break loose in the center of town. Chuck and I were walking down the street drinking a couple of Mexican beers. There was no age limit to drink alcohol in Mexico. About that time a bottle went flying over our heads and through a bar window right behind us. Startled, but laughing like crazy, we jumped behind a trash cart sitting nearby and watched the action unfold. It was like the wild-wild west. After the trash cart in front of us was set on fire and a pump pick-up truck with firemen hanging on to the back came and put the fire out, everything went right back to normal, like nothing ever happened.

A little while later we got into a conversation with a young Mexican kid about our age and the jest of it was that he was going to show us around. We started following him and before long we found ourselves on a dimly lit stone stairway going up the side of a cliff. By the time we got to the top of the stairs we were surrounded by at least ten locals each one grabbing a separate belt loop. One older fellow was pointing his finger at me and yelling 'you fingered, you fingered' whatever that meant. I certainly didn't feel that I had any control over the situation as we stood there next to the edge of a cliff, overlooking Nogales Sonora on Mexican Independence Day.

They started to search us (or rob us) and proceeded to take off my jacket, but I resisted as it was getting cold. One of them didn't care for that too much and I remember him punching me in the stomach. It didn't hurt one little bit and I guessed it was because the adrenaline was pumping. The entire mood changed rather quickly after this and they became friendlier, they let me keep my coat on and let go of all the belt loops. Maybe it was because we didn't have much money on us so they eventually ended up letting us go. They also let us keep our identification and keys. We immediately walked back to the U.S. side of the border and when we got back to the house we went straight to bed, and did not tell a soul about what had happened. I did thank my guardian angel for keeping an eye on me that evening.

It wasn't until morning before I realized I was in some pain and bleeding a bit on the sheets. Turns out I had a two inch slice across my abdomen. I didn't need stitches but did have a scar for a couple of years. I never told any adults about it but certainly bragged about it to all my friends. I wore that scar like a big badge of courage. However, I learned an important life lesson that day: *Be aware of your surroundings at all times. Try to anticipate all possible scenarios to any situation you might find yourself in before it actually happens.*

~ ~ ~ ~ ~ ~

It wasn't until my late thirties when I had my first eye operation (RK with a scalpel, before Lasik with a laser) before I became certified to scuba dive. After traveling the Caribbean and Central America for a while I started to run out of dive buddies that I wanted to travel with. Traveling alone was my only option but at least I could go where I wanted to. The first place I chose was Cuba, however, I had to sneak in through Canada to get there.

Cuba

It wasn't against the law to go to Cuba in the 1990s B.E. (Before Elian), but it was against the law to spend American dollars there. The way around this regulation

was to be sponsored by a Canadian company and let them handle the expenses in Canadian dollars. The Cubans would not stamp American passports and encouraged us touristas to spend all the American dollars we could. The irony did not escape me that it was free America putting all the restrictions on me and communist Cuba imposing very few.

This particular trip included a layover in Havana and then a few days on the 'Isle of Youth' at a dive resort called Hotel El Colony. Isla de la Juventud (Isle of Youth) is the second-largest Cuban island and the seventh-largest island in the West Indies. The island was called the 'Isle of Pines' (Isla de Pinos) until it was renamed in 1978.

Little is known of the pre-Columbian history of the island though a cave complex near the Punta del Este beach preserves 235 ancient drawings made by the native population. The Caves at Punta del Este are half-buried amid overgrown brush and greenery and contain significant examples of early pre-Columbian art pointing to an established culture on the island as early as 900 AD. These paintings are said to be among the few remaining traces of the Siboney who were among the first inhabitants of Cuba, and who arrived from South America via other Caribbean islands between three and four millennia ago. They are thought to have died out shortly after the paintings were made.

The six caves, only two of them accessible, were discovered by accident at the turn of the twentieth century by a north American named Freeman P. Lane who disembarked on the beach and sought shelter in one of them. The discovery made archeologists reconsider their assumption that the Siboney culture was primitive as the paintings are thought to represent a solar calendar, which would indicate a sophisticated cosmology.

On March 22 each year the sun streams through a natural hole in the roof of Cave One, the largest of the group, illuminating the pictographs in a beam of sunlight. Being linked to the vernal equinox, the effect is thought to celebrate fertility and the cycle of life and death. When bones were excavated here in 1939 it became apparent that the cave's function was not only ceremonial; they had also been used for habitation and burial. The main geometric design being displayed in these caves is that of the circle, believed to represent the stars and the heavens. This suggest to me that these early people associated cosmology with spiritualism, both being one in the same.

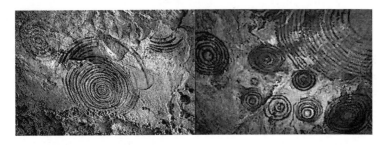

The island first became known to Europeans in 1494 during Christopher Columbus's second voyage to the New World. Columbus named the island 'La Evangelista' and claimed it for Spain; the island would also come to be known as Isla de Cotorras 'Isle of Parrots' and Isla de Tesoros 'Treasure Island' at various points in its history.

Pirate activity in and around the area left its trace in English literature. Both Treasure Island by Robert Louis Stevenson and Peter Pan by J.M. Barrie are rooted in part on accounts of the island and its native and pirate inhabitants, as well as long dugout canoes which were often used by pirates as well as indigenous peoples.

On a side visit during my stay on this comma shaped island, I went to see the remains of a prison that once housed Fidel Castro. From 1953 to 1955, Cuban leader Fidel Castro was imprisoned in the Presidio Modelo on the Isla de Pinos by the regime of Fulgencio Batista after leading the failed July 1953 attack on the Moncada Barracks in the Oriente Province. After the Cuban Revolution, the same facility was used to imprison

counterrevolutionaries and people allegedly otherwise opposing the revolution. The Presidio Modelo was a 'model prison' of Panopticon (circular) design. The prison was built under the President-turned-dictator Gerardo Machado between 1926 and 1928. The five circular blocks with cells constructed in tiers around central observation posts were built with the capacity to house up to 2,500 prisoners in humane conditions. It was modeled after the Statesville Correctional Center in Illinois that was built in 1925. What stood out to me was the fact that there were no doors on the cells, absolutely no privacy. The prison now serves as a museum and is declared a national monument.

Staying at the Hotel El Colony was like living on an 'I Love Lucy' movie set. Nothing has changed since it was made a hotel in 1958 after the Revolution. It was formerly the site of General Batista's summer villa. Interestingly, it was located adjacent to a small marina and a Cuban Naval Base where the soldiers would search the dive boat every day when it returned to the dock. The Cuban soldiers didn't like their picture being taken very much either. I also was told by the 'tourist guide' that missiles during the Cuban Missile Crises were hidden nearby.

The most important thing that happened to me on this trip was meeting two emergency room doctors who I would spend the next decade traveling with to the most obscure places on Earth. We got along well and they kindly invited me to join their like-minded scuba group of various nationalities. Anyone that travels will tell you, nothing ruins a good adventure more than someone who doesn't travel well. My Cuba trip turned out to be one of those destiny altering moments.

For the next fifteen years I was fortunate to be able to travel to about thirty different countries and never duplicating the same place twice. The strange and unique experiences however continued including being on an Egyptian dive boat called the Greta (re-named the Re-Greta after the trip) that just happened to be on the Red Sea at the moment the American Naval ship 'USS Cole' was bombed in Yemen, not too far south of us. The Egyptian crew was very tense and they all reacted to things as if they had heavy chips bearing down on their shoulders. One morning an American diver asked for some juice at breakfast and all hell broke loose until the attendant calmed down after realizing the diver said juice, not 'Jews.'

Early on, my travel bucket list included anywhere I could experience close encounters with wild animals. There was always a special connection I experienced with animals and they seemed to be drawn to me as if I was one of their own. No matter where I went the animals would seem to always find me first, before I found them, and we would always meet eyeball to eyeball. The other thing that was on my travel short list was anywhere that included ancient civilizations and ruins I could explore. I figured it was my early fascination with Erick von Daniken's 'Chariots of the Gods' that instilled this insatiable desire.

My first experience with Mayan ruins came on a dive trip to the Mexican Riviera at a place called Akumal. Not only did I get to drift dive at night which I relate to being able to fly, but I got to dive in an actual 'ceynote' or water cave called the 'Taj Mahal.' My understanding is that the Mayans regarded ceynotes as very spiritual and connected directly to the gods.

When I looked at the ruins at Tulum I could feel the energy emitting from the site. I could not see it, nor touch it, but I was positive it was there. Where does this energy come from? How did the Mayan people build something like this and who helped them do it? It was like the structure was built to somehow harness or even resonate with the Earth's own energy, maybe produced by the waves crashing on the rocky shore. It looked to me as a very symbiotic relationship between man and the natural world. What did the people of Tulum know that we haven't figured out yet?

Copan Ruinas

The first real mystical place I had the chance to come across was the ruins of Copan deep in the Honduras mountains. Often termed 'The Athens of the New World' or 'The Paris of Maya Cities,' Copan features some of the Mayas most impressive accomplishments in architecture, astronomy, and in civic organization. This was on a side trip on the way home after a week diving off Roatan, an island off the coast of Honduras. Copan is the easternmost city-state in the Maya World. It is famous for the artistic quality and the magnificence of the carved stone stelae standing on its main plaza. It is also known for having the longest Maya inscription discovered thus far in the Maya World in its 'Hieroglyphic Stairway.'

For me, the very first thing I noticed was the palpable energy coming off the ruins. I instantly knew why the Mayans decided to build here when I saw the beautiful mountains that surrounded the ruins on all sides. Some of the ridges were shaped like jaguars and other sacred animals. It was situated in a natural bowl encompassed by mountain ridges, very similar to Clover Hollow.

It is not known exactly when the first dwellers of the Copan Valley settled in the region. Below the great Acropolis, archaeologists have found evidence of dwellings suggesting occupation started as early as the Late Pre-Classic period around 400-100 BC. However, evidences of previous settlements have been found by archaeologists. It is possible that the first people who lived in the Copan Valley arrived here during the early Pre-Classic period, between 2000 and 1000 BC. The city we know today as Copan started thriving as a large ceremonial center around 300 AD. The founder of the Copan dynasty, Yax Kuk Mo, rose to power in 426 AD.

There is one difficulty in determining when the ancient Maya of Copan first settled the Copan Valley and it has to do with a strange phenomenon that is seen at ceremonial centers among the ancient Mayan cities where new rulers tend to 'erase' the presence of older rulers by defacing, destroying, relocating, reusing, or even burying monuments that held references to their predecessors. This is known as the 'Iconoclastic' Phenomenon and it can be seen in some of the monuments at Copan where some of the sculpted characters have broken noses. I would come to find that this was true in many other cultures around the world as well.

In the construction of new buildings it was very common for the ancient Maya of Copan to deface a building commissioned by a previous ruler and to build their own new facade or crest and make new additions to the buildings on top of the old. This is how the Maya attained ever taller, bigger, and more impressive buildings. One may say they recycled the old to build the new. You may witness this Iconoclastic Phenomenon all around Copan. It literally means the destruction of icons of most of the structures with the notable exception of Rosalila. Rosalila is located beneath Structure Sixteen and was a temple so sacred to the Maya of Copan that they buried it completely and with exceeding care. This was a clear tribute to their ancestors, the pure definition of spiritualism and a belief system in an afterlife.

The Maya of Copan were natural born artists; the art found within the City exhibits a greater level of expertise and commitment to artistic expression than at other sites around the Maya World. Copan is best known by the quality and quantity of their carved monuments. Their artists had a unique grasp of working stone to give life to the scenes they depicted. They experimented starting with a base relief style of carving such as is seen in the earliest monument at Copan Stelae Sixty-Three which is characterized by the rigidity of the main character in the sculpture. With time, their style of carving evolved, becoming more realistic and elaborate. By the time of Waxaklajuun Ub'aah K'awiil, Copan achieved its artistic climax as evidenced by the large amount of buildings he ordered built but especially by the stelae that name and portray him. The sculptors of these stelae made use of a bold new technique using a three dimensional approach.

Architecture, sculpture, and nature, merged into one and served as a scenario for the rulers to perform their ceremonies for the public. From the Early Classic Period, everything including artistic expression was carefully articulated as a part of an ever increasingly sophisticated ruling apparatus. The facades of buildings were richly adorned with mosaic sculpture often depicting the use of the building it adorned, with the added benefit that no two buildings had the same decoration.

The Maya used a numerical system based on the number twenty, which included the concept of zero, an accomplishment achieved by only two other civilizations before, the Babylonians and the Hindi. The system was based on dots and bars where one dot represented one and a bar represented five. This bar-dot system, similar to the one used today by computers (1 and 0) is called a binary system. Using these in different positions, the Maya were able to make complex calculations including certain astronomical operations which they computed with great precision. Are we to believe that they came up with this knowledge on their own? I think not.

The ancient Maya were mathematical geniuses, a gift they often used that had formidable uses, mostly for their religious purposes and to keep track of time which they perhaps thought of as sacred itself. The Maya devised calendars of great precision. Mathematics also had a number of other worthwhile applications including engineering and design. The astounding scientific discoveries made by Maya astronomers included their knowledge of different constellations and the calculation of Venus' precise orbit around the sun. Also, the Maya themselves did not invent writing but they did develop the most complex mixed-scripture writing system called the Logo Syllabic, made up of over eight glyphs. I don't believe for a second they figured all this out by themselves. But, who could have helped them? Someone, or a higher being not from this world I would surmise. I also noted that the Mayan calendar was developed as a round or circular mathematical system.

As far as their religion goes, since Pre-Classic times, the Maya conceived the Cosmos as a structure divided into three superimposed levels: That's three different dimensions occupying the same space; The Upper World composed of thirteen heavens; the Middle Level represented by Witz, the Sacred Mountain and is the natural level we live in, which is the source of sustenance to the living and where the sacred maize was cultivated as nourishment; and finally the Lower Level which related generally to the water world, with nine levels of Underworld. This is where the dead go when their natural lives are over.

The Maya took a Shamanistic approach to religion. The Ceiba Tree was sacred to the Maya. This tree's towering heights lead the Maya to believe that its branches supported the Heavens while its deep roots were the means of communication between the world of the living and the Underworld. Religious elements may be observed in burials. The Maya always showed a special respect for the dead and placed funerary offerings which they considered useful for the dead in the afterlife. The body was placed in an extended position with the head to the North. Depending on social status, the body was buried with offerings of polychrome ceramics and sacred objects made of jade, obsidian and shells. In Maya sites, temples resemble sacred mountains and the tombs of rulers were placed in their interior so that in their afterlife they were to serve as mediators between the Gods and their people.

The caves were considered as the means of communication with the Underworld and the bodies of the dead were placed in the cavities of limestone where they began their final journey. Interesting to note that limestone is the petrified remains of living organisms and is believed to have its own spiritual essence still attached. Rulers were

183

deposited with their offerings which would be useful in the nine levels of Underworld and to their final destination. The Maya paid great reverence and homage to their ancestors. All this reiterating the connection between man, nature, and the heavens.

Time and space were of vital importance to the Maya. The maize cycle, the cycles of seasons and those of human life all shaped their world vision shared by rulers and commoners alike. Their world vision or cosmology was related to the creation myths and their religious belief system as it was linked to celestial bodies and animals that had great powers such as the Sun-Jaguar duality and their subsequent transformation into supernatural deities. Religious beliefs and reverence towards main deities dating back to the Pre-Classic Period are evidenced and were consolidated through their artistic manifestations such as sculpture and painting. Double-headed serpents, the Jaguar God, jester gods, celestial birds and caverns, representing the Earth-Underworld symbiosis concept, are also found in other Mesoamerican civilization's artistic expressions since remote times. The Maya linked a specific color with each of the four directions; red for east, white for north, black for west, and yellow for south.

My take on the Maya's art, architecture, and religion, is that it's all connected and was designed to show the symbiotic relationship of man, Mother Nature, and Father Sky. I suspect the stone buildings, temples, and stone glyphs, were created to connect with the natural energy of Mother Earth to create a vortex or portal to make contact with other worldly dimensions in which they may have succeeded in doing so with the help from some unknown higher source.

The Trail to Machu Picchu

In 2005, just a few years after obtaining the Clover Hollow property and disguised as a graduation gift to my girlfriend, I arranged a trip to Peru that I always thought I would make. What started out as a dive trip to the Galapagos Islands off the coast of Ecuador turned into a visit to Ica, Peru, a flyover of the Nazca Lines, and then hiking the Inca Trail to Machu Picchu.

The highlight of the trip to the Galapagos Islands was a visit to Darwin's Arch which is a giant limestone arch sitting on top of an underwater seamount. Strong currents passing by create up-swellings of nutrients which draw in hammerheads and whale sharks that feed off this highly active natural energy field. It reminded me curiously of 'Natural Bridge' back in Virginia.

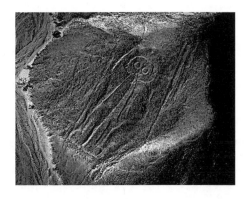

Ever since reading 'Chariots of the Gods' when I was twelve years old, I have had a fascination, if not an infatuation with the possibility that extraterrestrial life does exist and I was convinced the Nazca Lines were the proof of that existence. What I knew about the Nazca Lines from my research was that they were a series of ancient geoglyphs located in the Nazca Desert in southern Peru. The high plateau stretches more than eighty kilometers (fifty miles) between the towns of Nazca and Palpa on the Pampas de Jumana, about two-hundred and fifty miles south of Lima. Scholars believe the Nazca Lines were created by the Nazca culture between 400 and 650 AD. The hundreds of individual figures range in complexity from simple lines to stylized hummingbirds, spiders, monkeys, fish, sharks, orcas, and lizards. Also, you can only see them from the sky.

The designs are shallow lines made in the ground by removing the reddish pebbles and uncovering the whitish or grayish ground beneath. Hundreds are simple lines or geometric shapes and more than seventy are zoomorphic designs of animals such as birds, fish, llamas, jaguars, monkeys, and even an ancient astronaut. Other designs include phytomorphic shapes such as trees and flowers. The largest figures are over two-hundred meters (660 feet) across. Scholars differ in interpreting the purpose of the designs but generally ascribe religious significance to them. Are they trying to communicate to their Gods?

To get to Ica, we had to layover in Lima and then take a short flight down to Ica for the day and then return to Lima that evening. Once we got down to Ica, we found the charter that was going to fly us over the Nazca Lines. After a twenty minute flight over desert we arrived at the desert plateau. On each pass the pilots would fly over the lines and then take turns tipping each wing down so the passengers could take better pictures of the figures below. The flight lasted an hour or so before we flew back to the Ica airport.

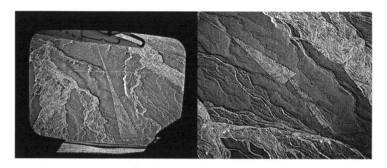

The first thing that really jumped out at me was that these images had to be put there for a purpose, but it also looked like other symbols and lines had been placed right on top of the older more recognizable glyphs. This suggests to me that we are talking about multiple cultures pancaked on top of one another. There were areas that looked like runways placed perfectly on the tops of ridges. To put these runways there, the very tops of the ridges had to be removed. Pretty much impossible even in today's standard. In addition, there was no rubble around the cliffs from the leftover tops. It is now theorized that the tops of these ridges were removed in a mining process with extraterrestrial technology. This explanation rang true for what I could see.

The giant geoglyphs depicting animals and other figures look to serve a different purpose. They appear to be some sort of signal to the heavens above, especially since you can only see them from the sky. An overwhelming notion flowed over me that these giant geoglyphs were an attempt to make some kind of contact with their ancestral spirits

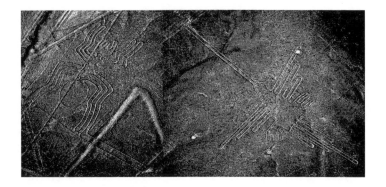

who reside in the heavens. The Nazca people were definitely trying to signal other worldly beings maybe for the help with things like reversing drought conditions or maybe for a better harvest. But ancestral contact would be the foundation of their spiritual beliefs.

We had some time to kill before our flight back to Lima so we decided to make a visit to the Regional Museum of Ica to look at some elongated skulls we had heard about. The first thing I ran across that peaked my interest was the strange and mysterious Ica Stones. In the 1960s, a local farmer tried to sell some rocks he had found in caves and gorges near the city of Ica, Peru.These stones are composed of andesite and vary in size from pebbles to boulders. They are shallowly engraved with a variety of images including carvings of humans, advanced medical procedures, advance technological instruments such as telescopes, flying machines, animals, dinosaurs, and even humans fighting dinosaurs.

Over the years the farmer had acquired thousands of these stones. Eventually, the archeological community heard of these rocks and began to investigate. The farmer was arrested and confined by the government of Peru for selling national treasures and upon his release, he recanted his testimony and confessed that he had carved them himself.

The scientific community holds to the farmer's confession of forging the stones himself, however, it has been shown that these ancient stones have a varnish over them that is formed over hundreds or thousands of years. When the varnish is removed the lighter colored lines appear. When the carvings on the stone were examined it was found the carvings themselves, have some varnish on them as well indicating that the carvings are also of ancient origin.

The mainstream scientific community cannot let the fact be known that these stones are authentic because it would make everything we are taught in school and instructed to believe one enormous fib. What I then noticed about the stones, were that some of them had the same images I had just seen from the air a couple of hours ago over the plains of Nazca.

This begs the question, which came first; the chicken or the egg? Did the same artist who carved the Inca stones carve the original Nazca Lines, or were the lines copies of images found on the stones? Whatever the case, the real hidden history of the world is not exactly what we are all led to believe. It did appear that this was another example of the Mother Nature and Father Sky, spiritual relationship. Spiritual here refers to a belief system in an afterlife.

This realization hit me like a ton of bricks as I explored a little further into the museum. What I came across next was very hard to swallow. Staring me in the face was the skull of an ancient extraterrestrial with red hair. The archaeological line is that these elongated skulls were the result of 'ritual deformations' where the skulls were bound as a child and made to grow that way. Really? I don't buy it. These skulls come mostly from Paracas which is located in the Pisco Province in the Inca Region on the Southern coast of Peru and the home of the ground breaking discovery in 1928 by Julio Tello of a massive graveyard containing tombs filled with the remains of individuals with elongated skulls now known as the famous Paracas Skulls.

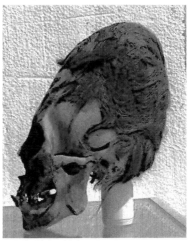

They are said to be approximately three-thousand years old and initial DNA analysis of them has revealed that they may not have come from humans but from a completely new species, according to Paracas Museum assistant director, researcher, and author, Brian Forester. Here is the apparent quote from the geneticist who did the testing: 'Whatever the sample labeled 3A has come from, it had mtDNA with mutations unknown in any human, primate, or animal known so far. The data is very sketchy though and a lot of sequencing still needs to be done to recover the complete mtDNA sequence. But, a few fragments I was able to sequence from this sample 3A indicate that if these mutations will hold, we are dealing with a new human-like creature, very distant from Homo Sapiens, Neanderthals, and Denisovans. I am not sure it will even fit into the known evolutionary tree. The question is, if they were so different, they could not have been interbred. Breeding within their small population may have degenerated due to inbreeding. That would explain buried children that were either low or not viable.'

It's always been thought that the skulls were a result of cranial deformation where the head is bound or flattened to achieve the shape. Many authors state that the time period to perform this shaping was approximately six months to three years but the practice is no longer performed, which makes it hard to really know. According to Forester 'From the doctors that I have spoken to, they have said that you can alter the shape of the skull but you cannot increase the size of the skull. The skull is genetically predetermined to have a certain volume. These skulls can hold up to fifty percent more volume than the human skull.'

Cusco, Peru

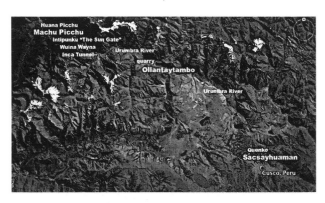

To start the Inca Trail segment of the trip, we made our way over to Cusco, Peru. Cusco was the capital of the Inca Empire (thirteenth century-1532). We are led to believe that the entire Inca infrastructure from Cusco to Machu Picchu was built in a few hundred years by the Inca, starting in the 13th century.

We stayed in Cusco for the first few days to acclimate ourselves to the altitude. We chewed on coca leaves to relieve any altitude sickness symptoms before we started our Inca Trail trek. I did have some free time to investigate some of Cusco's hidden secrets. The first thing you will notice in Cusco is the distinctive architecture used throughout the city. It's actually three different cultures built on top of each other; Spanish on top of Incan, on top of Pre-Incan. The stone walls found in the Incan Empire consisted of five different types:

The Rustic or Pirka: Made of carved rough stones that were placed without much care. The empty spaces were filled with small stones and a great amount of mud. This type was used for the construction of terraces, storages, and houses for common people.

The Cell Type: It has an aspect similar to the structure of a honeycomb made of small polygonal shaped limestone.

The Enchased Type Made of Igneous Stones: The examples of this type are the Main Temple in Ollantaytambo, and the Three-Window Temple in Machu Picchu,

The Sedimentary or Imperial Inca: It consisted of mean stones of a regular height positioned in horizontal lines that appear to be rectangular. They make perfect and polished junctures, 'where it is impossible to slip a razor blade or even a sheet of paper.'

The Cyclopean Type: Also known as Megalithic. This is the Pre-Inca type that is beyond explanation. They are giant stones that fit perfectly together.

Most Inca buildings were made out of fieldstones or semi-worked stones set in mortar, while others had adobe walls, usually with stone foundations. But, some of the buildings attributed to the Incas use precisely cut and shaped stones closely fitted without mortar, yet not even a knife blade can

be inserted between them. Sometimes, more or less rectangular (ashlar) blocks were used, but instead of being straight, each side is usually wavy, yet fits snugly with the neighboring block.

The most advanced stonework makes use of polygonal blocks with as many as twelve angles or more which interlock perfectly with all neighboring blocks, and some of the polygonal blocks are truly cyclopean, sometimes weighing at least one-hundred tons. Such stonework staggers the imagination. In many instances, the snug lateral fit extends through the entire thickness of the wall just as the bedding (horizontal) joints do. Such walls are essentially earthquake-proof. The fact "Inca" walls tend to incline inwards by three to five degrees also contributes to their stability.

To cut, shape, and dress stone blocks the Incas are believed to have used hammer stones such as river cobbles, mostly made of quartzite weighing up to ten kg. The masons allegedly achieved a perfect fit between adjacent stones mainly by trial and error. First they shaped a block on the ground and then they placed it in the wall to check the fit and then lowered it again to chip off more rock. This process was repeated again-and-again until a perfect fit was achieved. Other researchers argue that once the first block had been carved and fitted in place, the masons somehow suspended the second boulder on scaffolding next to the first one and traced the shape of the first onto it so that it wouldn't need to be repeatedly lifted into place and lowered again; this technique is known as "scribing and coping."

No sane person can believe that a twenty-ton stone was pecked here and there, dropped into position, hoisted out and trued, and then cut over-and-over again until a perfect fit was obtained. Even if we can imagine such endless herculean labor being performed it would have been impossible in many cases because the stones are locked or dovetailed together.

Although some of the stones are fairly square or rectangular with six faces, many are irregular in form and some have as many as thirty-two angles. The only way in which such complex forms could have been fitted with such incredible accuracy was by cutting each block to extremely fine tolerances, or by means of a template, a process which would indicate that these prehistoric people possessed a thorough and advanced knowledge of engineering, and the higher mathematics.

Many stones in Inca walls have strange protuberances or bosses of several shapes and sizes which appear to mar the beauty of the masonry. They are called maneuvering protuberances. They are generally found on the lower part of blocks that have been fitted. It is commonly assumed that they were used in handling the blocks, perhaps by attaching ropes to them or applying levers against them. Blocks at the quarries tend to have large protuberances, whereas blocks that have been fitted or are found lying around at Inca construction sites, or were abandoned along the route from the quarry, have much smaller protuberances. The latter could not have had ropes tied to them; what's more, the positioning of the protuberances seems rather random. Since they were clearly not needed for transportation or for handling the blocks at the building sites and were not always removed once the blocks were in place, they may have had some symbolic function.

Hiram Bingham roamed South America in the early 1900s and is credited with rediscovering Machu Picchu in 1911. He relates the following; 'The modern Peruvians are very fond of speculating as to the method which the Incas employed to make their stones fit so perfectly. One of the favorite stories is that the Incas knew of a plant whose juices rendered the surface of a block so soft that the marvelous fitting was accomplished by rubbing the stones together for a few moments with this magical plant juice.'

Saksayhuaman

Many researchers have commented on how 'Inca' stones look as though they have been cut like butter to produce perfect fits. Some see the fact that certain stones fit into concave depressions in the rock beneath as a sign that they did not have the same hardness during construction. The faces of many stones, particularly at Saksayhuaman, show strange circular or rectangular indentations and 'scrape marks' that might have been made when the rock was softer. It has also been suggested that the cup-shaped, square-shaped, and trough-shaped 'work marks' mentioned earlier were made after the surface had been softened.

Saksayhuaman, pronounced 'sexy woman' by the local guides, was definitely the most mysterious site I have ever visited up to this point. The work of geopolymer expert Joseph Davidovits is relevant to the discussion of stone softening. He has put forward compelling arguments that the ancient Egyptians built some of their major pyramids and temples using reagglomerated stone. Soft limestone was soaked in water to turn it into slurry and was then mixed with ingredients such as kaolin, natron salt, and lime. The concoction was then poured and compacted into moulds where it hardened into synthetic stone blocks, ninety-five percent of whose weight consisted of natural limestone. But, whereas fossil shells in natural limestone tend to lie flat, in reconstituted limestone, they are randomly oriented. Synthetic limestone blocks show varying densities with the topmost layer being the least dense. They sometimes contain air bubbles and organic fibers as well. Samples of pyramid blocks examined under an optical microscope appear to be natural rock and it is only under an electron microscope or during X-ray analysis that evidence of synthetic constituents emerges.

Given the very short life of the Inca Empire, many have wondered how the Incas managed to undertake such a vast construction program. This is based on the assumption that all 'Inca-style' architecture was the work of the Incas. But, it is quite possible that the Incas took over older sites and repaired, rebuilt, and added to existing structures made by earlier cultures. Maybe the result of more Iconoclastic phenomena.

Percy Fawcett put it this way: 'The Incas inherited fortresses and cities built by a previous race and restored them from a state of ruin without much difficulty. Where they themselves built with stone, in the regions where stone was the most convenient material, for in the coastal belt they generally used adobe, they adopted the same incredible mortarless joints that are characteristic of the older megalithic edifices, but made no attempts to use the huge stone masses favored by their predecessors. I have heard it said that they fitted their stones together by means of a liquid that softened the surfaces to be joined to the consistency of clay.'

David Hatcher Childress writes: 'That the Incas actually found these megalithic ruins and then built on top of them, claiming them as their own, is not a particularly alarming theory. It was a common practice in ancient Egypt. There are numerous legends in the Andes that Saksayhuaman, Machu Picchu, Tiahuanaco, and other megalithic remains were built by a race of giants.'

Commenting on the different architectural styles in and around Cuzco, he writes: 'The most recent style is Spanish. Perhaps the most primitive of all, it is characterized by the masonry and tiled roofs so common throughout colonial South America. The Incan construction of five-hundred to one-thousand years ago is evident on top of the larger, more perfect, and more ancient works. This Incan technique is easily recognized by its square or rectangular blocks, typically weighing from two-hundred to one-thousand pounds. Beneath it we find the megalithic construction of odd-angled blocks weighing from twenty to two-hundred tons, all perfectly fitted together.' He thinks the latter construction may date back to between 7000 and 3000 BC. but, some of it could be far older.

Referring to the polygonal, cyclopean style of masonry, archaeologist *A. Hyatt Verrill* commented: 'Ordinarily, all of these walls and buildings are referred to as Incan, but in reality the true Incan masonry was of an inferior type. The stones used were much smaller than those used by the pre-Incans and they were more carelessly and loosely fitted together, and not infrequently, mortar or cement was used between them. In many places the later Incans' work covers the ancient masonry of their predecessors and in such cases, where a portion of the more recent masonry has been removed, the contrast between the two types is very striking.'

Saksayhuaman is one of the wonders of ancient South America. It is one of the most magnificent edifices ever constructed anywhere in the world. Resting on top of a high hill, one side of the complex runs along a cliff with a commanding view of Cuzco. On the opposite side are three terraces, supported by three imposing megalithic walls up to twenty feet tall, made of cyclopean, perfectly fitting, polygonal blocks, which zigzag across the plateau for nearly twelve-hundred feet, resembling three lightning bolts.

Some writers believe that the zigzag outer walls imitate the distant mountain chain or that they symbolize 'Illapa' the deity of thunder and lightning. They are also said to represent the three levels of the Andean cosmos; the underworld, earth's surface, and sky, which are identified with three sacred animals; the snake, puma, and condor respectively. Another representation of Heaven, Hell, and Earth. But, it also represents a tribute to the natural world, the place where ancient people all over the world believed was where their ancestors now reside.

Various types of rock were used including massive diorite blocks from nearby for the outer walls, Yucay limestone from more than 1ten miles away for the foundations, and a dark andesite, some from over twenty miles away, for the inner buildings. Although the gigantic stones are fitted together with an almost ridiculous degree of accuracy, their faces have been deliberately left rough and many bear odd impressions and 'scrape marks' so that they look unfinished. There is therefore a stark contrast between the perfectly shaped and smooth (hidden) sides, which fit together seamlessly, and the crude, rough outer faces, maybe symbolizing spirit and matter respective. This is another example of the spirit and nature relationship.

The overwhelming notion that these megalithic stones that made up the lightning bolt walls at Saksayhuaman were somehow trying to communicate with me seemed very real. The rough outer side of the walls with so called 'maneuvering protuberances' and 'scrape marks' looked more to me like facial expressions trying to express their will. Could this be another attempt by an ancient culture trying to contact their gods and pay tribute to their ancestors through stone carvings in some way?

The idea that the entire temple complex of Saksayhuaman was built just a few hundred years ago using nothing but primitive tools is simply unbelievable. No records have been left describing when and how it was built; only guesswork and opinion from self proclaimed experts is all we have to go by. For all anybody knows, the outer walls could be hundreds of thousands of years old. The Incas may merely have repaired the upper sections of the zigzag walls and built the lesser structures that are within the walls.

On the flattened hilltop within the walls were various fine ashlar buildings including the circular tower of Muyu Marca and two rectangular towers, but today only the foundations remain. Muyu Marca was over one-hundred feet tall with three concentric walls, the outer one being about seventy-five feet in diameter. Some say it was an imperial residence and is said to have been covered with golden plates. It had a constant supply of fresh water carried up through an elaborate system of finely cut stone channels from a subterranean aqueduct leading to a spring two miles away. According to some, the various towers were connected to one another by underground tunnels (chincanas).

As I stood there staring at these humongous megaliths, I could feel the pulsating flush of chill bumps explode up a down my spine. It's hard to describe a feeling that you can't see or touch or offer any physical evidence that it exist. These chill bumps are not generated by trepidation but by excitement. It's as if my spine is vibrating like a tuning fork when exposed to some neighboring force. Like sympathetic frequencies vibrating together in harmony, the very definition of acoustic resonance seemed now to apply to every cell in my body as they were reacting to Saksayhuaman's natural vibrations.

This has been a reoccurring event all my life. First experienced it in the Saltpeter Caves in Greenville as a kid, maybe a Grateful Dead concert or two, the ruins of Copan, encounters with wild animals, and definitely overlooking the old Price mill and dam in Clover Hollow. I attributed these sensations as having mostly to do with natural occurring events. Scientifically speaking, physics offers one explanation for the above mentioned phenomena and they call it the Piezoelectric Effect.

Piezoelectric Effect

Definition: The generation of an electric charge in certain non-conducting materials such as quartz crystals and ceramics when they are subjected to mechanical stress or the generation of vibrations in such materials, when they are subjected to an electric field. Piezoelectric materials exposed to a fairly constant electric field tend to vibrate at a precise frequency with very little variation, making them useful as timekeeping devices in electronic clocks, wristwatches, and computers.

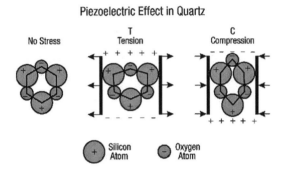

Piezoelectric Effect in Quartz

We can see that whoever or whatever created this complex at Saksayhuaman picked out very specific pieces of stone, yucay limestone for the foundations and channeling water, dark andesite for the inner buildings, and massive diorite blocks for the outer walls. It is my contention that these stones had very specific vibrational qualities. These stones could be shaped to produce whatever vibrational frequency was required by this ancient civilization.

This obviously would require a lot more knowledge about frequencies and vibrational theory than modern man could figure out in another one-thousand years. If it can't be measured and scientifically proven with our current technology, then it must not exist, nor ever have existed, as I have been taught. But, my intuition says otherwise. What if they knew how to transform a frequency to a specific vibration using natural material? They then could use naturally occurring stone with specific sympathetic vibrational qualities to convert naturally occurring frequencies into anything they wanted. If they could convert any natural frequency into anything they wanted, then they could turn the Earth's natural energy at a given location into a form of energy they could use like electricity, antigravity, lasers that could melt through stone, communication devices, spaceships, or any other technology we can't imagine. Having this type of knowledge would certainly be conducive to intergalactic or inter-dimensional travel.

Here's how I think they did it. With the help from a higher knowledge, most likely extraterrestrial; they had the ability to reshape and move massive stone blocks to make the outer walls. My theory would be that when they started building the massive cyclopean walls, they first started with one large diorite stone and by shaping and removing stone they created a piezo device that had a very specific frequency, or vibration, that would resonate when exposed to naturally occurring frequencies from the Earth's energy-field. They may have fine tuned this 'cornerstone' by removing parts of the stone by carving or pounding as can be seen in the bottom stones of the wall in the way of indentions, marks, and cups. Once they had this 'cornerstone' fine tuned where they wanted it, they began to meticulously fit other stones around it, creating their cyclopean masterpieces that altogether would vibrate at a certain frequency when exposed to Earth's naturally occurring forms of energy. Maybe carving facial expressions in the stone somehow regulates the vibrations being emitted. Pretty soon, by adding stone after stone, they had a huge wall structure which resonates the same frequency as that of the first stone, but now is greatly amplified. The entire Saksayhuaman complex could have been a giant extraterrestrial mining operation designed to export the Earth's natural energy to their home planet, or for some other purpose.

One mechanical analogy of reshaping or fine tuning a physical object so that it would resonate to a specific frequency when subjected to an external force would be the manufacturing process of a steel drum, a musical instrument from Trinidad. The Trinidadians would first cut off the top portion of a fifty-five gallon steel drum that they would find littering their Island. They would pound and flatten the top until they could reproduce a certain musical note when an outside force like a small rubber mallet would bang against it at a certain spot. Musical theory and vibrational frequency show a very close and mathematical relationship to each other. I have read that some have determined that Earth's naturally occurring magnetic field has a vibrating frequency of 438 HZ, which would be close to the musical wave form of the note A.

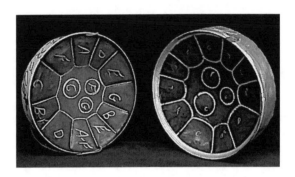

In scientific terms, the giant lightning bolt shaped wall structure of Saksayhuaman could be described as being one incredibly powerful transducer. According to Wikipedia; 'A transducer is a device that converts a signal in one form of energy to another form of energy. Energy types include (but are not limited to) electrical, mechanical, electromagnetic (including light), chemical, acoustic, and thermal. While the term transducer commonly implies the use of a sensor or detector, any device which converts energy can be considered a transducer.'

We don't know what type of energy they were trying to create, whether it was some sort of physical energy like electricity or maybe more of a spiritual energy that would help them travel or communicate between other dimensions, or other realms of the unknown. It would only be pure conjecture to suggest that maybe an ancient alien colony of tall redheaded elongated skull colonist once called this their home.

It is a scientific fact that water amplifies the Earth's magnetic field. This would explain the channeling of water from nearby springs and aquifers through and over Saksayhuaman's limestone foundations which effectively boost or amplified the power grid of their cyclopean, lightning bolt shaped, polygonal, and naturally structured wall of transducers.

Ollantaytambo

On the way to our next destination of Ollantaytambo, we passed by the ruins of Tambo Machay. Tambo Machay is a site used by the Inca for ritual bathing and consists of massive stone walls with elegant niches and a series of water fountains cascading from channels hidden within the structure. The water still runs today. It may be that these polygonal walls were constructed for their healing properties resulting from the energy created by the running water through the mysteriously shaped walls. This is another major example of a symbiotic relationship between humans (possibly extraterrestrials), Mother Nature (the physical universe), and Father Sky (the heavens that surrounds everything). It was also evident to me that Tambo Machay is multicultural with one culture piling on top of the other.

Our next stop, Ollantaytambo, is located fifty kilometers from Machu Picchu at the northern end of the Sacred

Valley. It comprises a town planned on a grid, a royal estate, and a ceremonial center. The ceremonial center, commonly called the 'fortress' takes the form of a vast amphitheater of terracing extending up a steep, concave hillside to a flat ridge three-hundred and sixty feet above. A series of stairways lead to the top of the terrace complex where the site is divided into three main areas; the temple sector to the south, (left); the middle sector directly in front of the terraces; and the funerary sector to the north, (right)

204

This is the most other worldly place I have ever seen. These are massive laser cut stone structures sitting atop a terraced mountainside like radar dishes facing toward the unknown. The outstanding polygonal cut-stone masonry of the temple sector contrasts with the buildings in the other two sectors which are made out of fieldstones and mortar. The temple sector is accessed via a stairway that ends on a terrace with the 'Wall of the Unfinished Gate,' and the 'Enclosure of the Ten Niches,' a one-room building. Behind them there is an open space with the 'Platform of the Carved Seat' and two unfinished monumental walls (the 'First and Second Walls).'

Higher up is the main structure of the whole sector, the 'Sun Temple.' This unfinished building features the 'Wall of the Six Monoliths,' which has been called 'The Jewel of Ollantaytambo.' The unfinished structures on 'Temple Hill' and the numerous stone blocks (some weighing over one-hundred tons) that litter the site, indicate that construction was still in progress at the time the site was abandoned. Some of the blocks have clearly been removed from finished walls showing that major reconstruction was taking place. The Incas used Ollantaytambo as a fort to guard the entrance to Cuzco from the Urubamba Valley but

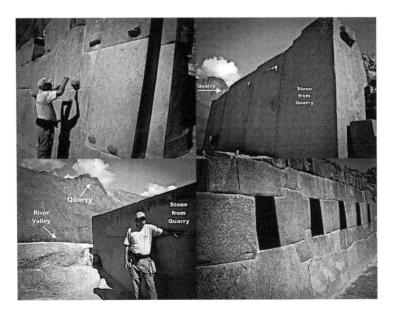

there is no reason to believe that the entire complex was built by them in the fifteenth century. It is far more likely that as at Saksayhuaman, the Incas merely adopted, remodeled, and added to buildings that were already in place.

We are led to believe that these one-hundred plus ton monoliths were brought here from a quarry a few miles away from on top of a mountain and then lowered down a sheer vertical face, and then transported over the Urubamba River, and then dragged up a steep concave hillside 250 feet to the top of the ridge, put in place using levers against the maneuvering protuberances, and then pounded to extreme tolerances using stone hammers. Not too long ago a group of scientific researches wanted to prove that this could be done so they decided to move a one ton boulder from the quarry. Well, the ropes broke and the rock fell to the bottom. They then tried to carry it across the river with rafts but it fell off and to this day, is in the middle of the river. They still use this as proof that it can be done.

Urubamba River Valley

The next travel segment brought us through the Urubamba River Valley and along the river. It reminded me of the New River just a few miles from Clover Hollow. The water was shallow with some rapids scattered along the way. The river valley was the heart of the civilization that called this home for thousands of years. It is here where the four day trek to Machu Picchu begins.

One can't help to notice the similarities between the Urubamba River Valley and the New River Valley where Clover Hollow exist today. However, it is somewhat hard for me to wrap my mind around the fact that the New River Valley rolling through the Appalachian Mountains is a much more ancient river system than the one here cutting through the Andes.

The Inca Trail

The Inca Trail was even more beautiful than I could have imagined. It was a four day trek with a guide and porters, hiking across the Andes on our way to Machu Picchu. Most of the hiking was over stone steps that crossed over the mountains, becoming difficult to climb at times. We would have to crisscross back and forth across each step in order just to get up them. Of course the porters would have no problems and would sometimes run and have races, just like the Inca used to do. All I had to carry was my camelback and my camera. Everything else was supplied by the porters and they would set up camp each night and cook the meals.

The thing that stood out most for me was the absolute harmony between man, Earth, and the heavens above. It appeared to me to be a complete cooperation between humans and nature, where each not only survived, but thrived, as they depended on each other. The Inca and those that came before built their structures and the trail itself with a certain thoughtfulness and cooperation with Mother Nature who they believed was the connection to their gods and ancestors.

I could see now what the ancients saw. You felt a lot closer to God and the heavens above in a way that was more than just having a closer proximity to them. The beauty of the mountains that jutted up all around you left you with no doubt that this wasn't random and there definitely was some kind of higher consciousness behind it all. It is no wonder the Inca saw these mountains and the animals that lived here as representative of the manifestation of the spiritual world.

The Andes Mountain chain is estimated to be about twenty-five million years old, a youngster in terms of age in the mountain building process. You can see their tall jagged peaks being pushed up over thirteen-thousand feet by currently active plate tectonics. This is in stark contrast to the four-hundred million year old Appalachian Mountains which have risen and worn down until flat, rose again, and then worn down again. Their peaks have been lowered and the tops rounded down to elevations mostly under three-thousand feet.

It did seem odd to me that the Andes, this relatively young mountain chain, was covered with ancient civilizations when the much older Appalachian Mountains had nothing but a hunter gatherer human past, or at least that's what we are led to believe. Could it be that there is ancient, if not extraterrestrial evidence yet to be found in the Appalachians? At some point over time, everything wears away, turns to dust, and disappears into oblivion. The longest lasting evidence would be that of stone and its susceptibility to erosion.

What I noticed in the architecture along the Inca Trail was the Inca's technique of blending their structures and walls to fit meticulously to the existing substrate and bedrock. It was like they were fused together, not unlike the cyclopean walls at Saksayhuaman.

The Power of Machu Picchu

After climbing a flight of steps that were carved into the side of a mountain, I walked through a great stone gateway called 'Intipunku' or 'The Sun Gate' and found myself on top of a mountain ridge looking out over Machu Picchu down below. The air of mystery and supernatural was thick and it surrounded you from every direction as you gazed out over Machu Picchu nestled into the next ridge over.

steps leading to the "Sun Gate"

Machu Picchu as seen from "The Sun Gate"

The Sun Gate

as seen from Machu Picchu

For me, it was obvious that Machu Picchu was the focal point of more than one ancient civilization. The oldest inhabitants appear to be the most creative and animistic of the cultures. Spiritualism must have been their primary focus as seen in the broad type of petroglyphs they created depicting the surrounding mountains, birds, and animals. They believed the natural world around them contained the spirits of their ancestors.

This suggests to me they were animistic by nature and believed nature and the spirit world were one and the same. It was like they were paying tribute to their gods whose spirits they believe live in every natural thing. One thing that I noticed was that the surrounding mountains and sky looked as if they were faces staring back at you. Maybe there is something to 'The Spirits in the Mountains.'

Sitting in the center of the Machu Picchu are some highly creative sculptures that look to me to have extraterrestrial connections because of the technology that must have been used to create them. Many appear to be perfectly smooth as if cut by a laser. It looks as though most of the stone buildings and walls were built around the previously existing abstract and creative stone sculptures.

The Andean condor that is carved on the rock floor in the very center of Machu Picchu is full of intrigue. The first thing you notice, once you realize it's a condor, is that it has no wings. Why would anyone carve just the torso of this sacred bird knowing the magnificence of a ten feet wingspan?

All you have to do is step back and look at the big picture. You can now see the massive wings in stone towering in the background. If you look closely you will see that they are carved to look like wings and notice that the wing on the left is not touching the ground.

As I stood there at the Sun Gate, gazing over Machu Picchu down below, an epiphany of monumental clarity washed over my body. It was now clear to me as the the day was bright, what exactly the ancient Peruvians saw when they stood on this exact spot. There is no doubt in my mind that these ancient people equated the spiritual world as one-in-the-same with the natural world. They believed the Gods created the natural universe, making it the connection back to the heavens where their ancestral spirits now reside. Everything they did, like their art and architecture, was devoted solely and in reverence to their natural surroundings, it was a tribute to honor their ancestors

214

Chapter 10 The Seventh Step

When I bought this little piece of property in Clover Hollow in 2002, I thought it was just a small house near the campus of Virginia Tech that my girlfriend could live in while she went to Vet School. Who would have thought the very first owners of record for this property were my direct ancestors and the original colonists, founders, and forefathers, of the New River German Settlement. The idea that I am the eighth generation grandson from three different bloodlines connected to this property I now own, boggles my mind. This extremely personal and unexpected connection to this little spot on Earth was having a profound effect on me.

The dam my house overlooks was built around 1840 by David Price Jr, grandson of Michael Price, my first-generation grandfather, a founding member of the New River German Settlement and one of the first European settlers to the area. David Price Jr's grandson, Robert Price, built a home nearby after the Civil War, only to come by hard times and have to sell his home and the Price Mill to his uncle, who then later sold it to Mr. William Echols.

By 1890, Echols had built my house for the manager of the mill, Ben Kendrick, using lumber from local, now three-hundred year old white oak probably cut at the mill at the bottom of the hill. This two rooms on two rooms, white oak plank structure, stood just on top of the hill overlooking the mill and dam. Frank Sibold, the grandson of Jacob Sibold, my fourth generation grandfather who is buried here on Clover Hollow Mountain, owned the property for many years. Electricity and plumbing were added to the house over the years. Furthermore, a bathroom and another bedroom were put on at different times. One of its best features is the eight foot wraparound concrete porch with iron railings, all under a tin roof. In the 1970s, I was told that they used dynamite to blow out the basement from the limestone bedrock directly beneath the house.

The miller's house sits on the side of a hill at the apex of three mountains; Sinking Creek Mountain, John's Creek Mountain, and Clover Hollow Mountain, all the while overlooking the dam on Sinking Creek. The running and rushing water over the dam could be mistaken for the ocean if you had your eyes closed. Certainly, it was my little piece of Heaven and how I came to be here completely befuddled my inner soul. This surely did not happen by some random coincidence.

I also knew the house was within a rock's throw from the old Indian trail that Mary Ingles, her Shawnee captors, and William Preston, traveled across that fateful day, July 8, 1755, when William Preston's uncle, Colonel James

Patton, on his sixty-third birthday and the day before 'Braddock's Defeat,' was assassinated by Shawnee Indians. Nothing but but a bunch of random coincidences? I don't think so. The historical and genealogical imprint on this little piece of land has been incredible if not unbelievable.

The house by the time I moved in needed tons of work. All the carpeting needed to be removed and replaced with hardwood flooring, and it all had to be cleaned and painted. The outside landscape wasn't much better, it was completely overgrown and I had no idea what would be found underneath all the ground-cover and brush. The previous tenants were an earthy bunch and left the remnants of a fire pit and a makeshift chicken coup to clean up. It could have been much, much worse.

After I had pulled up all of the nasty, old, wall to wall carpeting and two layers of faded linoleum, I came across my first clue to the secrets of Clover Hollow. Purposely placed for someone to find one day was the front page of the Roanoke Times dated March of 1952. I assumed the reason might be to mark the date of a new owner or the date the home was updated to include running water in the kitchen. At one time, an outhouse was out back. I left the newspaper in place for somebody else to find it one day. This all brought to mind what else might be found buried around the house. Was this newspaper a clue to something hidden nearby?

It became obvious very quickly what the hardest and most time consuming restoration project would be. It was the steep set of steps leading upstairs that were covered in multiple layers of carpet and multiple layers of paint. After scraping away layer after layer of everything, I discovered that the base wood was beautiful, bookmatched planks of old white oak, probably from a local tree that grew nearby. The only trouble was, I had to hand-scrape with brute force each layer of paint down until I reached bare wood. With dedication, two steps per weekend could be completed. There were twelve steps altogether so it would take me about six weeks to complete the job. Evidence that you had scraped down far enough into the wood was clear when you could smell the green bare wood like the three-hundred year old white oak was cut fresh that day. It was as though the oak planks took their first breath of fresh air in 125

years. The notion of bonding with the natural white oak seemed like a welcomed reacquainting.

Everything was going fine until a little bit of time was spent on stair number seven. Every time I would stand or sit on this particular step, the wave of goosebumps would start pounding up and down my spine. If I moved up a step, the pulsations would stop. If I moved down a step, they would also go away. This event could be recreated anytime I wanted. The feeling was intense and the sensation would always come on cue. It was decided to skip step number seven until the rest of the stairs were completed.

Once all the stairs were completed, a compulsion to study everything that could be found on the subject of ghost hunting became my current urgent reality. Ghost busting 101 suggested the use of an EMF (electromagnetic field) meter and an EVP (electronic voice phenomena) recorder to start documenting all the spooky spots. The first time I used my EMF gauss meter app on step number

seven, it spiked tenfold above normal at one particular spot right above the seventh stair tread. It didn't make much sense to me why this one stationary spot created such havoc with my insides. There are no wires or anything electric anywhere near this particular spot. I could find no source responsible for an electromagnetic field. It was as though something was trying to get my attention. I'm thinking it might be the mill manager's ghost giving me clues as to where he might have buried some gold or treasure. It really didn't feel like a haunting though, I didn't sense any danger, no foreboding, only pure exhilaration. The distinct feeling at the time felt more like a communication event happening than anything else. It was as though something intelligent was deliberately manifesting itself into something only I could pick up and make note. Christian upbringing tells us that ghost are actually demons representing themselves as lost love ones, however, it really didn't feel like a haunting of any kind.

The next thing to do was to use my trusty new digital recorder app on my iPhone to see if I could pick up some chatter from beyond. That's what they do on all the ghost shows I was thinking. Just as I reached the top of the steps with the app on, and while asking who may be trying to contact me, I received a startling noise on the machine. I could not hear it at the time but did notice the movement of the bars on the meter. It wasn't a human voice at all, but more like an electronic squelch. I made a mental note that this was not a human voice, but more like something trying to get my attention by purposely interfering with my recording device in some way.

My next ghost catching instrument I purchased was an eighty dollar Panasonic infrared video camera to see if my new etheric visitors wanted to make their stage debut on film. Honestly, I did not expect to see what I saw on step number seven. It was clear to me now I had some new friends.

Video 2 posted at www.virginiarockart.com

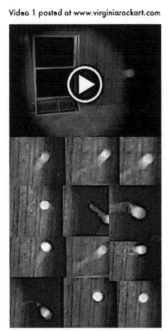

Video 1 posted at www.virginiarockart.com

The only word I can find to adequately describe what I have captured on infrared video would be the word 'ectoplasm' described as a supernatural viscous substance. As I panned up and down over step number seven, two frames would drop and go black, and on the third pass, an orb like material morphed and literally jumped off the step, clearly wanting to be seen. It happened so fast you had to play the clip in slow motion to see the lightning leap. In reviewing the clip, the ectoplasm could only be seen in three frames, which means the jump took a total of one-tenth of a second to complete. But it did happen at the exact spot the EMF meter had gone off. While I was filming this clip, I was at a heightened emotional state and this

222

excitement seemed to have an effect on the phenomena. Again, I had the distinct feeling that whatever this is, is manifesting itself in a form that I could recognize with my eye or equipment.

It didn't feel like ghostly encounter in the general sense as there was not any fear or foreboding like you would normally expect when there is a haunting taking place. It certainly was not old man Kendrick lamenting about what happened to his mill. It had more of an ancient Indian spirit kinda vibe going on as far as I could tell. This made the EVP make a little more sense, since I didn't record a human voice or a language I could understand. It seemed more like an attempt to interfere with the electronics and get my attention, like a message being sent.

I was actually happy and excited and it felt like something was trying to directly communicate with me, trying to show me or tell me something. Whatever it is, it's very cooperative in showing themselves and I just have to figure out what they are trying to say. Something compelled me to take some more video, upstairs this time. Maybe the mill manager will try to show me where he kept the payroll hidden, but I didn't really think so.

The next video was different from the first one in that the entity was taking the shape of round orbs as opposed to ectoplasm morphing into different shapes. Standing there in the dark room my jaw dropped as I could see round orbs flash continuously across the video display. Maybe they have changed into orbs because that's the shape I now expected to see them in, watching all the TV ghost shows that I was.

The next documented encounter happened during the beginning of a snowstorm in early January that year which laid down about a foot of snow overnight. I took a few high resolution photographs of the snow when it first started to fall, mainly because the snowflakes appeared enormous. It was only later when looking at the high resolution photos that I noticed that there were more than just snowflakes dancing around. The realization that this was not all snow hit me like a ton of rocks.

Okay, it looks as though I have some new friends and they don't appear to be ghostly apparitions, but more like first howdy-do's with your neighbors when moving to a new town. All I can say for sure is that they appear to be of an intelligent, energetic, natural, etheric form or entity, and they were purposely making themselves visible to me. The odd thing was the feeling that all this was really happening and it wasn't a case of an overzealous imagination or a dip into insanity. There it was, documented on film, proof that I wasn't sitting in the front seat of the short bus wearing my helmet on the way to the loony bin.

To start making some sense out of this, I started a physical search of the entire property. One odd item that I had found when I first bought the place was a large rock, painted white, and was being used as a garden stone. It caught my eye because it looked like a big white fish, and I immediately thought it might have been carved that way by Indians who lived in the area. Other explanations went through my head such as it being a stalagmite or a stalactite, or even part of a pillar from a nearby cave. Maybe it was a weight used at the mill; however, it still looked like a rock carved like a fish to me. I spent some time removing the multiple layers of paint to see what exactly I had, much like the removal of paint from the stairs. It created more questions than answers when this object appeared to be even more mysterious than I had first imagined. It still looked like a fish.

I was a man on a mission at this point and I was keeping my eyes open for anything and everything that might come my way. It felt like I was being fed clues one by one. If one was solved, or followed in the right direction, it seemed I was given another. Maybe, whatever is trying to reach out to me, doesn't want to overwhelm me all at once. Too late!

After the electromagnetic field disruptions on the seventh step stopped, I decided to start testing other places around the house. To my amazement, I found large electromagnetic field distortions all along the front porch iron railings with my gauss meter. To confirm the gauss-readings, I used a compass to pinpoint areas that had the largest distortions and these spots would make the compass needle rotate on its axis. Also, I fashioned a pair of divining rods out of copper wire to see if I could make them cross, and that's exactly what they did.

It felt as if now, I was being purposely led outside of the house to continue the next phase of 'Operation Have No Clue.' I did start to notice that every time there was a weather event like rain or snow, the magnetic field disruptions on the front porch would spike even higher. This clue inspired me to find a high definition video camera that would film in visible, infrared, and ultraviolet light. Every time it would rain, and right after dusk, when the magnetic field spikes would be at their highest point, I would film over the porch railings in the infrared and ultraviolet spectrum. As if this is what I was supposed to do, I was rewarded with supernatural visits from etheric entities of unknown origin. It was obvious they were appearing to me on purpose and apparently on command. They traveled at a high rate of speed and the only way to capture their image was to search the video, frame by frame. They seemed to be feeding off the electromagnetic field off the front porch railings.

They came before me in all shapes and sizes; as orbs, ectoplasm, mist, cones, cylinders, vortexes, glowing wave patterns and an assortment of other strange and sparkly creatures. It was like they had just stopped in for a visit and to give me their howdy do's. They were showing themselves to me for a particular reason, but I still had no idea what it was. There is no giving up, I am now all in, and I'm in it for the long haul. I was wondering what was next on their agenda. All I really had was strange photographs of things with no explanation.

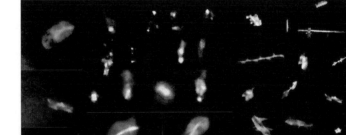

Chapter 11 The Faces of Clover Hollow

My research on Price's Mill confirmed that my house (the miller's house) stood somewhere within a stone's throw of the old New River Indian Trail. This ancient trail would have been used for thousands of years as it was the only passage through the Appalachian Mountains heading west anywhere in the area. Price's Fork and the German New River Settlement sat at the crossroads of the New River Trail, Southern Trail, and the Great Valley Road not seven miles down the mountain from my house.

After studying topographical maps for years, it was evident to me that the trail either crossed over my property or ran alongside where the road was now cut in down by Sinking Creek. When the mill was built on top of the dam sometime by 1840, a road was cut in and built alongside the mill and Sinking Creek. To cut the road in, they had to drill out the bedrock and remove part of the mountainside directly in front of my house. I've heard stories that an old road used to pass somewhere up behind my house, somewhere further up the mountainside maybe. More than likely I thought, was that the entire Indian trail was covered up and lost when the road and mill were first built one-hundred and seventy-five years ago.

However, one snowy morning in February 2013, I was standing out on the front porch enjoying my morning coffee when I realized my senses were at a heightened peak of awareness and I was trying to be conscious of everything around me. As I was standing there looking out over the porch railing enjoying the wonders of this place, there it was, staring me right in the face was a faint outline of a path or trail. It was heading right across my yard and along the side of the mountain. The path stood out because of the contrast between the lightly scattered snow and the bare dead leaves covering the ground. It took a little while before it started to sink in and the chill bumps started to multiply. Just twenty feet off the side of the front porch, I could clearly see a trail crossing over my property and then come to an abrupt stop overlooking Sinking Creek, the dam, and the road they had cut into the side of the mountain a long time ago.

Before the snow had melted completely, I followed the path to its end. This specific spot at the end of the trail along the steep mountainside, appears to have been completely hidden and blocked off ever since the road was cut in one-hundred and seventy-five years ago. At the end of the trail, where it came to a sudden stop, I noticed an odd looking rock that looked like an old pioneering trail-marker, maybe used by an early surveyor like Christopher Gist, James Patton, William Preston, or George Washington. They all could have easily passed over this spot I was thinking. It was oddly shaped rock and it was sticking out of the ground blocking a fifteen foot drop down to the road.

I could now see that the only section of the old Indian trail still in existence today runs across my yard and comes to abrupt stop overlooking the road, creek and dam. This overlook appears to have been unchanged for thousands of years. I photographed the trailhead area and the trail marker rock so I could study the photos later. It looked to me that this 'trail-marker' had a series of hack marks cut in all across the face and maybe somebody's initials or survey marks crudely cut into the stone.

After I cleaned some of the lichen and moss off the 'trail-marker' I took some additional photographs of the terrain and rock formations along the newly found path. These photos captivated my attention for hours, if not days, sometimes seeing carved initials and occasionally I would see the infamous 'Hooked X' but ended up blaming

229

it all on my out of control imagination. There has to be some meaning to all of this and it definitely warrants further investigation of the entire area. At the newly discovered trailhead, I noticed the convergence of three different cultures; the ancient, meets the old, meets the new. They looked like they were pancaked on top of each other just like Nazca, Saksayhuaman, Ollantaytambo, Cuzco, and Machu Picchu in Peru. In Clover Hollow, it was the ancient Indian trail, covered up by the early colonist, and then modern man with their paved highways.

One of the first things I realized when I went back to the trail head to take a better look, was that the mountainside along the trail was very steep, literally crumbling away and was hard to get a foot hold. As I was taking all this in and gazing down at a rock that appeared to have fallen down the cliff's side at one time, I noticed an extremely odd looking rock sitting on top like it was placed there for me to find. When I picked it up, it appeared to be carved on one side, and resembled a piece of petrified dinosaur bone on the other. I put it in my bag for further study.

The trail comes to a complete stop here as it overlooks a fifteen foot drop to the road below. On the other side of the road is where the dam remains today and at one time, the Price Mill. It may be that the last humans to cross over this trail, before it was cut off from the rest of the world, were those Shawnee warriors and their kidnapped hostages, including Mary Ingles, escaping from Draper's Meadow, July 8, 1755.

When I got back to the house, I pulled out the strange rock from my bag and cleaned it up to take a better look. This is definitely the strangest thing I have ever found. First, it's perfectly weighted to hold in your hand like a wand, scepter, or tool. The part you hold is the part that looks like petrified bone, maybe a dinosaur bone, you can even see what looks like bone marrow in the cross section. It also seems to have a different appearance or look, depending on what side you are looking at, like it had multiple personalities. You can see the carved marks throughout, and it appears to me to be very anthropomorphic and zoomorphic. Meaning, whoever did this, carved human and animal features into it.

For the next year and a half, I hacked, pulled, cut, and dug out all the brush and ground cover within a thirty yard radius of the house. Over the years, the property had become completely overgrown and covered in six feet of heavy brush, which hid everything below. What I discovered once the ground cover was removed was completely amazing. The following pages will be very controversial and all I ask is that you approach it with an open mind and imagination.

Pareidolia

Before we continue our journey, we need to understand the phenomenon of pareidolia to get a clearer picture on what's really going on here. Wikipedia defines pareidolia as: 'Pareidolia (parr-i-doh-lee-ə) is a psychological phenomenon involving a vague and random stimulus (often an image or sound) being perceived as significant, a form of apophenia.' A common example includes seeing images of animals or faces in clouds, the man in the Moon, the Moon Rabbit, and hearing hidden messages on records when played in reverse.

'The word comes from the Greek words para (beside, alongside, instead). In this context, meaning something faulty, wrong, instead of.' Pareidolia is a type of apophenia, seeing patterns in random data. This definition implies that the phenomenon of pareidolia is a delusional behavior. You are not really seeing these images; they are just figments of your imagination made from random data. There are a number of theories as to the cause of this phenomenon. Experts say pareidolia provides a psychological determination for many delusions that involve the senses. They believe pareidolia could be behind numerous sightings of UFOs, Elvis, the Loch Ness Monster, and the hearing of disturbing messages on records when they are played backwards.

Pareidolia often has religious overtones. A study in Finland found that people who are religious or believe strongly in the supernatural, are more likely to see faces in lifeless objects and landscapes.

Carl Sagan, the American cosmologist and author, made the case that pareidolia was a survival tool. In his 1995 book, 'The Demon-Haunted World – Science as a Candle in the Dark,' argued that this ability to recognize faces from a distance or in poor visibility was an important survival technique. While this instinct enables humans to instantly judge whether an oncoming person is a friend or foe, Sagan noted that it could result in some misinterpretation of random images or patterns of light and shade as being faces.

Sagan claimed that the human tendency to see faces in tortillas, clouds, cinnamon buns, and the like, is an evolutionary trait. He writes: 'As soon as the infant can see, it recognizes faces, and we now know that this skill is

Example of Pareidolia from the Galapagos Islands

hardwired in our brains. Those infants who a million years ago were unable to recognize a face smiled back less, were less likely to win the hearts of their parents, and less likely to prosper. These days, nearly every infant is quick to identify a human face, and to respond with a goony grin.'

A 2009 magneto encephalography study found that objects incidentally perceived as faces evoke an early (165ms) activation in the ventral fusiform cortex, at a time and location similar to that evoked by real faces, whereas other common objects do not evoke such activation. This activation is similar to a slightly earlier peak at 130ms seen for images of real faces. The authors suggest that face perception evoked by face-like objects is a relatively early process, and not a late cognitive reinterpretation phenomenon. An MRI study in 2011 similarly showed that repeated presentations of novel visual shapes that were interpreted as meaningful, led to decreased MRI responses for real objects. These results indicate that interpretation of ambiguous stimuli depends on similar processes as those elicited for known objects.

These studies help to explain why people identify a few circles and a line as a 'face' so quickly and without hesitation. Cognitive processes are activated by the 'face-like' object, which alert the observer to both the emotional state and identity of the subject, even before the conscious mind begins to process, or even receive the information.

Leonardo Da Vinci wrote about pareidolia as an artistic device. 'if you look at any walls spotted with various stains, or with a mixture of different kinds of stones, if you are about to invent some scene, you will be able to see in it a resemblance to various different landscapes adorned with mountains, rivers, rocks, trees, plains, wide valleys, and various groups of hills.'

He's talking about using your mind as a tool to increase your imagination and creativity. That's the best way I found in dealing with the sudden reality that I may be looking at hundreds of anthropomorphic petroglyphs carved by an unknown and ancient civilization that once lived in the Appalachian Mountains here in Clover Hollow. I'm seeing images of faces carved all over every rock formation I have uncovered so far.

Some people could argue that these images are natural rock formations and that I suffer from a severe case of pareidolia. All the evidence that I have developed and laid out in this book tells me that these carvings were deliberately put there using a specific method and theme applicable to all the designs. All this takes place on a few acres of land on the side of a mountain. It would have taken a highly skilled and creative civilization many years to carve every rock; if that's the way you think it all went down. Maybe it's just hundreds, if not thousands of natural coincidences, and it was really all done by Mother Nature. Either ways, put your pareidolia hat on, turn on your imagination and creativity, and enjoy the ride.

The Petroglyphs

Visits to ancient ruins has altered my perspective on the concept of life and the afterlife. All cultures I have noticed have their own but similar creation story. The Cherokee believed that the 'Great Spirit' created the physical universe for people to enjoy and be its keeper. It was believed to be the Great Spirit's way of communication to the physical dimension of mankind. Just as in Peru, the early people created their art using the natural world as their canvas to communicate back to their gods. Since the beginning of time, the people of every culture have used their art to express their most personal thoughts to whoever might gaze upon it, regardless of time and language. These were the thoughts streaming through my mind as the jumble of hack marks in front of me slowly formed into a giant face gazing up at the sky. At that exact moment, I was thinking 'oh yeah, I see what you are trying to do here.' It was a mind meld of epic proportions when I realized I was identifying with someone else's thought process made thousands of years ago.

My property is mostly limestone karst jutting from the ground and covering the steep mountainside. Karst is a landscape formed from the dissolution of soluble rocks including limestone, where the hardest of the lithographic rock remains. After I was convinced that I was not suffering from extreme pareidolia and wasn't hallucinating, I began to dig out a few of the outcroppings from the dirt, brush, moss, and lichen that covers them all.

The first rock megalith that stood out to me was on the cliffside standing there as if it were a sentry or guard post for the old Indian trail. You could stare at these rock formations twenty-four hours every day, and from every angle, and never see the artistic masterpiece that lay in front of you. The secret was to capture a single moment of time on a photograph, from that exact point of view, the sudden thrill of understanding slaps you across the face. Once you experience this epiphany of discovery, all the pieces of art distributed across the mountainside sharpen into focus. Also noticeable is the crumbling effect of erosion that has taken place since the Appalachian Mountain building process began millions of years ago.

One rock formation, fifteen yards from the front porch, is one of the most alien looking ones of all. It looks completely different depending on what side or angle you are looking at. This is a major trait common to all the carvings. Overall, it looks like an alien creature with flippers, and upon closer examination, has hundreds of smaller components, all with their own facial expressions. It's as if this rock has hundreds, if not infinite. personalities.

Every rock outcropping I have uncovered, exhibits a similar artistic approach and expression of overall method, which seems to primarily depend on the original, natural shape of the rock. Or, maybe it's more than just the shape of the rock, and more of an attempt to communicate, or pay tribute to their ancestral spirits and gods they believe live within the natural universe and these rock formations that surrounds them.

Panels

Large panels, or sections of rock, were completely covered with petroglyphs that exhibit weird, abstract, and complex stone work that completely baffles me. Searching for faces and animal shapes in every configuration does help me see some of the method in their madness and I certainly don't think I am looking at natural formations, random data, if you will. One rock panel seems just a little bit different then everything else I am finding. This rock outcropping sits up on the steep side of the mountain and I could just get close enough to use my telephoto lens. It may be that multiple cultures have added to this ancient piece of artwork.

Buried around the base of every rock formation were portable and artifact size rock carvings apparently placed there as if they were offerings to the gods. They came in all sizes, from very heavy, down to talisman size that would fit in the palm of your hand. They also, exhibit the same technique of 'images within images' and 'different images seen at different angles.' They were carefully placed around the base and in every nook and cranny, but the largest and most ornate pieces were buried at the center point of the megalith's base. The rock in the next four photo's is the same rock.

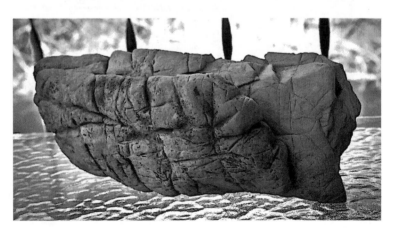

Unidentified Swimming Objects

Now that I have been able to spend a lot more time observing the weird behavior of Clover Hollow, I have started to notice unusual things happening in the waters of Sinking Creek. Whenever it would rain, the creek would bubble up like a witch's cauldron at the peak of incantation. There is a number of springs that empty into Sinking Creek at this exact spot depositing minerals of all sorts which may be reacting with the falling acid rain. This spot on the creek is thirty miles as the crow flies from the mineral and hot springs of Monroe County, West Virginia.

These events prompted me to film Sinking Creek after a rainstorm when the water started to react. The water would always start to erupt right on cue. One of the first recordings showed strange objects swimming around at incredible speeds. This brought to mind that strange and

242

alien beings might be the culprits that are playing havoc with Clover Hollow. It made more sense to me then thinking that they were water ghost. Honest to God, it appeared to me as some type of plant, flower, or natural form that moved with purpose and intelligence through the water. Could I maybe have discovered some new species of some sort?

Ok, I was getting creative now. I was so fascinated by this last clip; I decided to wait for the right opportunity to videotape the water's edge after dusk, after a thunder shower, and in full spectrum video. I wanted to see if the bubbles, or this off-gassing, had more to it than just a chemical reaction. I was surprised to capture colorful orbs of different sizes and shapes rising from the creek. These were different from the orbs and objects I was videotaping from the front porch. Could these be the Indian spirits that call Clover Hollow home?

Video 6 posted at www.virginiarockart.com

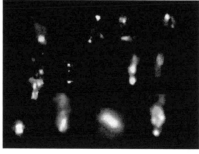

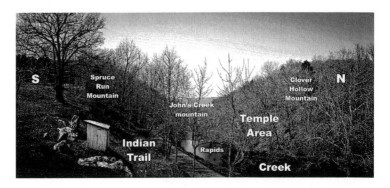

Clues to the mysteries of Clover Hollow have now revealed a lot about themselves. What would normally be considered pure coincidence and random circumstance have evolved into a box of puzzle pieces waiting to be put together. To understand what this finished puzzle may look like, one has to imagine what this spot in Clover Hollow looked like before my European ancestors and colonists reached Clover Hollow and built their mill and dam.

Removing the mill, dam, and millpond, would reveal a V shaped passageway, or water gap, through the Appalachian Mountains heading northwest. Sinking Creek would have been rushing rapids falling ten or fifteen feet in elevation as it flowed past this spot, very much like it still is today at the bottom of the dam. Both the south and north sides of Sinking Creek would rise steeply with rock formations covering both sides. A narrow ancient Indian trail would be winding itself along the south side of Sinking Creek, alongside the steep cliff, and the north side would be rising steeply toward the sky and unchanged from what it is today. The creation of the dam and millpond in the early 1800s effectively cut off the north-side of Sinking Creek from any human contact since. The only thing that has changed on the north-side of the creek since the millpond was created is the water level. You can still imagine the steep slope of the creek side continuing further down under the water.

The accessible south-side of Sinking Creek where my house (the miller's house) sits, is also steep except for the small patch of terraced land that includes the house, carved outcroppings, and a small section of the Indian trail.

To make some kind of sense to what's going on in Clover Hollow, I had to come to grips with either one of two things. First, you can reasonably assume that all the rock carvings and supernatural activity is just that, completely and one-hundred percent naturally occurring. This would also mean that everything mentioned in this book happened randomly and was nothing more than thousands of weird coincidences with no connection to each other. Or you could believe what I do, that I have been brought here to maybe uncover an ancient culture before it was lost forever. There is overwhelming evidence that points to something far bigger than your typical ghost story and its origins appear to go back thousands of years.

The realization I faced now was to try to find some cultural evidence that may connect the rock carvings to the American Indian, although I have not found any identifiable domestic items of Indian origin as of yet. A cultural connection would imply that these rock carvings were created by an ancient North American east coast Indian tribe. A tribe is viewed, historically and developmentally, as a social group existing before the development of, or outside of, states. Many people used the term 'tribal society' to refer to societies organized largely on the basis of social, especially ancestral, descent groups. A customary tribe in these terms is a face-to-face community, bound by kinship relations, reciprocal exchange, and strong ties to place. By this definition, my German forefathers and the German New River Settlement could also be considered a tribe.

Ancient cultural influences detected at Clover Hollow include strange and mystical stone alignments. Facing each other across Sinking Creek are two rock outcroppings that are standing there like the piers of a gate. Their carvings are the same abstract facial features and artistic self expression as found on all the rock formations and appear stacked on one another like a totem pole. The south-side post is standing directly beside where the Indian trail once ran along and the stone post on the north-side is standing in the creek. The first moment that I realized these 'gatepost' were carved on purpose, the chill bumps rushed up my spine like the flashlight fish exploding out of the cargo hold in Papua New Guinea. I was visualizing a vast temple like area right out of an Indiana Jones movie.

There are other peculiar stone alignments that apply to all the rock formations. Only by studying photographs of the rock formations taken during the winter months when all the leaves were gone, did I notice that there were particular curious alignments shared by all the stone outcroppings. The stones on the south-side of Sinking Creek appear to be all facing a northerly direction toward one particular spot on the north side of the creek. In addition, all the stones on the north side of Sinking Creek appear to be aligned facing right, in the direction of the same circular stone alignment the stones on the south-side face. All of this was indicating to me a ceremonial, religious, ritual, or an archaeoastronomy purpose for the circular stone formation. This seemed to me to be about as cultural as you are going to get. On top of that, numerous portable carved stones have been found buried around the bases of the stationary petroglyphs as though they were put there in tribute to their gods, even more of a cultural ceremonial indicator.

Chapter 12 The Sibold Effect

Within a couple of weeks after uncovering the Indian trail and the first of the carved rocks, I contacted the department heads of Appalachian Studies and Indian Studies at Virginia Tech, and sent them some of the photographs of what I thought were Indian rock carvings. They responded almost immediately with interest and referred me to the state archaeologist at the Virginia Department of Historical Resources.

The State Archaeologist met me a few days later and spent three hours looking over the property. He seemed very interested as I tried to explain my theory that it was all about faces. He did let on that he has never seen a phenomenon like this but did note my enthusiasm on the subject. He showed particular interest in my 'T-Rex' rock. When I told him I thought it looked like a Tyrannosaurus, he gave me the 'that's impossible' look and then told me he thought it looked like a snapping turtle. I still think it looks like a T-Rex with the two little arms and the V shape top of the skull. Of course that would mean this rock was carved by someone who had seen one twenty-five million years ago.

He seemed more interested in the old mill and dam than what I was calling Indian rock carvings. He did tell me

of a National Historic Paleo-Indian village site that was right around the corner on Sinking Creek. When I casually mentioned the paranormal activity happening in Clover Hollow, he took particular interest, so I went over the various events in more detail. After telling him the story about the seventh step, he mentioned that there were some significant spiritual beliefs about the number seven and it had a long history in the supernatural. This definitely warrants further investigation.

As far as the rock carvings go, I could see that the archaeologist had no idea what he was looking at. It's very important to note that in order to recognize these rocks as petroglyphs, you have to look at high resolution photographs. It's hard to recognize them at all if you don't know what to look for. I admired him for not acting like he knew what was going on when he did not, and also not thinking I just fell off the turnip truck. You could see the interest, but not enough for the State of Virginia to use any resources to investigate the site any further. I realized that it was up to me now on how to handle and manage the site. He did suggest that I should work on only one rock outcropping at a time. We have kept in touch, but I had to look elsewhere for some additional expertise.

What to do now? The only thing that came to mind was to put some of the photographs and the paranormal video up on a website, that way, anybody interested could examine them. Once www.virginiarockart.com was up and running, the link was sent to whomever could be found that might have some idea or interest in what's going on here in Clover Hollow.

It was decided then to contact National Geographic and the Smithsonian Institute, and the link to the website was sent to each one. Very quickly I received a response from both. They were extremely pleasant and National Geographic told me they have no budgets for investigations like this, but said the way I am getting the information out there is the way to go. The Smithsonian immediately responded by thanking me for the information on my research and that they were going to turn it over to the anthropology department, but I never heard back.

My next step was to send the website link out to as many Indian relic experts that could be found and every archaeological department head that could be located an email address for. All of the American Indian experts responded relatively quickly and said that they were knowledgeable on modern Indian relics like arrowheads and pipes, but nothing you would classify as prehistoric. Hopefully, some of the archaeological department contacts may have this expertise.

Out of the dozens and dozens of queries that were sent out to archaeology departments around the world, only two replies were received; one from England and one from Australia. The weird thing was that these two professors had written a book together about the mysteries of Stonehenge, even though they had been contacted separately. Just another random coincidence one would presume.

Their responses let me know very quickly what I was up against. All I was looking for was someone who might have some expertise on the subject matter and might want to examine the evidence. At least they had very quick responses to my email. The professor from Australia immediately responded that he saw nothing cultural in the rocks and that they all appeared to be completely natural. This response surprised me; however, it did prepare me for the skepticism that lay ahead. I attributed his response to be somewhat based on his own discoveries of cave drawings in Australia that he did not want to be diminished.

The professor from a major university in England responded just the opposite than his friend in Australia. His opinion was that he recognized the carvings as 'petroglyphs of the broad type.' He suggested that there were probably a lot more around the area. It had been a few years since he had been to the mountains of Virginia but the photographs reminded him of that special fragrance that only comes from Appalachian earth. He was the only one that responded outside the box. He gave me some good advice about dealing with the academic community and their unwillingness to investigate anything outside the norms of current belief systems. He said that researchers can choose any site or area of interest to study that they want to or care to, and in lots of cases, many choose the same subject while other discoveries are never looked at by anybody.

There was a lot of interest coming in from paranormal groups, however, I started to realize that there was more to this than just a ghost story. I had to put a stop to one paranormal group that wanted to do an investigation because I sensed they were only interested in recording EVP's (electronic voice phenomenon) that I surmised were to be used to promote their own ghost hunting services.

However, I did record one EVP myself in particular. It was an unexplained noise I captured on video at the same time an unidentified light streaked across the frame. It was the only sound I caught on video tape that was directly linked to a visible paranormal event. I'm not sure the sound is the most pleasant sound I have ever heard, but it is very startling. If one were to describe to someone what this audible wave pattern sounded like, I would use terms like supernatural, inter-dimensional, and explosively energetic.

Video 7 posted at
www.virginiarockart.com

It was clear to me now what had to be done. There were no experts on this kind of stuff anywhere that could be found. No publisher or agent would touch this story with a ten foot pole and they all considered it pure fantasy. The only way this information was ever going to be made public and believed, was for me to publish the evidence myself. There's a whole lot more to the story than just a few rock carvings and some ghost flying around. My only publishing experience comes from technical bulletins and programs used for training purposes. Maybe not such a bad way to tell this story and explain my reasoning.

So, the rest of this book is going to offer a few explanations that are based totally on my own opinion, research, photographs, video, and the facts on the ground, as they happened, and in the order they happened. The following pages will be controversial, contentious, disputed, disputable, debatable, arguable, but strictly based on the documented evidence. You can make your own mind up whether there is substance behind the evidence, or just chuck it up to a boatload of random coincidences.

The Sibold Effect begins to unravel the twisted mound of seemingly unrelated coincidences and molds them into a coherent and purposeful story. The pile of documented evidence and clues that have accumulated in Clover Hollow must be sorted, analyzed, and connected, in order for it to make any sense at all. God has given us the power of reason to come up with conclusions of our own. I have divided up the evidence into five categories; the historical record, the archaeological record, the terrestrial connection (of this natural Earth), the extraterrestrial connection (not of this Earth), and the supernatural (spiritual) connections.

The Historical Record

First and foremost, I am the eighth generation grandson of John Michael Price, John Phillip Sibold, and John Phillip Harless, who traveled together with their families to escape religious persecution in their homeland of Germany and arrived on America's shore aboard 'The Winter Galley' on September 5, 1738. All three families became founding members of the German New River Settlement and were the first owners of record for my property in Clover Hollow. The odds that I would stumble across this property, sight unseen, and having no knowledge of the history connected to this little piece of land is incalculable.

There is no doubt that the historical record connected to my property in Clover Hollow is a heavy one. Thanks to Lucy Lee Lancaster and her collection archived at Virginia Tech, the genealogical record is clear. My first generation grandfather Michael Price was the first German colonist to survey my property for a future mill site. His grandson David Price Jr. completed the construction of the mill and

A GUIDE TO THE LUCY LEE LANCASTER PAPERS, 1915-1989

A COLLECTION IN
SPECIAL COLLECTIONS
COLLECTION NUMBER MS1990-069

dam by the 1840s and it is believed slaves were used to build the concrete dam, some of who are buried on Sinking Creek Mountain just on the other side of the road. My house was built for the mill manager, Ben Kendrick, by Mr. Echols who owned the mill in the 1880s.

My fourth generation grandfather, Jacob Sibold, who built his log cabin on Clover Hollow Mountain by 1840, reared two of my fifth generation grandfathers, George Washington Sibold and John Franz Sibold in Clover Hollow, before they both moved to Monroe County, West Virginia. Jacob Sibold also had a grandson named Frank W. Sibold who owned my property and house for many years in the 1900s.

Also connected to this property through the historical record and detailed in this book are, Christopher Gist, William Preston, James Patton, George Washington, Paleo-Indians, Cherokee and Shawnee Indians, Drapers Meadow Massacre, New River German Settlement, French and Indian War, Revolutionary War, and the Civil War.

If it is true that significant historical events can leave long lasting residual energy embedded in the ground at the point where they occur, then my little piece of property on the side of an Appalachian mountain has the equivalent energy of a nuclear power plant. The energy level at my house is not only palpable through the center of your bones but also measurable by numerous manmade devices.

The Archaeological Record

According the Virginia Department of Historical Resources, my house in Clover Hollow is listed on the National Historic Registry, but only for its architectural significance in the community. They had no record or information regarding the Price Mill site, the miller's house (my house), the concrete dam that still remains, nor the mill itself that burned down in the 1960s. Virginia archaeologists have identified a Paleo-Indian village site right around the bend on Sinking Creek from my property and have listed it as a national historic site.

The German New River Settlement was considered a 'lost' settlement by early writers in the area. I have discovered in the historical record that David Price Jr built the concrete dam using local slaves in the area and which still stands strong today. There is a slave graveyard along with part of the foundation of a cabin just up on Sinking Creek Mountain overlooking my property and dam. The mill that stood here was a three level white oak plank construction building and it burned down in the early 1960s. You can still see the three-hundred year old white oak planks in the rafters of my house. They most likely were cut from local oak trees at the mill less than a hundred yards down the hill on Sinking Creek.

Price's Mill 1957   Same Spot 2012

Recent discoveries in Clover Hollow threaten the very fabric that our history books are written on. The rock petroglyphs suggest an ancient culture far older than the establishment of the East Coast North American Indian Tribes. Highly creative and artistic sculptures are spread across an Appalachian mountainside proclaiming 'We are here, don't forget us.' There is growing evidence that now can be revealed that this lost tribe or colony is still relevant today and must be examined closely to find out exactly who we are today as a people. Evidence now shows the possibility of a spiritual center and temple area almost completely buried on the steep mountainside, not unlike Machu Picchu before its discovery in the early 1900s. What was known about my property in Clover Hollow before the first white Europeans and my ancestors colonized the area, is very little to nothing at all. Undiscovered was the ancient Indian trail that cut across the property as it passed through this water gap in the Appalachian Mountains. This small passageway was also very strategic to the migration patterns that developed in the area. Any traffic going east or west in the area would have to cross over at this point.

It is clear to me now that my German ancestors settled Clover Hollow and unintentionally built their mills, dams, and cabins directly on top of another colony or tribe that existed there thousands of years before. There may be three different cultures pancaked on top of one another in Clover Hollow; the Germans, the American Indian, and possibly their ancestors. Not unlike the Spanish, who built on top of the Inca, who had built on top of the pre-Incan societies of Peru. You can see this iconoclastic phenomenon at the bottom of the dam.

If you believe the mainstream scientific community, you would have to believe that these petroglyphs, if they are petroglyphs, and all the portable size artifacts were created by a band of hunter gatherers no older than the Paleo-Indians of the area. In this vein, they could have been ancestors to the North American Indian tribes. The problem with this theory is that no Paleoindian domestic artifacts or tools were found around the petroglyphs in the way of scrapers, weapons, points, or any kind of basic utility items. This might indicate this site was a specifically used for religious or spiritual purposes.

The rock carvings cannot be matched up to any known archaeological discoveries and distinguish themselves from others with their artistic creativity. This indicates to me that this may be the remnants of a lost tribe or culture unknown to history that settled the same spot my German ancestors did thousands of years later. The irony does not escape me that my German ancestors may have unknowingly placed their colony on the exact spot where another ancient colony once made their home thousands of years before. The Germans did to this ancient lost colony what the Incan empire did to the pre-Incan civilization and almost covered up this lost settlement forever. Although it must have been done by complete accident.

It wasn't until the summer of 2014 before the old Price Mill dam site provided me with a possible answer to the secret that was buried some one-hundred and seventy-five years ago. All the recent supernatural phenomena seem to be directing my attention away from the house and yard, down toward the dam, mill pond, and creek. From the bubbling water and unidentified swimming objects, to mysterious orb like manifestations, Sinking Creek now had my complete focus.

One hot summer morning I awoke out of bed with a compelling urge to climb down to the bottom of the dam since there hadn't been much rain and the water was barely falling over the dam. Normally this wasn't happening because the water flow was usually very strong. I grabbed my camera and climbed, and slid, down the bank to the bottom of the dam.

The first thing I noticed was how well built and sturdy the dam was and especially how well German engineered it was. It looked as if it would last forever. The dam seamlessly blended into the rock bed below as if they were now one, reminding me of the Inca structures along the Inca Trail. But, the rocks below the dam that morning seem to be trying to get my attention, almost yelling at me for some yet unknown reason. I could swear they had been shaped and formed by somebody even though they have been mostly underwater for a very long time.

This dam used a turbine instead of a water wheel and the man made dam abutments were made of stone. Some of them looked as though they were from the creek bed and were carved like the petroglyphs on the surrounding mountain side.

Sitting on a flat rock that has spent the majority of its existence submerged, was a very odd rock standing there in the dry creek bed like it was placed there for me to find that day. My attention was drawn to part of the rock that appeared to have a perfectly carved dolphin or fish head on one end. It was obvious beyond any possibility of pareidolia. On the other side of that rock was another unmistakable image of a beavers head. This is when it hit me that another ancient colony inhabited this spot long before the German New River Settlement and my ancestors did the same? That sealed the deal for me as everything started to make sense and fall into place. What was almost buried for an eternity, under the old Price mill, has now revealed itself. If I had not ever made it to Clover Hollow for whatever reason, none of this would have ever been found and completely lost to history forever.

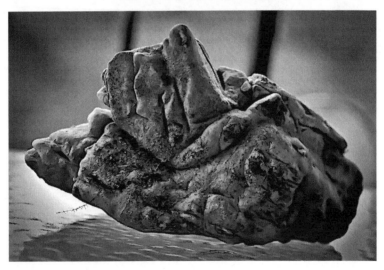

The links are solid and the evidence is sound, and it all indicates the existence and remnants of a lost colony of emigrants of unknown origin buried on the side of an Appalachian mountain. I have read stories based on folklore and mythology about a long ago interplanetary colony from the planet Procyon, a star system in the constellation Canis Minor, that settled somewhere in the eastern United States. It has been said they settled in North America a very long time ago and were the ancestors to the North American East Coast Indian.

As far back as Paleo-Indians, the Appalachian Mountains around Clover Hollow have been considered sacred hunting grounds. Could it be that these mountains were considered sacred for other reasons? Perhaps this was the sacred burial ground of the American Indian's ancestors? Maybe the East Coast American Indian was directly descended from this lost colony of Clover Hollow. It's very possible, modern Native American's animistic and shamanistic approach to their spiritual beliefs were passed down through the ages, from their own first-generation colonist grandfathers. The irony does not escape me that my first-generation German grandfathers also settled this exact same spot. As with the sacred sites of Peru, Clover Hollow could also be considered a multi cultural site.

Some would call the parallel events that have happened in Clover Hollow simply serendipitous, or even just coincidental. There has to be a connection between this early and possibly extraterrestrial colony, the American Indian, and my German ancestors who also colonized and settled the same spot thousands of years later.

I still believe more than ever, there are no coincidences, everything happens for a reason, and everything is connected. However, that's not quite the end of the story. There also must be a connection, or answer, as to why I was brought to Clover Hollow, the land where my ancestors are buried, and the land of two lost colonies.

The Terrestrial Connection

The evidence here indicates that my property in Clover Hollow sits on an active geodesic zone, meaning that this spot is an extremely active Earth energy hotspot with multiple geological sources contributing to the release of electromagnetic energy. This electromagnetic energy could also be a generator or an energy source for the supernatural events taking place. You could make the argument that all of the visualizations of orbs, ectoplasm, mist, and other etheric flying objects are just random electromagnetic energy discharges. However, I was sure they were intelligent and acted with purpose, but seem to be connected, if not projected, from my own personal consciousness.

In physics, energy is a property of all objects, transferable among them via fundamental interactions like work and heat which can be converted into different forms, but not created or destroyed. Isaac Newton's Third Law of Motion states 'To every action (force applied) there is an equal but opposite reaction (equal force applied in the opposite direction). This pretty much describes the physical transference of energy between objects. A good example is how the Price Mill and dam transferred energy from the water in Sinking Creek falling over the dam to the millstones which ground the corn and meal. This is what we know, energy is a measure of the ability to do work, it comes in many forms and can transform from one type of energy to another, but cannot be created or destroyed. Examples of stored or potential energy include batteries, and water behind a dam. Objects in motion are examples of kinetic energy. Charged particles, such as electrons and protons, create electromagnetic fields when they move, and these fields transport the type of energy we call electromagnetic radiation, or light.

Mechanical waves and electromagnetic waves are two important ways that energy is transported in the world around us. Waves in water, and sound waves in the air, are two examples of mechanical waves. Mechanical waves are caused by a disturbance of vibration in matter, whether solid, gas, liquid, or plasma. Matter that waves are traveling through is called a medium. Water waves are formed by vibrations in a liquid, and sound waves are formed by vibrations in a gas (air). These mechanical waves travel through a medium by causing the molecules to bump into each other, like falling dominoes transferring energy from one to the next. Sound waves cannot travel in the vacuum of space because there is no medium to transmit these mechanical waves.

Classical waves however transfer energy without transporting matter through the medium. Waves in a pond do not carry the water molecules from place to place; rather the wave's energy travels through the water, leaving the water molecules in place, much like a bug bobbing on top of ripples in water.

Electromagnetic Waves

Electricity can be static, like the energy that can make your hair stand on end. Magnetism can also be static, as it is in a refrigerator magnet. A changing magnetic field will induce a changing electric field and vice-versa, the two are linked. These changing fields form electromagnetic waves that differ from mechanical waves in that they do not require a medium to propagate. This means that electromagnetic waves can travel not only through air and solid materials, but also through the vacuum of space.

In the 1860s and 1870s, a Scottish scientist named James Clerk Maxwell developed a scientific theory to explain electromagnetic waves. He noticed that electrical fields and magnetic fields can couple together to form electromagnetic waves. He summarized this relationship between electricity and magnetism into what are now referred to as 'Maxwell's Equations.'

Heinrich Hertz, a German physicist, applied Maxwell's theories to the production and reception of radio waves. The unit of frequency of a radio wave, one cycle per second, is named the hertz, in honor of Heinrich Hertz. His experiment with radio waves solved two problems. First, he had demonstrated in the concrete, what Maxwell had only theorized, that the velocity of radio waves was equal to the velocity of light. This proved that radio waves were a form of light. Second, Hertz found out how to make the electric and magnetic fields detach themselves from wires and go free as Maxwell's Waves, electromagnetic waves.

The terms light, electromagnetic waves, and radiation, all refer to the same physical phenomenon; electromagnetic energy. This energy can be described by frequency, wavelength, or energy. All three are related mathematically such that if you know one, you can calculate the other two. Radio and microwaves are usually described in terms of frequency (Hertz), infrared and visible light are referred to as wavelength (meters), and x-rays and gamma rays in terms of energy (electron volts). This is a scientific convention that allows the convenient use of units that have numbers that are neither too large nor too small. We know they are mathematical in nature and follow the laws of physics.

The waves which do not require any medium for propagation are called electromagnetic waves. Electromagnetic waves have a continuous wavelength. These wavelengths are starting from gamma rays which are short, to radio waves that are long. The orderly distribution of wavelength of an electromagnetic wave is called the electromagnetic spectrum wavelength.

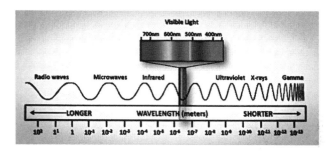

The wavelength spectrum is explained by the spectrum of electromagnetic radiation. The electromagnetic spectrum extends from low frequencies, to almost infinite higher frequencies. The low frequencies results in a very large wavelength, and we know that wavelength and frequency are inversely proportional to each other. This may be one explanation for the wave like images I was capturing in the infrared and ultraviolet spectrum at night off the front porch. They might be visible energy discharges in the ultraviolet and infrared frequency of light. But, they sure did act like they had a mind of their own.

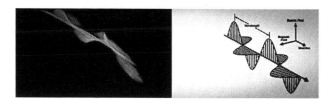

Frequency

The number of crests of the wave pattern that pass a given point within one second is described as the frequency of the wave. One wave, or cycle per second, is called a

Hertz (Hz), after Heinrich Hertz who established the existence of radio waves. A wave with two cycles that pass a point in one-second has a frequency of two Hz.

Electromagnetic waves have crests and troughs similar to those of ocean waves. The distance between crests is the wavelength. The shortest wavelengths are just fractions of the size of an atom while the longest wavelengths scientists currently study can be larger than the diameter of our planet.

Energy

An electromagnetic wave can also be described in terms of its energy in units of measure called electron volts (eV). An electron volt is the amount of kinetic energy needed to move an electron through one volt potential. Moving along the spectrum from long to short wavelengths, energy increases as the wavelength shortens. Consider a jump rope with its ends being pulled up and down. More energy is needed to make the rope have more waves.

All of this tells us the following:

All forms of energy contain wavelengths.
All wavelengths contain a frequency.
Thus, anything that contains energy has a frequency.

This would of course include *all* matter. Einstein showed us that all matter is energy and vice versa, which has helped us come to understand much about the world in general and life in particular. A key outcome of Einstein's insight is the notion that nothing is still, everything is vibrating. Every vibration has its own frequency. This would suggest that brainwaves are also a form of energy, including thought and consciousness.

The Earth's Magnetic Field

A magnetic field is the magnetic influence of electric currents and magnetic materials. The magnetic field at any given point is specified by both a direction and a magnitude (or strength); as such, it is a vector field. The term is used for two distinct, but closely related fields

denoted by the symbols B and H, which are measured in units of tesla and amp-per-meter, respectively. B is most commonly defined in terms of the 'Lorentz force' it exerts on moving electric charges.

Earth's magnetic field, also known as the geomagnetic field, is the magnetic field that extends from the Earth's interior, to where it meets the solar wind, a stream of charged particles emanating from the Sun. Its magnitude at the Earth's surface ranges from 25 to 65 microtesla (0.25 to 0.65 gauss). It has the same properties as that of a simple bar magnet. When I tested the magnetic field on the front porch I was getting around 57 uT (micro-teslas) in a non-active area and when I was at a precise spot above the center of one of the iron porch railings, the magnetic field would spike tenfold and set off the alarm.

The Earth's magnetic field is believed to be generated by electric currents in the conductive material of its core, created by convection currents due to heat escaping from the core. However, the process is complex and computer models that reproduce some of its features have only been developed in the last few decades. The Earth and most of the planets in the Solar System, as well as the Sun and other stars all generate magnetic fields through the motion of highly conductive fluids. The Earth's field originates in its core, according to scientist. This is a region of iron alloys extending to about 2,100 miles (the radius of the Earth is about 4000 miles). They tell us it is divided into a solid inner core with a radius of 758 miles, and a liquid outer core. The motion of the liquid in the outer core is driven by heat flow from the inner core. This is the mainstay of the mainstream scientific community.

According to National Geographic, scientists now know that the Earth's magnetic field also changes with time, like a giant jigsaw puzzle with its pieces constantly changing. These fluctuations in Earth's magnetic field are known as 'Secular Variation.' Secular Variation happens over decades to centuries and some geophysicists think it may play a role in the mysterious reversals of Earth's magnetic field that takes place every half million years or so. Supporters of the dynamo theory think Secular Variation occurs because of circulation patterns within Earth's liquid core. Since drilling to Earth's core is a technical impossibility, Secular Variation is the only evidence scientists currently have that Earth even has an active core.

In a new paper, published in the New Journal of Physics, Northwestern University's, Ryskin, argues that Secular Variation may instead be due to circulating seawater. It's well established that ocean currents, such as the Gulf Stream in the Atlantic form the circulatory system of the seas. These currents bring up nutrient-rich cold water from the ocean depths and carry it to different parts of the Earth. The Humboldt Current that passes by the Galapagos Islands is the major cause for the up-swelling of nutrients that bring the Whale Sharks in to feed.

It's also known that dissolved salts in seawater conduct electricity and as ocean currents move within Earth's main magnetic field, they generate their own secondary magnetic field. Hmmm, this kinda changes everything I thought I knew about the Earth's magnetic field and what's going on in Clover Hollow. Could it be that water is the main influence on the Earth's magnetic field? It's not the energy released from the movement of the liquid core of molten iron, but the energy released from movement of the Earth's water supply that is creating the real Earth energy grid.

Just as the salty waters of Earth's ocean currents create electromagnetic energy, so does the movement of acid rain and water traveling through the limestone karst springs, creeks, caves, fissures or any underground drainage areas. The release of energy from Clover Hollow can easily be measured by different devices such as EMF meters, dowsing rods, and the erratic movement of a compass's needle.

Earth's Energy Grid

Video 3,4,5, posted at
www.virginiarockart.com

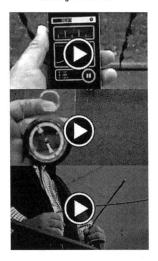

Topography is the study of Earth's surface shape and features, or those of planets, moons, and asteroids. It is also the description of such surface shapes and features. Planetary Energetic Grid Theory falls under the heading of pseudoscience. It operates through geometric patterns called Sacred Geometry. These are grids that meet at various intersecting points forming a grid or matrix. This is equivalent to the acupressure points on our bodies. These grid points can be found at some of the strongest power places on the planet.

Plato recognized grids and their patterns, and devised a theory that the Earth's basic structure evolved from simple geometric shapes to more complex ones. These shapes became known as platonic solids; cube (four), tetrahedron (three), octahedron (eight), dodecahedron (twelve), and icosahedrons (twenty). Plato associated each shape with one of the elements, earth, fire, air, ether, and water. The Earth's energy grids, from the beginnings of its evolutionary course, have evolved through each of these shapes to what it is today. Each shape, superimposed, one upon the other to create a kind of all encompassing energy field that is the very basis of Earth holding it all together. This explains why everything that is physical, is also mathematical by nature. In other words, Sacred Geometry is the math or basis of all things natural.

The radiation (energy) emitting out of the earth is commonly referred to as Earth's rays, and these rays are what influences and makes up the Earth's energy grid. There are many theories of what this energy grid consist. This Earth radiation, or Earth rays, are a supposed form of radiation, emitted outwards from the earth, possibly from (or diffracted by) water veins, and ostensibly only detectable by means of dowsing.

There are various folklore beliefs that hold that lines of energy on the surface of Earth can affect health, for example, Feng Shui and Mana. The idea was revived by several western writers and researchers such as Carl Reichenbach (Odic Force), Alfred Watkins (Ley Lines), Gustav Freiherr von Pohl, Manfred Curry and Ernst Hartmann. They described a mystic force field affecting the health of living creatures that supposedly covers the Earth at regular intervals, and may be detected by using divining rods. This belief is especially common in Germany and Scandinavia. The vast majority of scholars in geophysics believe that the theory of Earth radiation is nothing but pseudoscience or even a hoax.

When the dowsing rods were used on the front porch of my house in Clover Hollow, the rods made of copper would cross each other every time they passed over the iron railings. It was if they were crossing through an invisible barrier. The Earth's energy grid can be thought of as a web that holds, or links the Earth together. The energy grid is affected by many influences like electricity, magnetism, light, color, heat, sound, and matter.

Curry lines are a global grid network of electrically charged lines of natural origin. These lines run diagonally to the poles and were first discovered by Dr. Manfred Curry and Dr. Whitman. There is some disagreement between authorities how wide apart these lines are, but the consensus seems to be approximately three meters or ten feet, although most experts recognize that this can vary. The lines themselves are not seen as a problem, only the points where they cross, and obviously lines which run in this way will have numerous intersecting points. As the lines are electrically charged, the intersecting points are either, double positives, double negatives, or one of each. The Hartmann net consists of naturally occurring charged lines, running North-South and East-West. It is named after Dr. Ernst Hartmann, a well regarded German medical doctor, who first described it soon after the Second World War. Alternate lines are usually positively and negatively charged, so where the lines intersect, it is possible to have double positive charges and double negative charges, or one positive and one negative charge, just as in Curry lines. It is the intersections that are seen to be a source of potential problems. The Hartmann Net appears as a structure of radiations rising vertically from the ground like invisible, radioactive walls, each twenty-one centimeters (nine inches) wide. The grid is magnetically oriented, from north to south, and they are encountered at intervals of two meters (six feet six inches), while from east to west they are two-and-a-half meters (eight feet) apart. Between these geometric lines, lies a neutral zone, an unperturbed micro-climate. This network penetrates everywhere, whether over open ground or through dwellings. This is another example how everything natural follows the laws of physics, or the mathematics of nature.

The Hartmann net has been defined using the Chinese terms of Yin and Yang. The Yin (North-South lines) is a cold energy which acts slowly, corresponds to winter, and is related to cramps, humidity, and all forms of rheumatism. The Yang (East-West lines) is a hot, dry, rapidly acting energy. It is related to fire and is linked to inflammations. The points formed by the intersection of these lines, whether positive or negative, are dynamic environments sensitive to the rhythms of the hours and the seasons.

Schumann waves are naturally occurring, beneficial electromagnetic waves that oscillate between the Earth and certain layers of the atmosphere. They were first identified in 1952 by Professor W. O. Schumann, a German scientist. He found that these waves have similar, almost the same frequency as brain waves, and follow a similar daily pattern. It has been suggested that these waves help regulate the body's internal clock, thus affecting sleep patterns, hormonal secretions, the menstrual cycle in women, and so on. The American space agency, NASA, became interested in this phenomenon when the early astronauts returned to Earth only after a short time in space feeling distressed and disoriented. Subsequently, NASA installed equipment to generate Schumann waves artificially in their spacecraft. Some modern buildings with reinforced concrete and metal roofs can inadvertently shield occupants from these beneficial waves. Part of the reason people suffer from jet lag is that Schumann waves are much weaker at normal airplane altitudes, and this effect is further weakened by the metal fuselage.

Ley lines are generally recognized as man-made phenomena, occurring where 'sacred stones' which have somehow been charged energetically, are laid in a straight line. Ley lines appear naturally and spontaneously, and at least five such stones are placed in line within a distance of twenty-five miles. The stones can be large or small, and the method of charging is thought to be activities such as heating, or impacting with considerable force against other rocks. Other methods could also include ritual washing with spring water (as seen in Peru) or vibration through the influence of sound or energy.

All the Earth rays can be influenced by another source of energy, geopathic stress. Geopathic stress is mainly caused by narrow paths of water about two-hundred to three-hundred feet below ground and also on top of mountains. The narrow water path creates an electromagnetic field which distorts the earth's natural vibrations as these pass through the water. It is in particular the 7.83Hz (cycles per second) which are beneficiary and which we have lived with for millions of years. This is also the optimum part of the Schumann waves and Alpha vibrations. It has been confirmed by NASA that the 7.83 Hz vibrations are incorporated into spacecrafts and otherwise the astronauts could only live in space a short time. Could all the underground springs flowing into Sinking Creek be causing geopathic stress in the form of electromagnetic radiation in Clover Hollow?

Certain mineral concentrations, fault lines, moving underground plateaus, and underground cavities can also disturb the natural earth vibrations. Strong geopathic stress can cause the body's vibrations to rise as high as 250 Hz. The U.S. scientist George Lakowsky confirmed in the thirties that humans (as well as animals) have less chance of fighting bacteria, viruses and parasites above 180 Hz, as they love humans and animals that vibrate at high levels.

And then you have telluric current (from Latin tellus, Earth), or Earth current, an electric current which moves underground or through the sea. Telluric currents result from both natural causes and human activity, and the discrete currents interact in a complex pattern. The currents are extremely low frequency and travel over large areas at or near the surface of the Earth.

Geomagnetically induced currents (GIC) affecting the normal operation of long electrical conductor systems are a manifestation at ground level of space weather. During space weather events, electric currents in the magnetosphere and ionosphere experience large variations, which manifest also in the Earth's magnetic field. These variations induce currents (GIC) in conductors that operate on the surface of Earth.

So, our physical world is in a constant state of flux, juggling and reacting to an infinite amount of Earth radiation or energy that is bombarding us always. All this energy is just sitting out there, free wireless energy, we just don't know how to harness it. The key to unlocking the secrets of free energy lies somewhere in the phenomena called resonance.

Resonance

My understanding of the term resonance is simply the ability of one physical system to sympathetically vibrate in harmony with the natural vibration of a neighboring system. Thus, producing frequencies that together are greatly amplified. A perfect example of acoustic resonance is when a guitar is set into its vibrational motion at its natural frequency when a person hits, strikes, strums, plucks or somehow disturbs the strings. Striking the A string can cause sympathetic vibrations of other strings, causing those strings to vibrate at their natural frequency which are called harmonics. Resonant systems can be used to generate vibrations of a specific frequency (e.g. musical instruments) or pick out specific frequencies from a complex vibration containing many frequencies (e.g. filters).

In a thoughtful and noble experiment, Nikola Tesla attached a small oscillator (vibrator) to an iron column in his New York City laboratory and started it pulsating. At certain frequencies, specific pieces of equipment in the room would jiggle. If he changed the frequency, the jiggle would move to another part of the room. Unfortunately, he hadn't realized the fact that the column ran downward into the foundation and beneath the building. His vibrations were being disseminated all over Manhattan.

Although Tesla was not the first to uncover the phenomenon of resonance, he was totally obsessed with it and created some of the most incredible examples of it ever seen. He studied both mechanical and electrical versions. In the process, he created an artificial earthquake, numerous artificial lightning storms, knocked an entire power plant off line in Colorado, and nearly caused the steel frame of a sky scraper under construction in Manhattan to collapse. Tesla realized that the principles of resonance could be used to transmit and receive radio messages well before Marconi. Many knowledgeable sources now credit Tesla as the inventor of radio rather than Marconi. This includes the Supreme Court which in 1943 ruled that Tesla's radio patents had preceded all others including Marconi's. Tesla never realized notoriety and died a pauper. Maybe the 'powers to be' put a stop to his crazy notions of free wireless energy for everybody.

Karst

Clover Hollow lies in a karsistic area of the Appalachian Mountains and the people there live over the remains of the largest mountains (above the ocean) ever recorded. These ancient mountains were thrown up in massive plate movement with accompanying volcanoes. The limestone rock, shale, coal, silt and clay layers laid down millennia ago have been thrust up into a tangled and contorted mess. In many places the strike of the rock is contorted, folded, and may go past vertical.

Karst is a landscape formed from the dissolution of soluble rocks including limestone, dolomite and gypsum. It is characterized by sinkholes, caves, and underground drainage systems. Nearly all surface karst features are formed by internal drainage, subsidence, and collapse triggered by the development of underlying caves. Rainwater becomes acidic as it comes in contact with carbon dioxide in the atmosphere and the soil. As it drains into fractures in the rock, the water begins to dissolve away the rock creating a network of passages. Over time, water flowing through the network continues to erode and enlarge the passages; this allows the plumbing system to transport increasingly larger amounts of water. This process of dissolution leads to the development of the

275

caves, sinkholes, springs, and sinking streams typical of a karst landscape.

The long and complex tectonic history of the Appalachians has produced a substrate of folded and faulted sandstones, shales, and carbonate rocks, leaving aside the metamorphic and igneous core. The Appalachian fluviokarst is an evolving landscape developed on the carbonate rocks. The erosion of surface streams competes with dissolution processes in the carbonate rocks and both compete with tectonic uplift of the eastern margin of the North American plate. The Appalachians have undergone erosion since the Jurassic and three to ten miles of sediment have been removed. It is remarkable that there is anything left at all of the petroglyphs in Clover Hollow. They are highly eroded and crumbling, and without studying high resolution photographs they would have never been found.

This brings us to the connection between my property in Clover Hollow and the Earth's natural energy. To understand this phenomenon, I had to understand the topography first. My house sits on limestone bedrock and is centered at the apex of three different mountain ranges. It sits next to and overlooks Sinking Creek which flows southeast to northwest, diagonal to the poles. The movement of the stream through and across the limestone bedrock produces its own highly charged magnetic field.

Numerous known and unknown underground springs empty into Sinking Creek at this exact location and all produce their own magnetic fields as they collide and merge with all the other magnetic fields in the area. These underground streams also add to the geopathic stress, which is another form of energy being released at a frantic pace.

This particular spot in the Appalachian Mountains is a confluence of a multitude of energy systems and their rays. To top it off, there is the dam that is generating large amounts of mechanical energy when the water falls ten feet upon limestone bedrock. This collision of water and limestone is generating additional radiation from the geopathic stress. Also, Sinking Creek is olive green indicating large amounts of iron with its own magnetic properties are adding to the witches brew.

Sinking Creek is constantly being energized by its own limestone magnetic fields mixing together with the emptying spring's magnetic fields into the creek itself and then add to the mix a dose of geopathic stress, telluric current, geomagnetic induced current, Curry and Ley Lines, the Hartman Net and Schumann waves. You then have a highly charged amalgam of reactive energy. If any of these energy systems resonate with each other, the amplification of the energy released can be drastically increased. Also, there is positively charged acid rain that is coming into contact with highly charged limestone creek water that can produce gases anywhere from carbon dioxide to sulfuric acid, which could account for the bubbling reaction in Sinking Creek. With all these energies being released, colliding, and interacting with each other, it has created a highly charged natural energy hotspot.

A good example of the Earth's energy reactive nature would be my iron front porch railings. Here we have an unintentional man made energy system that effectively amplifies the Earth's energy or radiation at that particular spot. This was achieved by using an iron rod bolted to limestone concrete which sits on top and therefore connecting physically to the limestone bedrock which contains multiple sources of energy. The iron rod or rail has now become a transducer that resonates with the natural energy from below and amplifies it exponentially. This is exactly what I believe is happening at other ancient hotspots all over the world. Examples would be the stone monoliths at Stonehenge, The Great Pyramid of Giza, the lightning bolt shaped cyclopean walls of Saksayhuaman, and the laser cut one-hundred and fifty ton blocks at Ollantaytambo, among others. All were made to resonate with Earth's natural energy and convert it to usable energy for some unknown purpose.

The last and probably most important point to make about the terrestrial Earth is that if your belief system is that God created the physical universe (as mine does) then this would mean that everything on Earth that is natural falls under the providence of God and operates according to his will.

There is more than enough evidence collected around the world that extraterrestrials did in fact visit planet Earth a very long time ago. It was so long ago, the only thing left to remember them by is the work they created in stone, stone that hasn't yet turned to dust. Since we don't have the ability to determine the age of stone, nor able to measure the natural energy emitting from the stone, we can only look at how the stone was manipulated, shaped, formed, or moved. We can tell by looking at the ancient stone structures all over the world that only an extreme technologically advanced race of beings could have created them. Common sense tells us that what we are taught in school, that indigenous humans, not much more than hunter-gatherers, created all these man-made wonders of the world simply cannot be true.

If we assume that ancient extraterrestrials did visit our planet, then we can also assume they had the expertise and technology to travel from their planet by either spaceship, or some inter-dimensional means to get to Earth in the first place. This also would mean they would have to have a complete understanding of the natural universe and the ability to tap into its abundant natural resources.

There are many places on earth where there is unexplained stone work. As mentioned earlier, the Nazca people carved giant animals and even an ancient astronaut in the desert floor that can only be seen from the sky. And those that came before the Nazca people carved dinosaurs into the Ica Stones for some unknown and mystical reasons. Maybe it was for the purpose and objective to give us a heads up. At first thought this concept of extraterrestrials visiting Earth doesn't fit into the normal teachings of theologies that say that humans are the only intelligent life in the universe. But if you believe as I do that God created the universe, than the concept of alien life seems more than likely. If they had made it to Earth than it is highly likely they were technically advance and understood the laws of nature (Sacred Geometry) in order to make the trip.

As reported on ancientliensmap.com
The top 49 ancient alien hotspots listed by popularity are:

Golden Flyer
Machu Picchu (Peru)
The Money Pit (Oak Island)
Bermuda Triangle
Pharaoh Akhenaton
Band of Holes (Peru)
Derinkuyu Underground City
Ancient African Gold Mines (Stone Circles)
Serpent Mound (Ohio)
Carnac Stones
Saksayhuaman (Peru)
Lake Titicaca (Peru and Bolivia)
Lost City of Dwarka
15 cm Humanoid Alien
Atlantis
Suicide Forest (Aokigahara)
Baltic Sea UFO
Joan of Arc
Dragons Triangle
Zone of Silence
Zuni Indians
Wow! Signal (Radio Signal from Space)
Alien Baby
Underwater City of Khambhat

Stonehenge
Roswell UFO Incident
Christopher Columbus UFO Sighting
Dyatlov Pass Incident
Zorats Karer
The Annunaki
Valley of Death
Yonaguni Monument
Dogu Figurines
Great Pyramid of Giza
Great Sphinx of Giza
Pumapunku (Bolivia)
Nan Madol
Nazca Lines (Peru)
Göbekli Tepe
Piri Reis Map
Trojan War
Pic de Bugarach
City of the Dead
Saqqara Bird
Nabta Playa
Svalbard Global Seed Vault
Hall of Records
Sumerian Language
Sumerian People

The elongated skulls found near Ica Peru and the ruins of Ollantaytambo would be some other choices I would have included in the list. Maybe one day, Clover Hollow might be considered. The one common denominator between most of these ancient alien hotspots is their proximity to rich natural resources and energy deposits. These locations would have been prime targets for recovery with advanced extraterrestrial technology. If they were able to travel from one planet to another, they certainly had the ability and knowledge to pinpoint Earth's energy fields.

It is believed by some, that the Annunaki used humans as slaves to mine gold in Africa, and that the complex at Saksayhuaman in Peru was used as a giant gold smelter. The sheared off tops of Nazca mountains that have been removed in what appear to be mining operations can only be attributed to our extraterrestrial forefathers as no ruble around the operation was found. They must have had the technology and advanced knowledge to transform the natural energy of the Earth to suit their own needs. If aliens could scan the Earth for minerals and natural energy resources, then they probably came across Clover Hollow in the Appalachian Mountains on their first pass. But what they left behind is all we have to go by and we can only take a guess at who they were.

Carved in Stone

A quick internet search pulled up dozens of ancient languages carved in stone which have been found all over the world. The differences in these writing systems to each other suggest that they came from different cultures and must have taken thousands of years to develop. Since I can't believe these written languages were created by hunter-gatherers or a primitive culture of any kind, one has to believe they must have evolved from extraterrestrial colonist (or colonialist) a very long time ago.

Experts today say that the early writing systems that emerged in Eurasia by early 3000 BC were not a sudden invention. On the contrary, they were a development based on earlier traditions of symbol systems that cannot be classified as conventional writing but do have many characteristics strikingly similar to writing. These systems are described as proto-writing. They used ideographic and, or, early mnemonic symbols to convey information, yet were probably devoid of direct linguistic content. These systems surfaced in the early Neolithic period, as early as 7000 BC.

An ideogram or ideograph, from the Greek words 'idea' and 'grapho' (to write), is a graphic symbol that represents an idea or concept. Some ideograms are comprehensible only by familiarity with prior convention; others convey their meaning through pictorial resemblance to a physical object and thus may also be referred to as pictograms. Maybe a face or two was used.

A mnemonic, or mnemonic device, is any learning technique that aids information retention. Mnemonics aim is to translate information into a form that the brain can retain better than its original form. Maybe the form resembling a 'face' could work as a mnemonic device?

The differences in the Clover Hollow stone carvings to the previously mentioned writing systems are striking. Mainly, the Clover Hollow carvings are not cut into flat and smooth pieces of stone. Also, the Clover Hollow writing or art is aligned to the contour of the stone, there is no horizontal and vertical. This might have something to do with the 3D aspect in the writing technique.

The Clover Hollow carvings do meet the requirements for being a 'proto-writing' system since they use ideograms, ideographs, and pictographs. They also use mnemonic devices by matching the same type of rock and surface with the same type of image carved. In other words, they let the medium dictate what kind of technique, personality, and image that would be created.

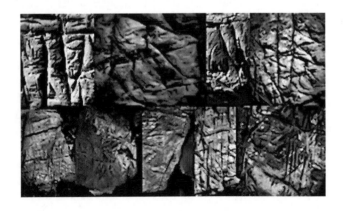

If this is Clover Hollow's written language, it appears also to be integrated completely into their art. Could this mean that the written language of the Clover Hollow colonist, and I don't mean my German ancestors, is the same thing as their art and an example of their creative expression? Maybe they carved images reflecting their culture, history, and ancestry into an Appalachian mountainside. Maybe they are offering a form of communication to their gods and ancestors.

There are also similarities between rock carvings in Clover Hollow and other supposed extraterrestrial colonies around the world like Machu Picchu for instance. Some of the anthropomorphic style carved rock outcroppings that I saw ten years ago in Peru, are strikingly similar to some of the stone petroglyphs in Clover Hollow.

Machu Picchu   **Clover Hollow**

There is this one panel on one side of a large rock outcropping that I can't stop staring at. It appears to be abnormally creative and I see different images every time I look at it. There is no way this could have been made by an indigenous primitive culture and if you look very closely and open your eyes wide, you can pick out some other-worldly artistic expression and creativity, and maybe an alien or two. The artistic creativity exhibited at Clover Hollow is astounding. This is one of the reasons I consider all this to be extraterrestrial in origin. Although the rocks are extremely ancient and crumbling, you can still recognize some of the technique used to design and carve these pieces of art.

'dee spirits had brot ju dare'

Having recently resigned from my job of twenty-six years to finish the research and prepare to tell the tale of Clover Hollow, I had to find a way to pay my bills. Becoming an Uber driver solved this dilemma. This offered me a way to work when I wanted to and work on the book whenever I got a chance. Luckily, I could receive Uber rides straight to my house, however, I had to be ready at moments notice to answer the call. It was like Batman leaving the Batcave when the ping came in.

The reason this is brought up is to mention one ride in particular that has great meaning to this book. For three days in a row I was called to a nearby assisted living complex to pick up one of the caretakers. She was a lovely older lady from Kenya who had been in the states for less than a year. I originally and erroneously first guessed that she was Jamaican because of her British influenced English accent. We immediately bonded and started a conversation about our heritage and ancestral background. Riter was from the Kalenjin tribe, one of forty-two tribes of Kenya still in existence. Her's was the fifth largest tribe in Kenya and she talked about her ancestors and the stories she was told as a child.

The conversation on the third day evolved into my story of purchasing a piece of property sight unseen and how it was connected to three of my first generation grandfathers. After I told her the story, she looked up at me with very wise eyes and a broad smile and exclaimed 'Ahh, dee spirits had brot ju dare.' In one short sentence she summarized the answer that I have finally come to grips with. This is the answer as to who brought me to this little piece of the Appalachian Mountains. I now knew for sure; the spirits have brought me here. My only question now is why?

The Supernatural Connection

Supernatural is that which is not subject to the laws of physics or more figuratively, that which is said to exist above and beyond nature. In philosophy, popular culture and fiction, the supernatural is associated with the paranormal, religions, and occultism. In all religious belief systems, supernatural activity refers to the manifestation of spiritual entities directly related to an existence from beyond the grave. Therefore, supernatural activity is evidence of an afterlife, the pure definition of spirituality.

Okay, the spiritual connection to the property in Clover Hollow is based around one simple yet profound truth. If it's believed that my ancestors had something to do with bringing me to Clover Hollow, then that would suggest that my ancestors, or their messengers, have made contact with me from beyond the grave. This would infer the real existence of an afterlife. And if an afterlife does exist, it would then suggest of course the existence of a 'spirit' world, a place where our spirit or soul goes after our physical body dies and we leave this world behind. This premise is the foundation for all religions and their belief systems.

For this discussion, the spirit world will be defined as just that, another world or dimension that is inhabited by spirits. You can contemplate that there are multiple dimensions or worlds which occupy and share the same space. Oh, our physical, natural universe, the home of the living, created by the Creator, is just one of those multiple dimensions.

So, if I really have been guided to Clover Hollow by my ancestors, then they must have done it for a reason. Was it just to find this lost colony, if that's what it is? There just seems to be a little bit more to the story and it requires a little bit more digging.

~ ~ ~ ~ ~ ~

Almost immediately, I came across the research of Masaru Emoto, who claims that human consciousness has an effect on the molecular structure of water. Something told me this might be the answer I was looking for. Emoto has stated 'Water is the mirror that can show us what we cannot see. It is a blueprint for our reality which can change with a single, positive thought. All it takes is faith, if you're open to it.' He believes that energies or vibrations of thought can change water physically and structurally. Again implying brainwaves and thought are a form of energy.

Emoto's water crystal experiments consist of exposing water in glasses to different words, pictures, or music, and then freezing and examining the aesthetics of the resulting crystals with microscopic photography. Emoto makes the claim that water exposed to positive speech or thoughts (intention) will result in 'beautiful' crystals being formed when that water is frozen, and that negative intention will yield 'ugly' frozen crystal formations.

Emoto also claims that different water sources produce different crystalline structures when frozen. For example, he claims that a water sample from a mountain stream when frozen, will show structures of beautifully shaped geometric design, but those structures will be distorted and randomly formed if the sample is taken from a polluted water source.

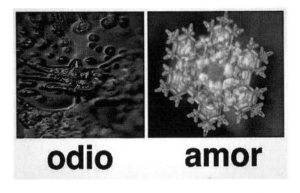

odio   amor

His results and findings were literally earth shattering news for me. If his findings are correct, it proves that good and evil intent really does exist and they have their own distinctive energetic vibrations. This supernatural energy shows that human consciousness or intent, does exist and their vibrations have an effect on, and a direct relationship to the natural physical world, in this case water, one of nature's elements. It would appear that water crystals exposed to the higher vibrations of good intent, sync and resonate harmoniously with the water crystals to form beautiful geometrical shapes. When evil and bad intent are focused on the water crystals, there is still resonation happening but in a destructive way, and the energetic waves are deformed, disrupted, and distorted, to form ugly and non-symmetrical images which appear unnatural.

This convinces me that a spiritual dimension in the form of human consciousness really does exist and it has a direct connection and relationship with the natural universe. The proof that intent or thought has it's own supernatural energy regulated by good and evil is reinforced by the fact that it does not matter what language is used when the water crystals are subjected to written words. No matter what language is used, amor and odio, love and hate, the results are the same. It's the intent behind the words that can be measured in the frozen water crystals. This gives true meaning to the power of a hug. This energetic etheric realm that can differentiate between good and evil stimulus must be the dimension that spiritual entities operate from and where they can make contact with the physical or natural world. This leads me to some profound truths:

Intent, or consciousness, has it's own energetic vibration or frequency and it has a direct impact on the physical universe that it comes into contact with.

This realm of etheric good and evil, energy and thought, must be the same space occupied by any spiritual existence.

Anything created with thought and intent like architecture and art will always retain an energetic imprint of the artist's consciousness from the time of creation.

This explains the magic of the Mona Lisa and fills in more dots in the understanding of a spiritual realm. It must be a nonphysical dimension or reality that is occupied by etheric spiritual beings, where good and evil intent exist in an energetic form, a Heaven and Hell if you will. Since I believe spiritual entities, possibly ancestral spirits, somehow guided me to Clover Hollow, then they must have had the ability to travel between the dimensional realities of the spirit world and the living natural world, in order to communicate with the living. Also, you would have to assume that if a spirit world does exist, it exist for everyone and everything, and would apply to any extraterrestrial colonist and the American Indian as well. It wouldn't be discriminatory.

The channel spiritual beings are said to connect to the living world is through manipulations of the natural universe. Their messages and guidance can be found in numbers, signs, symbols and Sacred Geometry, or in the way planets move around the galaxy known as archaeo-astronomy. It is believed they communicate with us through human consciousness and subconsciousness in the form of dreams, intuition, creativity, and art. Many believe these subtle messages are everywhere and we just need to learn how to read them.

The biggest epiphany here for me is the connection between the natural and the spiritual. As shown in the water crystals of Masaru Emoto, when nature resonates with good intent, the natural energetic vibrations are at a higher and harmonious level, creating beautiful wave patterns. But, when nature vibrates after being exposed to evil intent, it resonates at a lower vibrational level and can be visualized as deformed and distorted wave patterns in our physical reality.

This convinces me that the etheric supernatural energy of good and evil intent that resides in human consciousness has a direct effect on the natural universe, and this must be the realm that spiritual realities exist, and there appears to be a symbiotic relationship between the spiritual and natural, the world of the supernatural.

A perfect example of the nature and spirit relationship lies in the idea of 'Sacred Geometry' or the 'math of nature.' Sacred geometry is used as a religious, philosophical, and spiritual term to explain the fundamental laws of the natural universe covering Pythagorean geometry and the perceived relationships between geometrical laws and quantum mechanical laws of the universe that create the geometrical patterns in nature. In other words, the math of nature is that all things physical are mathematical or symmetrical in nature, and all things natural, follow the laws of Sacred Geometry, God's blueprint of creation if you will.

In Sacred Geometry, symbolic and sacred meanings are ascribed to certain geometric shapes and certain geometric proportions. The belief that God created the universe

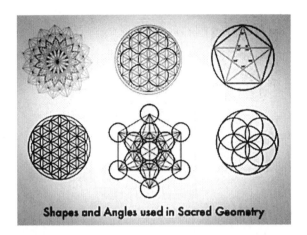

Shapes and Angles used in Sacred Geometry

according to a geometric plan has ancient origins. Plutarch attributed the belief to Plato, writing, 'Plato said God geometrizes continually.'

Some believe that the study of sacred geometry has its roots in the study of nature and the mathematical principles at work therein. These sacred shapes and angle relationships are clearly seen in the crystalline formations of Masaru Emoto's water crystals when exposed to positive and spiritual stimuli.

Just as nature is a physical manifestation and creation of the spirit world, Sacred Geometry, the sacred math of nature, is the key, code, or language that connects the Heavens and Earth together. In other words, where physics is the math of the physical universe, Sacred Geometry is the connection between our physical reality and the supernatural world of our ancestors. Maybe this is one of the secrets to inter-dimensional travel, something ancient extraterrestrials must have known.

Ancient extraterrestrials who visited Earth a very long time ago used archaeoastronomy and sacred geometry in everything they did. They must have developed supernatural technology based on this sacred math of the heavens in order to master the mechanics of inter-dimensional travel. This would be a more likely and more efficient means of travel than in conventional spacecraft. They also would be able to use this inter-dimensional technology not only to travel to Earth, but use it to locate and process Earth's energy resources in all its forms and locations.

Some recent occurrences related to sacred geometry are the sudden overnight appearances of Crop Circles. UFO and Alien enthusiast will gladly tell you that these circles are examples of Aliens trying to contact us. But, what if I were to suggest that these circles might be positive sacred messages from other heavenly dimensions in the language of sacred geometry?

A Circle with a Horizontal Line

The one geometric symbol that has been rolling around in my head since the first time I visualized it while looking at the 'Devil's Writing Table' in the Saltpeter Caves in Greenville, West Virginia, was a circle with a horizontal line. What I found researching the spiritual meaning behind this symbol, if there was one, completely astounded me.

It seems the circle divided by a horizontal line is a structure often found on rock carvings all over the world. In early Chinese calligraphy it represented the sun. In the Greek alphabet, the structure is used to signify the letter theta. The sign is used in at least ten different ideographic systems of natural science and in the new religion conceived by the late science fiction writer and philosopher L. Ron Hubbard half a century ago. It is a symbol for the individual human spirit.

The circle is the most common and universal sign found in all cultures. It is the symbol of the sun in its limitless or boundless aspect. It has no beginning or end, and no divisions, making it the perfect symbol of completeness, eternity, and the soul. My take is that it represents the spiritual kingdom that surrounds us at all times.

The horizontal axis represents the path from birth to death, beginning to end, and linear time. This axis represents life on earth as a binary, linear process, life to death, beginning to end, and the dual nature of human existence evidenced by our symmetrical shapes, left and right, male and female, good and evil. In other words, it represents the human physical existence. The circle and horizontal line represents that human existence as surrounded by the spiritual kingdom. In other words, a spiritual existence is always there, before birth, during life, and after death.

The Number Seven

During the supernatural events that occurred on the seventh step during the remodel of my house in Clover Hollow, the message that I felt was directed straight at me revolved around the importance of the number seven. It seemed very important to me at the time. Since there are no coincidences, everything happens for a reason, and everything is connected, it warranted further investigation into numerology and its relationship to the mysteries of Clover Hollow.

Numerology is any belief in divine, mystical, or other special relationship between a number and some coinciding events. It has many systems, traditions, and beliefs. Today, numerology is regularly associated with the paranormal, alongside astrology and similar divinatory arts. Saint Augustine of Hippo (A.D. 354–430) wrote 'Numbers are the universal language offered by the deity to humans as confirmation of the truth.' Similar to Pythagoras, he too believed that everything had a numerical relationship and it was up to the mind to seek and investigate the secrets of these relationships, or have them revealed by divine grace.

We also now know that numbers, signs, and symbols, can be affected by the energetic vibrations of intent. Physical objects like music and art must also have their own vibrational properties. When I finally did research on numerology and the number seven, the first thing to come up was 'Number seven resonates with the vibrations and energies of the collective consciousness, faith and spirituality, spiritual awakening and awareness, spiritual enlightenment, spiritual development, mysticism, intuition, and inner-knowing.' Holy smokes!

The number seven seems to be a very important number in many cultures, especially concerning the psychological or spiritual traditions of those cultures. A quick internet search turned up the following:

The seven levels of consciousness
The seven chakras
The seven planets of astrology
The seven heavens
The seven metals of alchemy
The seven islands of Atlantis

The seven gateways
The seven cities
The seven stars
The seven golden candle sticks
The seven seals of the Apocalypse

It is my understanding that repeating sevens mean your spirit guides and angels are trying to communicate with you. While writing this section of the book on numerology and the number seven, I came to the point where I had to purchase an ISBN (International Standard Book Number) in order to self-publish this story. While studying about the number seven, this is the random number I received and the ISBN for this book: *9780990777717*

Another reoccurring number in this story is the number three. I am the grandson to three first-generation grandfathers, three different families, traveling together on the ship 'Winter Galley.' I share the first name of all three men, John. All three men are connected directly to this piece of property in Clover hollow.

According to the theories of sacred geometry, Pythagoras deemed the study of mathematics essential to understand the relationship of God, man, and nature (three). Mathematics was more than just adding and multiplying numbers, the numbers themselves had a spiritual meaning. The number three represents the trinity of God, man, and nature. In Pythagoras's 'Table of Ten Numbers' the number three, III, The Triad, the number three represents equilibrium. The triad is sacred because it is the outcome of adding one, the monad, and two, the duad (1 + 2 = 3). It is represented by the sacred triangle, the first shape to have a beginning, middle, and an end. The triad represents time as it is in the past, present and future. Three also represents creation, for it is symbolic of the monad, the Divine Father, and the duad, the Great Mother, and out of the two, the world was created. In this aspect, three represents the soul of man, or maybe the spirit of man.

The spiritual number three is the number of 'manifesting and manifestation' and carries the vibration of the ancestral spirits. In spiritualism, the number three can be an indication that your spirits are trying to get your attention. Your ancestral spirits want you to follow your intuition and inner-wisdom, so that you are able to take appropriate actions at this time. Again, Holy Smokes!

Three, as emblematic of the Trinity, has always been considered a sacred number and long before the Christian era, God was worshiped as a triple deity. This is true not only of the Assyrians, Phoenicians, Greeks, and Romans, but also of the ancient Scandinavians, the Druids, the inhabitants of Mexico and Peru, as well as the Chinese and Japanese. An animistic approach to the Trinity would be the reverence of Spirit, Man, and Nature.

Now was the time to dig a little deeper and past the scientific mainstream that doesn't believe in alternate realities, to get a clearer picture on who might be occupying this spirit realm, and who also might be paying Clover Hollow a visit.

The Spirit World

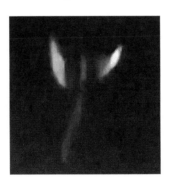

Before there were any organized religions, there was a worldwide view, including many cultures, in the natural instinct and belief in the anthropological construct of animism. Animism, from Latin animus, soul or life, is the worldview that non-human entities like animals, plants, and inanimate natural objects possess a spiritual essence. We see that this is true in the work of Masaru Emoto. The energetic wave patterns representing good and evil intent, are clearly seen in the frozen water crystals. These wave patterns are the physical visualizations of the spiritual essence.

Animism encompasses the belief that there is no separation between the spiritual and physical (or natural) world and souls or spirits exist, not only in humans, but also in animals, plants, rocks, geographic features such as mountains or rivers, or other entities of the natural environment, including thunder, clouds, wind, and shadows. Remember, Einstein stated that all matter vibrates with its own frequency. Is the frequency related to spiritual essence?

Some believe that animism consists of two unformulated propositions; all parts of nature had a soul and these souls are capable of moving without requiring a physical form. This leads to fetishism, the worship of visible objects as powerful, spiritual beings. The second proposition was that souls are independent of their physical forms. It gives rise to 'spiritism' or the worship of the souls of the dead and the unseen spirits of the heavens. In many animistic world views, the human being is often regarded as on a roughly equal footing with other animals, plants, and natural forces. Therefore, it is morally imperative to treat these agents with respect. In this world view, humans are considered a part of nature, rather than superior to, or separate from it.

Many animistic cultures observe some form of ancestor reverence. Whether they see the ancestors as living in another world, or embodied in the natural features of this world, animists often believe that offerings and prayers to and for the dead are an important facet of maintaining harmony with the world of the spirits. Animism was always considered by modern science and all the religions as well, as a primitive belief system, one associated with uneducated, uncivilized, tribal cultures. These 'tribes' had the belief system that revolved around the reverence of a spiritual existence, where mainstream civilization believes in the reverence of technological advancements and no spiritual existence.

Somewhere in the distant past, ancient extraterrestrials apparently understood the power of the natural and spiritual (dimensional) universe and incorporated that insight into advanced technology. It seems logical to me that at some time in the distant past, Earth was settled by numerous species of extraterrestrial life scattered across the planet. Some of these tribes or colonies were animistic or spiritual in nature and some were guided by their egos and quest for technological advancement. It's easy to surmise extraterrestrial colonies may have evolved into different races and disseminated around the world. One could believe an extraterrestrial colony may have originally settled in Clover Hollow and possibly evolved into the East Coast North American Indian, and may of had a strong animistic belief system.

Elementals

This all encompassing spirit world, according to ancient legend, folklore, and mythology, is occupied by many different forms of spiritual entities. One of these groups consisting of 'nature spirits' were sometimes called elementals. An elemental is a mythic being in the alchemical works of Paracelsus in the 16th Century.

According to Paracelsus, there are four elemental categories; gnomes, undines, sylphs, and salamanders. These correspond to the classical elements of antiquity: earth, water, air and fire. Aether (quintessence) was not assigned an elemental.

From what I can gather, the breakdown of the Elemental Kingdom starts with the four basic elements of nature; fire, air, earth, and water. Within each of the four elements are nature spirits that are the spiritual essence of that element. They are made up of etheric substance that is unique and specific to their particular element. The beings in the Elemental Kingdom work primarily on the mental plane and are known as 'builders of form.' Their specialty is translating thought-forms into physical-forms by transforming mental patterns into etheric and then physical patterns. Each of them is a specialist in creating some specific form, whether it is an electron or interstellar space.

It is said that elemental beings begin their evolution small and increase their size as they evolve. The elementals serving on planet Earth materialize whatever they pick up from the thoughts and feelings of mankind. This relationship was intended to facilitate the re-manifestation of 'Heaven on Earth.' My understanding is that the elementals take their orders from the 'Devas' and they do not remain individualized as humans are. Devas are animated by the thought power of angels and so they are thought forms of sorts. They may be etheric thought forms, yet they have etheric flesh, blood, and bones.

Supposedly, Devas live, propagate off spring, eat, talk, act, and sleep. They cannot be destroyed by material elements such as fire, air, earth, and water because they are etheric in nature. They are not immortal. When their work is finished they are absorbed back into the ocean of spirit. They do live a very long time, three-hundred to one-thousand years, from what I am to understand.

Elementals are said to have the power to change their size and appearance almost at will. They cannot, however, change elements. The Elementals:

Earth~~Gnomes

The nature spirits of the Earth are called Gnomes. I read somewhere that Gnomes have the ability to carve stone. Subgroups: Brownies, Dryads, Durdalis, Earth Spirits, Elves, Hamadryads, Pans, Pygmies, Sylvestres, and Satyrs.

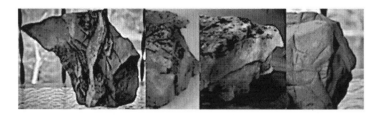

Fire~~Salamanders

The Salamanders are the spirits of fire. Without these beings fire cannot exist. There are many families of Salamanders, differing in size, appearance, and dignity. Some people have seen them as small balls of light, but most commonly they are perceived as being lizard-like in shape and about a foot or more in length.

The Salamanders are considered the strongest and most powerful of all the elementals. Their ruler is said to be a flaming being called Djin. Those who have seen him say that he is terrifying, yet awe-inspiring in appearance. They are greatly affected, as are all nature spirits, by human consciousness.

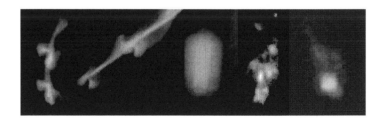

Air~~Sylphs

The sylphs are the air spirits. Their element has the highest vibratory rate of the four (air, earth, fire, water). They live hundreds of years, often reaching one thousand and never seeming to get old. They are said to live on the tops of mountains. The leader of the sylphs is a being called Paralda, who is said to dwell on the highest mountain of Earth.

Sylphs often assume human form but only for short periods of time. They vary in size from being as large as a human to being much smaller. They are volatile and changeable. The winds are their particular vehicle. They work through the gases and ethers of the Earth and are kindly toward humans. They are usually seen with wings, looking like cherubs or fairies. Because of their connection to air, which is associated with the mental aspect, one of their functions is to help humans receive inspiration. The sylphs are said to be drawn to those who use their minds, particularly those in the creative arts.

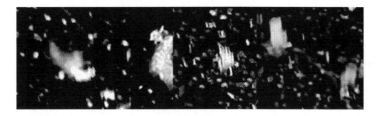

Water~~Undines

The undines are the elemental beings that compose water. They are able to control, to a great degree the course and function of the water element. Etheric in nature, they exist within the water itself and this is why they can't be seen with normal physical vision. These beings are beautiful to look at and are very graceful. They are often seen riding the waves of the ocean. They can also be found in rocky pools and in marshlands. They are clothed in a shimmery substance looking like water, but shinning with all the colors of the sea with green predominating. The undines also work with the plants that grow under the water and with the motion of water. Some undines inhabit waterfalls; others live in rivers and lakes. Every fountain has its nymph. Every ocean has its Oceanids. Subgroups: Limoniades, Mermaids, Naiads, Oceanid, Oreads, Potamides, Sea Maids, and Water Spirits.

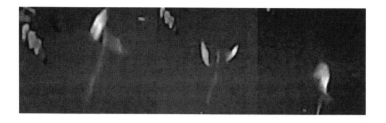

Angels, Guardian Angels, and Spirit Guides

My thought process on all the conflicting opinion that abounds on the subject of angels is to disregard them and rely on my own life experiences, intuition, and personal spiritual enlightenment. I would suggest that angels have existed since the beginning of time. These subtle beings come from Heaven and act as messengers from the higher level deities.

Higher deities in Heaven are said to speak in the language of light (a higher vibrational level) whereas humans speak in the language of sound (a lower vibrational level). So, the angels act like a step-down transformer when they carry messages from the deities in

Heaven to deserving humans in a language they can understand. It is believed that the primary medium used by angels to communicate to humans is by putting thoughts into their minds. Some believe the messages they deliver are generally about how to address a particular worldly issue and some angels are said to give worldly advice themselves.

On October 2, 2014, at the Feast of Holy Guardian Angels, observed by Catholics around the world, Pope Francis proclaimed 'I believe in guardian angels and everyone should listen to their advice.' Pope Francis has said he believes in angels, telling Catholics around the world to reaffirm their belief in holy guardians. Speaking to followers at the Vatican that Wednesday, the pontiff said every person has a guardian angel advising them in life. Stressing they were not imaginary; he said it was only pride stopping people hearing their voices. 'Do not rebel: follow their advice, no one walks alone and none of us can think that he is alone.'

My understanding is that everyone has a guardian angel, with no exceptions. This is the angel who constantly remains with you from birth, until your transformation back to Heaven. This angel's love for you is unconditional and larger than anything on this earth. Your guardian angel makes certain you are safe and guided always. Guardian angels are sometimes referred to as 'spirit guides.' A spirit guide is thought to be a loving being who has lived upon the earth in human form. Some say a spirit guide does not interfere with your free will or make decisions for you. The spirit guide is there to give you general advice, comfort, and at times warning and protection. They say most spirit guides are deceased loved ones, such as grandparents, siblings, beloved friends and parents.

Your spirit guide may have passed-away in physical life before you were born. However, this loving being was there at your birth and has been with you every day of your life since. Just as you will always take an interest in your family's future offspring, so do the deceased family members whom we may have never encountered in physical form.

Spirit guides are said to behave in the same capacity as guardian angels, in that they bring many rewards to our lives. Some believe that guardian angels, as differentiated from spirit guides, have never walked as mortals upon the earth, plus have a higher vibrating energy frequency. People who are empathic, who can 'feel' the sensation of a spiritual presence, can tell the palpable difference between an angelic and a spirit guide's appearance. Some clairvoyants see that guardian angels aura is bright white, whereas a spirit guide's aura is not quite as bright and may appear as a bluish-white.

Connection to the Blue Road of Spirit

Since the beginning of humankind, people believed in the extraordinary powers of animals. This belief originates in animism, the idea that animals possess souls and a consciousness. Early people around the world honored animals for having a spiritual life similar to their own and the spirit of the animal existed after death. They recognized their dependency upon the animal and respected the animal's superior strength, speed, and other qualities. Some cultures held the animal sacred because it was an important part of their lives. Various types of animals, especially snakes and birds, were held in great esteem by early peoples around the world and many cultures adopted prayers, rituals, and built temples in which to worship them. The ancient Egyptians, Greeks, Hindus, Buddhists, Aztecs and other cultures venerated and worshiped various animals, like birds and reptiles.

However, there is an important distinction between these cultures and the North American Indians. Most North American Indians were careful not to worship any part of creation, but held the whole of creation sacred. They constructed no idols or temples to worship animals, birds or reptiles, but made fetishes, art, and other creative works honoring their animal cousins. Could this be what this lost tribe of Clover Hollow left on the side of an Appalachian mountainside?

I've always considered encounters with wild animals as an adventure between kindred spirits. Animals were drawn to me as I was to them. From Flashlight Fish in the Coral Sea, Hammerheads in the Red Sea, and the Kingfishers on Sinking Creek, every experience brought peace and added to the quality of my spiritual existence.

According to the American Indian, you do not choose your animal spirit guide as your personal spirit guide. The spirit guide chooses you and they decide to whom they will reveal themselves and make you their friend. A spirit guide can be anything in Creation that speaks to a person through dreams, physical appearance, magnetic resonance (vibration); or by signs, symbols, words, or any other method or means of communication. It is said your animal spirit guide may reveal themselves to you three times to let you know who they are. It is up to us to recognize when this happens.

My spirit animal came to me during the summer of 2013 when I was in the midst of controversy concerning the rock carvings and their possible association to the Cherokee. This led to research on Cherokee folklore and their spiritual belief system. Having many animal encounters all my life, I was always looking out for those subtle qualities of the encounter that would enrich us both.

For three consecutive nights, right before dusk, a large Blue Heron would would make three passes before landing in the top of tall tree directly in front of where I was sitting on the front porch. The Blue Heron stayed for about five minutes each night and then flew away disappearing into the dusk. I immediately looked up the Indian medicine that a Blue Heron spirit guide can bring to your life.

According to Cherokee folklore regarding all of the Creature Beings of the Earth Mother, the coloring of the

Great Blue Herons feathers is significant, as each color carries with it special attributes unique to that creature. Blue in nature is a connection to Father Sky and also represents peace and tranquility. In esoteric thought, deep blue is also the color of the sixth chakra which corresponds to the third eye. Hence, insight and psychic vision are also emphasized here.

All of the 'Winged Ones' (birds) are believed to be messengers of the 'Great Spirit' and hence carry messages from the 'One Above' and of the 'Ancestors' to the minds and hearts of the two-legged who walk the 'Red Road of Physical Life.' Each Winged One has a specific task to perform as Messenger, for the Eagle, it is to bring illumination into the souls of humans, for the Crow, it is to assist those who are making the journey from darkness into light, and for the Blue Heron, it is the 'Medicine of Connection to the Blue Road of Spirit.'

In Earth Medicine, life is viewed as a sacred wheel (circle). We enter at the eastern point along this mighty wheel and traverse the hoop until our life path for that present incarnation has been filled. At this point, we once more cycle off the Red Road of Life to walk the Blue Road of Spirit. The Blue Road in Earth Medicine is the equivalent of what some traditional religions and philosophies may view as life after death, and is the place that our souls journey to after the physical body dies. On the Blue Road, relatives and loved ones who have crossed over previous await us there, as do the Ancestors and the Elders who guide the footfalls of the Earth`s inhabitants while we are encased in flesh.

For the Blue Heron, the significance is found once more in the coloring of his/her feathers, hence the link to the Blue Road of Spirit. The Blue Heron carries messages from those walking the Red Road of life to those who walk the Blue Road and vice versa, flying in between 'planes' and carrying with him/her contact between realms. Holy smokes, this says a lot to what is happening in Clover Hollow. Is this a sign of communication from my ancestors residing in another worldly realm?

The Great Spirit

According to shamanic teachings, every place on the earth carries the energetic imprint of what has ever happened in that location. The earth holds the stories of everything that has ever happened in its soils, in the waters, and in the air. There are stories of family, conflict, love, dreams, and those who lived there or passed through. Although we have long forgotten these stories, the earth still holds these secrets. In particular is Clover Hollow.

Human activity on the land leaves not only a physical imprint, but an energetic imprint as well. Human activity done in harmony with the land, maintains the sacred balance of place and can raise the vitality and carrying capacity of the land. The earth has an innate intelligence and is a complex living organism woven with an energetic matrix of vortexes, Ley lines, energy fields, and multiple dimensions which all work in harmony to support and nourish life.

The Earth is where spirit meets matter. Or, another way of saying this, spirit from Father Sky above, and matter from Mother Earth below, converges on Earth to create the miracle of life, our physical reality. First we must understand the Earth herself. The Earth is constantly moving toward balance and harmony. From a tiny bug to a giant earthquake, everything that happens is a part of the weave of life moving toward balance following a specific blueprint of creation. For example, a tsunami is the result of a shifting and rebalancing of displaced water created from displaced earth (an underwater earthquake) which was itself created by the tension being released between converging land masses.

When looking at the cosmology of the Earth, some believe there are two main categories of energies to be encountered, spirits, and fields in the landscape. Spirits are energies that have an individuality and personality. They are more likely to have a voice of sorts and communicate telepathically in some form. The undine (the water elemental) of a bubbling creek may communicate a request to remove an obstructing stone. In comparison, natural energy fields are said to be devoid of a voice or personality, yet they emanate a unique tonal quality which can be strongly felt and experienced. A mountain peak may have a quality of power and exhilaration. A vortex may have a quality of intensity or disorientation.

It is said that spirits and fields are layered upon one another, interwoven like a holographic image. The spirit of a mountain may communicate a message to you, yet simultaneously you experience the quality of its field which may be wisdom and power. All landscapes, both urban and wild, are said to be composed of this matrix of spirits and fields. It is believed that spirits can make themselves visible to you, if they desire, in any form, while they interact with the fields of energy, as they have in Clover Hollow.

American Indian spiritual tradition tells us that in the beginning, humans were created to be the custodians of the garden they called Mother Earth. The American Indian respected nature and they held all things of creation sacred. These people respected nature and accepted that they were only a small part of the whole circle of life. They knew each part of creation played a significant role in the contentment and survival of the other. They accepted the divine idea that all things were equal, and no animal, including man, held dominion over other parts of creation.

American Indians, who were also known as the 'People of the Land' traditionally and historically held a special knowledge of the land and its inhabitants. Intimate knowledge of the world surrounding the American Indian was possible because of a belief system that considered all things of creation equal and necessary, worthy of respect and honor. Some traditional American Indian teachings and beliefs are:

Never take more than we need.
Thank the Creator for what we have or what we will
receive.
Use all of what we have.
Give away what we do not need.
Everything on earth is alive.
Everything on earth has purpose.
Everything on earth is connected.
Everything on earth is to be embraced.

American Indian spirituality is characterized by the religious belief that spirits are present in all things, both animate and inanimate. These religious beliefs are centered around the environment and the natural world of animals, birds, insects, plants, herbs, trees, and natural phenomena such as rocks, mountains, rivers, lakes, clouds, and celestial bodies, such as the sun, moon, planets and the stars.

The indigenous people of North America believed that the living are intimately connected with the souls, or spirits of the dead. Religious practices were based on communication with the spirit world through mediums known as a Shaman or a Medicine Man, who also acted as healers. There are many stories, legends and myths about the Creator who is generally referred to as the Great Spirit. The Great Spirit is the Supreme Being and principal deity of the American Indian. The Great Spirit is the supernatural being conceived as the perfect and all powerful originator and ruler of the universe. The Supreme Being is often defined simply as 'God' in Western beliefs, and is used with this meaning by many other religions to refer to different deities.

The American Indian was characterized by an intimate relationship with nature. The creed or doctrine of these belief systems held that intelligent spirits inhabited all natural objects, and every object is controlled by its own independent spirit. Spirits inhabit the sky, stars, sun, moon, rivers, lakes, mountains, forests, animals, insects, fish, stones, flowers and birds. Some spirits are good and help those who please them, whereas other spirits are bad and liable to wreak havoc on people and on tribes. Animals, referred to as power animals, are singled out as powerful manifestations of the supernatural, including those seen in dreams or Vision Quests. Lesser spirits inhabit stones and plants and are viewed as 'spirit helpers.'

The native Indian concept of the Great Spirit varies from tribe to tribe who refer to the Supreme Being by a variety of different names. Some of their beliefs about the Great Spirit are derived from both patriarchal and matriarchal traditions. The Lakota Sioux believe that the Great Spirit is an amalgamation of a dominant Father Sky god and Mother Earth. The Great Spirit is seen as both male and female beings, separate, but part of one divine entity. Other tribes refer to the Great Spirit as Father, Old Man, or Grandfather, and in these cultures the Great Spirit is perceived to be a man, or an animal, with human thought and speech.

American Indians were a deeply spiritual people and they communicated their history, thoughts, ideas, and dreams, from generation to generation through symbols and signs, such as the Great Spirit symbol. Native American symbols used sacred geometry in geometric portrayals of celestial bodies, natural phenomena, and animal designs. The meaning of the Great Spirit symbol was to signify the divine power that created the world. The Great Spirit was the principal deity in the religion of many Native American peoples. Names for the Great Spirit are given by some Indian tribes. 'Gitchi Manitou' is the name given by Algonquian speaking tribes. 'Wakan Tanka' is the name given by the Sioux which translates as the 'Great Mystery.' The Blackfoot tribe refers to the Great Spirit or Great Mystery as 'Old Man' and 'Ababinili' is how the Great Spirit is known by the Chickasaw tribe. The Great Spirit symbol shows a depiction known in Western culture as the 'Eye of Providence' (or the all-seeing eye of God) representing the eye of God watching over humankind. In Western culture the symbol of the 'all-seeing eye' is usually depicted in a triangle as it appears on the United States one-dollar bill. This symbol is also associated with societies like the masons and Illuminati. The Great Spirit symbol is depicted within a four sided symbol symbolizing the cardinal directions, North, South, East and West. This is another example of the spirit and nature relationship.

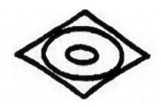

As mentioned before, the American Indian believed that the living were intimately connected with the spirits of the dead. They believed they were still connected to their ancestral spirits even though their physical forms were long gone. Shamanic teachings tell us that ancestral spirits consist of three types; ancestors of spirit, ancestors of place, and ancestors of blood. Herein lies the spiritual connection to Clover Hollow.

Ancestors of spirit are all those who inspire you, whose work you carry on in the world, those who built the tools and traditions you use in your life. They are behind the passion for things that you love, like music or art. All those that you have looked up to and have guided your life through thick and thin are with you always, wherever you go.

Ancestors of place include all the beings that once lived in the area you live. They extend beyond other human beings to include the animals who lived and died, and the plants who flourished and decayed. The ground you walk on is literally made out of the bodies of those plants and animals, those ancestors of place. This would also include all those who left an energetic or spiritual imprint embedded in Clover Hollow over the span of history (e.g. extraterrestrials, American Indians, and the early pioneers). Not to forget the limestone bedrock, which still retains the spiritual essence from the shells of organisms that were once alive.

Ancestors of blood are the people you're physically descended from. Their bones are your bones; their blood flows through your veins. You can imagine yourself as the bud on a branch of a great tree, with roots extending far into the past. You are the child and the grandchild, and the great-grandchild of people who survived at least long enough to reproduce. In my case it was a double dose of Sibold blood plus two other bloodlines, the Harless and Price families, who connect me to this place.

So, my ancestral footprint here is a heavy one. This imprint would include the spirits of this 'Lost Tribe of Clover Hollow' regardless of their origin. Their history is carved into stone, locking their spiritual essence into the fabric of time. This would be a significant energetic imprint that is still in flux today. My ancestors of place would include all those who crossed over this piece of earth since the beginning of time. This would include to a large part the American Indian, possibly the descendants of this lost colony and who made the land their sacred hunting grounds. This property would also hold negative Karma with harmful energetic imprints, like that of slavery, colonialism, or any connection to the 'Trail of Tears' and Indian removal from their ancestral homeland.

May I suggest that all my ancestral brethren of spirit, blood, and place, are now together in the spiritual kingdom of Heaven, and have conspired together to successfully bring me to Clover Hollow. Their reasons why they would have gone to this trouble have become much clearer.

Shamanic teachings tell us that ancestral spirits frequently attach themselves to a descendent for whom they have an affinity, or one who can hear or see them. As the descendent can recognize the ancestor through genetic memory, so the ancestral spirit is drawn to familiar genetic vibrations of a living descendent. A symbiotic bond is created when needs of both beings are satisfied in the relationship.

This I'm sure is my destiny. This is what I am supposed to be doing on this Earth. It's clear to me now why my ancestral spirits attached themselves to me when I was very young, probably while playing in the caves in Greenville. They have successfully guided me on my journey to a small piece of land in the Appalachian Mountains. It took a team effort between my ancestral spirits, guardian angels, spirit guides, spirit helpers, nature spirits, and animal guides, or whatever your belief system may call them, to draw me to this spot, and show me what's buried underneath. I can see three possible explanations why my ancestral spirits went to all of this trouble.

I

The first reason must have been for the specific purpose to discover and uncover this lost culture of Clover Hollow. It is clear now that this lost tribe or colony was completely buried and covered up, almost for eternity, by another colony belonging to my German ancestors, although it was surely unintentional. Maybe the tribal ancestors to the American Indian wanted me to find their beautiful, artful, mysterious, and possibly extraterrestrial culture, which is sure to enrich our lives if we take the time to understand it, before it was lost forever. I'm sure my German ancestral spirits would like to right the wrong when they inadvertently buried and built over the sacred site of their own ancestors of place. Now together in the spiritual realm, they have conspired together to bring me to Clover Hollow to uncover both lost tribes and to tell their story.

II

The second reason I was brought to Clover Hollow would be the opportunity for my German ancestral spirits to atone for sins they had committed during their lifetime on Earth. The American Indian believe that when you die, your spirit and individual personality move on to the spiritual kingdom. Your existence doesn't end there though; you can still atone for past sins or fulfill uncompleted charity to reach higher spiritual vibrational levels. The German colonists were pacifist in their religion, spirit, and way of life. They lived their lives trying to follow the golden rule and do onto others as you would have them do unto you. They were blood brothers with their Cherokee neighbors.

But, they still had to tow the line for their colonialist masters and even though they were not large slave owners, they did own some slaves and even used slaves to build the Price dam that sits on Sinking Creek today at the bottom of the hill below the house. Now that my ancestors share the Kingdom of Heaven with all ancestors of place associated with Clover Hollow, they can now atone for their sins and acknowledge any cruelty towards their fellow man that they may have been responsible. Not to long ago I climbed to the top of Sinking Creek Mountain, where some of the slaves that helped build the dam are buried and recited a prayer of respect and honor over their graves.

Even though they were blood brothers with the Cherokee, my ancestors were also guilty of taking Indian land in the way of their sacred hunting grounds, the very land I now own. They must have also felt some responsibility and anguish in the way their ancestors of place, the Cherokee Indian, were treated by the British and colonist during the colonialism of America, and by the United States of America's responsibility for the 'Trail of Tears.' I am sure they would want to acknowledge, apologize, and ask forgiveness for any harm or hurt they inflicted on their brother, their fellow spirits now in Heaven. To tell the story how the American Indian's ancestral homeland, where their first generation grandfathers are buried, and was taken from them, seemed very important for me to do. The need to honor and pay tribute to my ancestors of place, who now inhabit the spiritual kingdom, has now become destiny fulfilled as I tell their story. Many times, overlooking Sinking Creek, I have offered tobacco and recited a prayer of honor and respect to my Indian ancestral spirits.

III

The third and final reason I was brought to Clover Hollow, and more of a worldly message I suppose, is simply to get the message out to redirect the priorities of humankind and offer a little proof that an afterlife and spiritual existence really does exist for all and everything. There is a place we go after we die and when we leave this physical reality behind. We will always have the opportunity to atone for our sins and we will always have the chance for redemption as we continue our never ending journey along the circle of existence in the Kingdom of Heaven.

The early American Indian believed that their connection to the heavenly world of the Great Spirit lay somewhere within the land of their ancestors. They believed that when their ancestors passed on they became in someway part of the spiritual fabric of the natural world, the creation of the Great Spirit. To recite prayer and to honor the history of their ancestors, was to pay tribute and respect to the Great Spirit and bring them closer to their own spiritual destiny. In honor of my ancestors of spirit, place, and blood, this book is dedicated.

Affirmation

It was Saturday, February 28, 2013, and I was an emotional wreck. It had been two weeks since the discovery of the old Indian trail and the first of the rock carvings. It also had been two weeks since I quit my job of twenty-six years. Oh, it was also my dog's seventeenth birthday, he was my very much loved, Jack Russell Terrier, named Memphis, and I had lost him just a few months prior. My emotions were on a roller coaster climbing with sudden exhilaration thinking about the new discovery I just made and then dropping like a heavy rock in a pond when I would think about the loss of my best friend and companion for the last seventeen years. I had to seriously practice my breathing techniques I learned from scuba diving, just so I could keep my composure.

That day, I had uncovered a rock formation not twenty feet off my front porch that was hidden under dirt and brush for the last two-hundred years. When I realized what lay before me, like a wave pounding down on me, I suddenly came to the realization that every rock formation in sight on this property was also carved in the same manner. It also hit me that this rock formation was part of the same bedrock under the house that had been dynamited and buried beneath concrete in the 1970s. Curiously, it was the same time I was spending a lot of time in the caves in Greenville. The chill bumps were pulsating up and down my spine as the tears spilled down my face.

All at once and all of sudden, I understood why I had been brought here to the land where my ancestors are buried. It was to discover and uncover this lost ancient culture that my ancestors had covered up and hidden for almost an eternity. But what is more important than that, I had the sudden feeling that all that is happening, right here in the now, was a life changing spiritual event more so than an important archaeological discovery. At that instant, something told me to grab my iPhone and video tape the moment.

There is no doubt in my mind that what I captured on tape was the spirit of my dog Memphis tearing across the side of Clover Hollow Mountain, just like he would tear through the backyard as a puppy chasing a squirrel. This video is posted at www.virginiarockart.com. There was no doubt he was reassuring me that he would always be there and everything was going to be okay. Very clearly on the video tape you can see a small white light travel across Clover Hollow Mountain at a supernatural pace, obviously trying to be seen. It was all the confirmation I needed to know that there really is an afterlife, and our physical life here on Earth is only one segment in the circle of our spiritual existence. Just like the circle with a horizontal line.

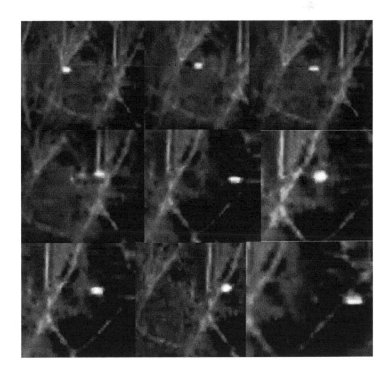

All video's mentioned in this book are posted at
www.thesiboldeffect.com

Made in the USA
San Bernardino, CA
28 March 2017